MW00812735

ADOPTION ACROSS RACE AND NATION

FORMATIONS: ADOPTION, KINSHIP, AND CULTURE
Emily Hipchen and John McLeod, Series Editors

Adoption across Race and Nation

US Histories and Legacies

Edited by Silke Hackenesch

THE OHIO STATE UNIVERSITY PRESS
COLUMBUS

Copyright © 2022 by The Ohio State University.
All rights reserved.

Library of Congress Cataloging-in-Publication Data

Names: Hackenesch, Silke, editor.

Title: Adoption across race and nation : US histories and legacies / edited by Silke Hackenesch.

Other titles: Formations: adoption, kinship, and culture.

Description: Columbus : The Ohio State University Press, [2022] | Series: Formations: adoption, kinship, and culture | Includes bibliographical references and index. | Summary: "Combines chapters on current practices of child separation, deportation, and immigration with chapters on the histories of transnational and transracial adoption, highlighting the legacies and correlations of adoption with race, nation, immigration, belonging, and citizenship"—Provided by publisher.

Identifiers: LCCN 2022030674 | ISBN 9780814215173 (cloth) | ISBN 0814215173 (cloth) | ISBN 9780814282601 (ebook) | ISBN 0814282601 (ebook)

Subjects: LCSH: Intercountry adoption—United States—History. | Interracial adoption—United States—History. | BISAC: SOCIAL SCIENCE / Race & Ethnic Relations | FAMILY & RELATIONSHIPS / Adoption & Fostering

Classification: LCC HV875.55 .A36353 2022 | DDC 362.7340890973—dc23/eng/20220818

LC record available at https://lccn.loc.gov/2022030674

Other identifiers: ISBN 9780814258576 (paper) | ISBN 0814258573 (paper)

Cover design by Nathan Putens
Text design by Juliet Williams
Type set in Adobe Minion Pro

∞ The paper used in this publication meets the minimum requirements of the American National Standard for Information Sciences—Permanence of Paper for Printed Library Materials. ANSI Z39.48-1992.

CONTENTS

ILLUSTRATIONS

FIGURES

TABLES

ACKNOWLEDGMENTS

I was fortunate to meet most of the scholars in this volume at a conference on the history of intercountry and transracial adoptions that I organized in 2017 at Kassel University in Germany. This event was generously funded by the German Research Foundation, the Alliance for the Study of Adoption and Culture, and the Society for the History of Childhood and Youth. I am grateful to these organizations for their support. The idea for this book grew out of the intriguing discussions we had on less known histories of transnational adoption, and its ongoing relevance to debates on nationality, citizenship, belonging, and identity, among other concepts.

Critical adoption studies is a dynamic and exciting field, and I consider myself lucky to be part of this scholarly community and to have participated in the last nonvirtual and virtual Alliance for the Study of Adoption and Culture conferences. At ASAC in Oakland in 2018, I had the opportunity to meet with Kristen Elias Rowley from The Ohio State University Press. Kristen has been a great supporter and editor along the way, and I am deeply grateful for her guidance and commitment. Many thanks also to the formidable editors of the Formations: Adoption, Culture, and Kinship series, Emily Hipchen and John McCleod. I would also like to express my appreciation and gratitude for the anonymous reviewers who offered valuable criticism and provocative questions as I pulled this volume together. Their valuable feedback helped and encouraged me to sharpen my ideas.

Next to the fantastic crowd of scholars who generously agreed to contribute to this volume, I am indebted to the following colleagues for their engaging discussions, productive feedback, and intellectual rigor: Cynthia Callahan, Kimberly McKee, Rachel Rains Winslow, Karen Balcom, Azziza Malanda, Philip Rohrbach, Tiffany N. Florvil, Nancy Nenno, Bettina Hitzer, Benedikt Stuchtey, Isabel Heinemann, and Juliane Hornung. At my academic home institution, the History Department at the University of Cologne, I am especially grateful to Anke Ortlepp for her continuous mentoring and support. For their last-minute work on formatting, I would like to thank research assistants Maria Wiegel and Max Gaida. My hope for this volume is not only that adoption scholars will find it useful but also that it reaches an audience beyond academia. I dedicate this book to adoptees around the world who may find traces of their own experiences reflected in the contributions collected here.

Histories and Legacies of Adopting Children across Race and Nation

SILKE HACKENESCH

Transnational and transracial adoption has become a phenomenon that is rapidly declining in numbers yet highly visible.[1] How adoptive families were and are made has come under intense scrutiny in critical adoption studies over the last two decades, especially with regard to international adoption.[2] Major debates in recent years have addressed the detention of children at the US-Mexican border and their subsequent adoption by American families, adoptees' citizenship issues and deportation, and the role of Black American families in international adoption since World War II. Many works explore adoption in the contested space between care and consumption, between rescue and self-fulfillment in deeply economically unequal global settings. They illuminate the tensions between legal and cultural citizenship, complicated notions of belonging, and the liminal status of adoptees. While modern adoption is considered child-centered and often framed as serving the "best

---

1. What we today call international adoption was at its beginning referred to as intercountry adoption and was often not only transnational but transracial as well. The terms *intercountry, transnational, international* all describe adoption across national borders. They obscure, however, the race and class dynamics inherent in transnational adoption.

2. See Balcom, *Traffic in Babies*; Briggs, *Somebody's Children*; Carp, *Adoption in America*; Dorow, *Transnational Adoption*; Graves, *War Born Family*; Herman, *Kinship by Design*; Kim, *Adopted Territory*; McKee, *Disrupting Kinship*; Melosh, *Strangers and Kin*; Oh, *To Save the Children*; Potter, *Everybody Else*; Rains Winslow, *Best Possible Immigrants*; Yngvesson, *Belonging in an Adopted World*.

interest of the child," the practice of proxy adoptions has been highly contested from its beginnings. Other works demonstrate that the experiences of transnational adoptees explain that questions of belonging and citizenship are racialized. Deportations of adoptees with a criminal record especially expose the fragile and precarious status of adoptee-citizens.

Looking at the history of transnational adoption and its emergence after World War II reveals that these contested debates are anything but new. In fact, exploring transnational/transracial adoptions from a historical perspective and taking contemporary issues into account, as this volume does, highlights the centrality of the categories *race* and *nation* in adoption discourse and practice. It also reveals adoption as a site of Cold War politics in the past and as a site for immigration and citizenship politics in the present.

The collection is interdisciplinary and multiperspective, bringing together historians, sociologists, anthropologists, and demographers as well as scholars from childhood studies and adoption studies to uncover the contours of adoption. It looks at adoptive parents, at adoptees, at birth mothers and adoption advocates.[3] It integrates well-known case studies of adoptions from Korea, China, and South America with less known ones, such as Black German adoptions. For instance, as Kori Graves shows, when Black Americans adopted Black Korean children during the Korean War, they relied on networks, practices, and news coverage that were in place since the end of World War II, when Black families had adopted Black German children to the US.

By approaching the issues at hand from a diversity of disciplinary perspectives, the essays provide novel scholarship on the emergence of transnational and transracial adoptions and illustrate the repercussions of the past in today's adoption controversies. All contributors address the close interconnectedness of adoption with race and nation, immigration, poverty, gender, border control, politics, and economics in the (un)making of families.

The Emergence of International Adoption

The late 1940s and early 1950s witnessed the emergence of transnational and transracial adoption to the US. These adoptions were regarded as deviant, unconventional, and revolutionary. They subverted the premise of "match-

---

3. Chapters in this volume distinguish between "professional social workers" and "nonprofessional" individuals and adoption advocates like Pearl S. Buck, Harry Holt, and Mabel A. Grammer. This is warranted, not least because it is a distinction that was important to both sides—the social workers in their ongoing critique of laypeople who seemingly did not understand the "science of adoption and family making," and adoption advocates who used terms like *professionals* almost derogatorily as a reference to red tape and unnecessary paperwork.

ing," a heretofore dominant paradigm in the social work profession. Matching meant that social workers should attempt to find a match between children and parents in terms of race, religion, or mental capacity.[4] Until the mid-twentieth century, social science had relied on what Ellen Herman called "kinship by design," namely creating families by adhering to processes of standardization and rationalization. These processes included matching children with adoptive parents in ways that should mimic "natural" families as much as possible; failure to do so would entail great risks for the families, social workers believed.[5] Since matching came under critical scrutiny in light of the transformations that orphaned children and "war babies" brought to the practices of adoption, Wayne Carp had described the Second World War as a "watershed moment."[6] Additionally, the internationalism of the postwar period as well as the galvanizing civil rights movement and a belief in colorblind social policies challenged these social work procedures.

The public discussions and controversies that intercountry adoptions elicited reflect the paradoxes inherent in American family formation and the formation of the American nation. On the one hand is a pluralist understanding according to which families can be made through voluntary association and a nation can be made through immigration and naturalization. On the other hand is a belief that blood ties determine belonging, into the family and into the nation. Transracial adoptions in particular touched on these notions in new and challenging ways.

The most common form of intercountry adoption has been the adoption of Asian, specifically Korean, children by white American families. White Americans were apparently more open to the idea of adopting a "biracial" Asian child from abroad than a Black American child because of the long history of racial segregation and so-called miscegenation in the US. Moreover, a pervasive culture of "Cold War Orientalism" made "racially mixed" families possible, with liberal and deeply religious white parents adopting Asian children to be educated and raised to American citizenship.[7] So, even though postwar America was deeply affected by a pronatalism that compelled many Americans to adopt a child, it was the Korean "orphans" who pushed the idea of domestic transracial adoption, resulting in an increased domestic diversity.[8]

---

4. McRoy and Zurcher, *Transracial and Inracial Adoptees*, 4.

5. Herman, *Kinship by Design*.

6. Carp and Leon-Guerrero, "When in Doubt, Count."

7. See Klein, *Cold War Orientalism*; Pate, *From Orphan to Adoptee*, 76–77.

8. On the construction of the social category *orphan*, see also Pate, *From Orphan to Adoptee*, 101; and Oh, "From War Waif to Ideal Immigrant," 42; as well as Rains Winslow, *Best Possible Immigrants*; see also Potter, *Everybody Else*, 14.

Korean adoptees were compelled to fully integrate into their white adoptive families, often by downplaying their Korean heritage. Adoptive parents of Chinese girls, in contrast, have tried to build a community of adoptive parents and actively tried to preserve (even if inauthentic or distorted) elements of Chinese culture by participating in Chinese cultural events.[9] Some families seem to honor the ethnic origin of their adopted children, and by celebrating and connecting through their differences, enable the development of a Chinese American identity, a practice Amy Traver describes as "quotidian transnationalism."[10]

Transracial adoption was framed as an antiracist act in this context. Intriguingly, race was downplayed and "overlooked" when white American families adopted Korean children—whereas Black American families often acted on color consciousness and emphasized the racial identity of the "biracial" children they adopted from Germany and Korea. Scholars such as Kim Park Nelson have analyzed Asians' proximity to whiteness and integration into white families as a misguided symbol of a colorblind society.[11] While these transracial adoptions have been presented as "an extension of whiteness" to (foremost) Asian adoptees, or an attempted incorporation of them into the category of white American citizenship, it has also firmly anchored "racially mixed" children as "Black" within the context of American racial logics in the 1940s and 1950s, thereby conforming to the so-called one-drop rule. Korean children were racialized, but as not-Black and thus as close to whiteness, what Arissa Oh has called "digestible diversity" for white families; Black German children, in contrast, were racialized as Black, and Black American couples were sought out as possible adopters for them. Whereas a belief in racial purity pressured birth mothers to relinquish these children in the countries of their birth, an increasing commitment to racial diversity, at least in official rhetoric, led to their adoption in the US.[12]

However, race as a socially constructed category depends heavily on context. Whereas the children were considered American in Korea, they were regarded as Asian in the US. Similarly, Afro-German children were identified as "Black" in Germany but were often perceived as "half-German" and light-skinned in Black communities. Still, Pamela Anne Quiroz and others have instructively critiqued the colorblindness and postracial utopianism that

---

9. Most notably on Chinese adoption is Dorow, *Transnational Adoption*; see also Traver, "(Ap)parent Boundaries."

10. Traver, "Adopting China."

11. Park Nelson, *Invisible Asians*.

12. Oh, *To Save the Children*, 67.

long defined studies of transnational and transracial adoption, for instance the Indian Adoption Project and the (rare) adoption of Black children by white couples.[13] This volume, instead, explores the complexity of racial identification, racial exclusions, and always shifting notions of identity and kinship.

In its early years, transnational adoption was popularized by prominent figures such as actress Jane Russell and writer Pearl S. Buck, or by activists who rose to prominence such as Harry and Bertha Holt and the Doss family. In response to the inaction of the US government to claim responsibility for the children fathered by US American members of the military forces, and the procedures implemented by social work professionals that critics perceived to be "red tape," celebrities, families, and individuals stepped in by attempting to "rescue" the children.[14] In postwar America, when domesticity was glorified by Cold War society, few would have doubted that the family belongs to a "private sphere," void of political matters and social forces.[15] However, this domestic space was political and shaped by geopolitical concerns, and transnational and transracial adoption was clearly a Cold War politics put into practice. The historical context of the establishment of international adoption underscored its political and humanitarian dimensions.[16] In its early stages in the wake of World War II and the Korean War, intercountry adoption was characterized as an act of humanitarian rescue in the face of destitution and poverty as well as racism, fascism, and communism.[17] Those who considered adoption could frame their actions as a colorblind, patriotic manifestation of Christian humanitarianism.[18] Yet while child rescue, racial equality, and progressive notions of modern families informed discourses on transnational and transracial adoption from early on, these adoptions affirmed and reproduced injustices and inequalities, especially between birth/first mothers and adoptive families and between sending and receiving countries.

The historiography of early transnational and transracial adoption to a large extent consists of remarkable studies on the adoption of Korean American children born to US servicemen and Korean women during and after

---

13. Quiroz, *Adoption in a Color-Blind Society.* On the adoption of Native American children into non-Native American families, see, for example, Jacobs, *Generation Removed.* See also Hübinette, "Post-Racial Utopianism."

14. Oh, *To Save the Children,* 73.

15. Tyler May, *Homeward Bound;* Coontz, *Way We Never Were;* Heinemann, *Inventing the Modern American Family.*

16. Oh, *To Save the Children,* 10.

17. On the "rescue" trope, see Briggs, "Mother, Child, Race, Nation"; and Choy, *Global Families.*

18. On "Christian Americanism," see Oh, *To Save the Children,* 79–84.

the Korean War.[19] However, Rosemarie Peña has reminded us that the children born to German women and Black American soldiers during the US occupation of Germany following World War II represent the first organized adoption efforts, primarily on the basis of race.[20] Why is it pertinent to bring analyses of Korean and German adoptions in conversation with each other, as this book proposes? What the German and the Korean examples share is not only the birth of children considered illegitimate and their birth mothers bearing the stigma of being framed as sex workers and as having fraternized with the occupational force, but also the existence of children with dual heritage in countries that believed themselves to be racially homogenous. In both instances, race is the mobilizing factor for their adoption.[21] Another aspect both share is the role of the media in popularizing adoption. For Korea, it was the mainstream press and Christian media outlets; for Afro-German children, it was the Black press and the writings of Pearl S. Buck. Black Americans following the news on Black GIs stationed in Germany in the Black press, on how Germany sought to integrate children of dual heritage, or even articulating a desire to adopt a Black German child practiced transnationalism.

The children from Germany and Korea were adopted by proxy, a contested procedure that the social work profession, most prominently the International Social Service (ISS) and the Child Welfare League of America (CWLA), critiqued vehemently. Adoptions by proxy meant that children were legally adopted by their prospective American parents through a representative before the children traveled to the US and met their adoptive mothers and fathers. In the absence of laws and regulations, or "best practices" for international adoptions, volunteer activism by individuals like Harry Holt, Pearl S. Buck, and Mabel A. Grammer could flourish.[22] Proponents supported proxy adoptions as a means to save children from war-torn countries and bring them to the US without lengthy formalities.[23] The ISS, however, emphasized that transnational adoption, too, needed a supervision of process, and that childless couples and abandoned children did not automatically "match" as a family. They were also concerned about the legal ramifications of proxy adoptions and documented the danger of this practice in their files.

---

19. See Kim, *Adopted Territory*; Pate, *From Orphan to Adoptee*; Hübinette, *Comforting an Orphaned Nation*; Graves, *War Born Family*.

20. Peña, "Remarks at Homestory Deutschland Exhibit Launch."

21. On race in Germany, see, among others, Fehrenbach, *Race after Hitler*; El-Tayeb, *Schwarze Deutsche*. For Korea, see Oh, *To Save the Children*.

22. Rains Winslow, *Best Possible Immigrants*, 7, 72.

23. Herman, *Kinship by Design*, 218.

Child welfare nonprofessionals were key players in bringing children to the US from both countries. As several chapters in this volume reveal, Black American women were also among these nonprofessionals, yet their involvement has not been sufficiently analyzed up to now. In general, Black Americans are less visible in the scholarship on modern adoption. This volume addresses this void and amends it by including chapters that focus on the adoption efforts of Black American couples as well as the adoption of Black children. Looking at international adoptions from Germany and Korea comparatively and transnationally thus complicates one's understanding of the early emergence of intercountry adoption. Putting both research areas into conversation is especially insightful with regard to configurations of race in postwar America in the wake of the Cold War and the civil rights movement. What adoptions of "racially mixed" and dual-heritage children share is their entanglement with Cold War politics and civil rights, their adoptions often having been framed as a statement of progressive racial views in the wake of democracy versus fascism and communism.[24] Yet while some have characterized these adoptions as charitable, noble, and humane, others—among them adoptees themselves—have come to see them as imperialistic, neocolonial, and self-serving, a privilege masked as benevolence. White American adoptive families often thought to act on liberal Christian beliefs and progressive motives, while Black American adoptive families were distrustful of domestic adoption agencies, which often discriminated against families of color and placed their action within broader civil rights struggles. Race turned out to be a decisive aspect in these historical examples.

Today, many adult adoptees seek out adoption communities for validation of their experiences and recognition. The question of national belonging, racial and ethnic identification, and cultural heritage continues to be relevant to many of them. In cases of precarious citizenship status, their Americanness is liminal, and they face possible deportation, as do other undocumented immigrants in the US. The repercussions of this history are vulnerable subject positions of adoptees and the privileging of American adoptive parents over nonwhite immigrant families. Moreover, the economic and political inequality between the sending countries and the receiving country are exacerbated. Several chapters explore the correlation of adoptees' racial identity and skin color with degrees of vulnerability, especially with regard to legal and cultural citizenship.

Studying transnational adoption means studying the US in its global context. Discourses and practices reveal that adoption destabilizes the nation and

---

24. Alvah, "'I Am Too Young to Die.'"

affirms it at the same time. The various contributions in this volume show that, in the words of Thomas Bender, "every dimension of American life [is] entangled in other histories."[25] This is certainly true for transracial/transnational adoption, which is shaped by neoliberal dynamics, foreign policy, individual preferences, and constructions of race and kinship. These are key topics in critical adoption studies, a dynamic, interdisciplinary field that has produced a large body of scholarship on modern adoption, the origins of transnational and transracial adoption, and contemporary practices for and legacies of adoption over the last three decades. This volume revisits the emergence of international adoption. It offers a series of case studies that illustrate the historical and contemporary confluences of race, nation, and kinship that shape and haunt adoption. While the volume certainly illustrates that there are continuities from the past to the present, it also uncovers distinct differences, especially with how adoptees (re)negotiated their sense of self and belonging and how recent American adoptive parents reimagined themselves as cosmopolitan. Many adoptees experienced a sense of liminality, not fully belonging in their countries of origin or in their new adopted homes. For others, their liminality gave them an opportunity to fashion new identities and engage in activism that advocated for more adoptee rights in the US, thereby challenging the definitions of citizenship.

About the Collection

This interdisciplinary volume seeks to interrogate the present conditions in connection to the early history of intercountry adoption. In the past as well as today, adoption, nation, and race continue to operate as relational categories with immediate effects on normative notions of family and kinship, belonging, the role of the state, and social welfare.[26] Chapters explore the complexity of racial identification, racial exclusions, and continuously shifting notions of identity and kinship. The nine contributions assembled in this volume affirm, reject, and enact different notions of nation, belonging, race, and gender. Adoption scholars come from a variety of scholarly disciplines. Most of the contributors in this volume are historians who go back to the origins of international adoption. They expose the long trajectory of child (dis)placement, revealing less known stories of transnational and transracial adoption.

---

25. Bender, "Introduction," 6.
26. See Myers, "Marking the Turn," 19; Rymph, *Raising Government Children.*

Other contributors tackle adoption by using ethnographic data and sociological methodology.

The political climate of increased border control and restrictive immigration policy is closely linked to the history of adoption in the US, as Laura Briggs insightfully discusses in her essay. It was the existing system of foster care, she argues, that allowed the violent separation of children from their parents and the placement of them into that system to its fullest capacity. This history has deeply humanitarian roots, as the chapters on Germany and Korea in this book demonstrate, but has also historically been used to break the political resistance of birth parents, and to assimilate "biracial" adoptees. This conflation of child rescue and child stealing has a history, and Briggs recounts that particular history with various examples, such as the adoption of Native American children, child rescue from fascist and communist countries, or the pressure to relinquish children on marginalized women of color. These examples provide a history of child separation that enables us to get a better understanding of the current political situation.

Pamela Anne Quiroz's contribution examines the blurring of the intersections of nation, immigration, race, and citizenship in the US as children of detained and deported parents are filtered into foster care and adoption. As the transnational "market" for children has changed over the years, US adoptive parents have faced potential ethical and pragmatic issues. At the same time, this development underscores the vulnerability of immigrant families of color who are deemed "unfit" to parent. Quiroz's chapter highlights the economics of adoption through the lens of adoptive and birth parents.

Eleana J. Kim and Kim Park Nelson examine "adoptee immigration privilege," that is, the contested and conflicted relationship between adoptees as immigrants, on the one hand, and the connection between citizenship and familial kinship, on the other. They focus their discussion on Korean adoptees, whose status as "honorary whites" has facilitated their integration into white American families; yet, because of the long history of anti-Asian immigration policies, "the gap between kinship and citizenship has been experienced as acutely painful," they write. They connect the category of "natural-born alien" that was created in response to the first transnational adoption and discuss the immigration legislation and the history of federal law in regulating adoption up to the present, when deportation of adoptees received wider media scrutiny.

Amy Traver's chapter focuses on contemporary issues. In her analysis of American adoptive parents of Chinese girls, Traver moves beyond the nation and applies the concept of cosmopolitanism to her data. She analyzes cosmopolitanism as an everyday practice, specifically to actualize adopted children's right to identity and community (specifically, the global orphan is a child of color who is offered a family of white Americans). At the same time, adoptive parents experience cosmopolitanism as a way of "internal globalization" through which they connect their local experiences with global concerns—a perspective that also applies to the ways in which early nonprofessional adoption and humanitarian activists framed their advocacy for adoption from Germany and Korea.

Quiroz and Briggs particularly show the vulnerability of birth families of color, where parents are seen as "unfit" or "unworthy" and the children in need of "rescue." Whereas Briggs's contribution highlights the precarious status of American Indian and Black American families, she and Quiroz also discuss the more recent exploitation of immigrant families and children. In this sense, both contributions are in conversation with Eleana J. Kim and Kim Park Nelson, who explore the close and complicated relationship between adoptee and immigrant status in the US. Further, Quiroz, like Amy Traver, focuses on the plight of birth parents, their economic and political vulnerabilities, while also offering fascinating glimpses into the narratives and rhetorical strategies of adoptive parents. In addition, Traver explores how the adoptive parents seek to transgress national, cultural, and ethnic boundaries by making an effort to celebrate difference, though they remain rather silent on the structural inequalities inherent in many forms of transnational and transracial adoption, in the past as well as today.

By focusing her discussion on two nonprofessional adoption advocates, Kori Graves's chapter highlights the adoption efforts of Black American couples and their attempts to bring Black Korean and Black German children to the US, thereby demonstrating that the experiences and actions of Black adoptive parents form a significant part of the early phase of transnational and transracial adoption. Graves's contribution illustrates that Black activism and involvement in transnational adoption was neither marginal nor surprising given the strong tradition of clubwomen's activism in Black communities. Graves discusses the similarities between clubwomen and nonprofessional adoption advocates and helps us understand why the establishing of informal structures in adoption seemed "natural" for these Black women.

My own chapter analyzes selected publications by Pearl S. Buck against the backdrop of 1950s colorblind discourses, on the one hand, and Buck's relationship to the Black American community and the Black press, on the other. Focusing on Buck's adoption of a Black German girl, the essay interrogates Buck's shifting, sometimes conflicting perspective on race and matching. It demonstrates that Buck's close connection to Black American activists contributed to her embracing transracial adoption, which she propagated as Cold War politics put into practice.

Born to a Black German adoptee mother with relatives in Germany and the US, Tracey Owens Patton interweaves her unique personal story through narratives by her mother and her grandmother with current scholarship on racial identification and national (un)belonging for Black German adoptees. By highlighting the stories of her maternal grandmother and her mother, she foregrounds the experiences of birth mothers whose voices are often absent in critical adoption studies and critically demonstrates that her grandmother chose a "life in whiteness" by relinquishing her Black children. Patton productively takes her own family history as a trajectory through which she explores the multilayered experiences of Black German adoptees as well as the history of hegemonic whiteness and anti-Blackness in the German and the US nation-states. Her narrative also touches on adoptee trauma by revealing that kinship may continue to be difficult and fraught to negotiate for adoptees even after reunion. Her experience complicates notions of belonging and helps us understand that any sense of belonging may be a privilege in itself.

According to Rosemarie Peña, adoptees searching for their original kin often discover other adoptees who share their context-specific circumstances in online social networks. Since the 1980s, searching Black Germans are collectively reconnecting with birth-family members and, concomitantly, with a globally situated, multigenerational, and multicultural Black German community—virtually, in discourse, and in practice. Peña focuses her discussion of Black German adoptees on forms of organizing and community-building in the US as well as adoptees' renegotiations of self, (racial) identity, national belonging, and social relations that the practice of re-kinning engenders. Like Patton's, her contribution illustrates that reunion and kinship practices can be an ongoing process that is seldom linear.

The four chapters that center the history and experiences of Black German adoptees to the US productively enrich our understanding of the early phase of transnational and transracial adoption. They demonstrate the heretofore overlooked, yet central role of Black Americans in the early years of transnational adoption; for them, adopting from Germany was a means to demonstrate responsible citizenship as much as a way to work around domestic adoption agencies and their discriminatory practices. For the adoptees, on the other hand, coming to the US often meant a shift in their racialized identities from "racially mixed" to Black. As the chapters by Patton and Peña aptly show, their experiences and struggles overlap with those of Korean adoptees, especially with regard to citizenship status, racial identity, and national belonging.

Finally, Peter Selman explores the demographic history of intercountry adoption from the Second World War to the present in a data-rich appendix. His tables help us understand adoption trends in relation to money, power, and neoliberal mechanisms, and that transnational adoption has become a response to a moment of crisis and an alleged "solution to a social problem."[27] Selman's chapter concludes with some reflections on the last seventy years of intercountry adoption in the light of earlier chapters and asks what we can learn from past experience, and how the story of intercountry adoption may be viewed in the years to come. Taken together, this collection gives testimony to the breadth and depth of critical adoption studies. It puts the works of well-established and emerging scholars into conversation, reflecting on major themes and newer trends in this vibrant field. The chapters demonstrate the wide-reaching impact and relevance of transnational/transracial adoption for understanding national belonging, immigration, legal and cultural kinship, cultural and familial kinship, racial identity, and cosmopolitan practices in modern America and beyond.

Bibliography

Alvah, Donna. "'I Am Too Young to Die': Children and the Cold War." *OAH Magazine of History* 24, no. 4 (2010): 25–28.

Balcom, Karen. *The Traffic in Babies: Cross-Border Adoption and Baby-Selling between the United States and Canada, 1930–1972.* Toronto: University of Toronto Press, 2011.

Bender, Thomas. "Introduction." In *Rethinking American History in a Global Age,* edited by Thomas Bender, 1–21. Berkeley: University of California Press, 2002.

Briggs, Laura. "Mother, Child, Race, Nation: The Visual Iconography of Rescue and the Politics of Transnational and Transracial Adoption." *Gender & History* 15 (2003): 179–200.

———. *Somebody's Children: The Politics of Transracial and Transnational Adoption.* Durham, NC: Duke University Press, 2012.

Carp, E. Wayne, ed. *Adoption in America: Historical Perspectives.* Ann Arbor: University of Michigan Press, 2002.

Carp, E. Wayne, and Anna Leon-Guerrero. "When in Doubt, Count: World War II as a Watershed in the History of Adoption." In *Adoption in America: Historical Perspectives,* edited by E. Wayne Carp, 181–217. Ann Arbor: University of Michigan Press, 2002.

Coontz, Stephanie. *The Way We Never Were: American Families and the Nostalgia Trap.* New York: Basic Books, 1992.

Dorow, Sara K. *Transnational Adoption: A Cultural Economy of Race, Gender, and Kinship.* New York: New York University Press, 2006.

El-Tayeb, Fatima. *Schwarze Deutsche: Der Diskurs um "Rasse" und nationale Identität 1890–1933.* Frankfurt: Campus, 2001.

27. Park Nelson, "Critical Adoption Studies," 20.

Fehrenbach, Heide. *Race after Hitler: Black Occupation Children in Postwar Germany and America.* Princeton, NJ: Princeton University Press, 2005.

Graves, Kori. *A War Born Family: African American Adoption in the Wake of the Korean War.* New York: New York University Press, 2020.

Heinemann, Isabel. *Inventing the Modern American Family: Family Values and Social Change in 20th Century United States.* Frankfurt: Campus, 2012.

Herman, Ellen. *Kinship by Design: A History of Adoption in the Modern United States.* Chicago: University of Chicago Press, 2008.

Hübinette, Tobias. *Comforting an Orphaned Nation: Representations of International Adoption and Adopted Koreans in Korean Popular Culture.* Seoul: Jimoondang, 2006.

———. "Post-Racial Utopianism, White Color-Blindness and 'The Elephant in the Room': Racial Issues for Transnational Adoptees of Color." In *Intercountry Adoption: Policies, Practices, and Outcomes,* edited by Judith L. Gibbons and Karen Smith Rotabi, 221–29. Farnham: Ashgate, 2012.

Jacobs, Margaret D. *A Generation Removed: The Fostering and Adoption of Indigenous Children in the Postwar World.* Lincoln: University of Nebraska Press, 2014.

Kim, Eleana J. *Adopted Territory: Transnational Korean Adoptees and the Politics of Belonging.* Durham, NC: Duke University Press, 2010.

Klein, Christina. *Cold War Orientalism: Asia in the Middlebrow Imagination, 1945–1961.* Berkeley: University of California Press, 2003.

McKee, Kimberly. *Disrupting Kinship: Transnational Politics of Korean Adoption in the United States.* Urbana: University of Illinois Press, 2019.

McRoy, Ruth G., and Louis A. Zurcher. *Transracial and Inracial Adoptees: The Adolescent Years.* Springfield, IL: Thomas, 1983.

Melosh, Barbara. *Strangers and Kin: The American Way of Adoption.* Cambridge, MA: Harvard University Press, 2006.

Myers, Kit. "Marking the Turn and New Stakes in (Critical) Adoption Studies." *Adoption & Culture* 6, no. 1 (2018): 1–49.

Oh, Arissa H. "From War Waif to Ideal Immigrant: The Cold War Transformation of the Korean Orphan." *Journal of American Ethnic History* 31, no. 4 (2012): 34–55.

———. *To Save the Children of Korea: The Cold War Origins of International Adoption.* Stanford, CA: Stanford University Press, 2015.

Park Nelson, Kim. "Critical Adoption Studies as Inclusive Knowledge Production and Corrective Action." *Adoption & Culture* 6, no. 1 (2018): 1–49.

———. *Invisible Asians: Korean American Adoptees, Asian American Experiences, and Racial Exceptionalism.* New Brunswick, NJ: Rutgers University Press, 2016.

Pate, SooJin. *From Orphan to Adoptee: U.S. Empire and Genealogies of Korean Adoption.* Minneapolis: University of Minnesota Press, 2014.

Peña, Rosemarie. "Remarks at Homestory Deutschland Exhibit Launch." Howard University, February 3, 2016. Accessed July 27, 2020. http://bghra.org/wp-content/uploads/2016/02/Homestory-Deutschland-at-Howard-University.pdf.

Potter, Sarah. *Everybody Else: Adoption and the Politics of Domestic Diversity in Postwar America.* Athens: University of Georgia Press, 2014.

Quiroz, Pamela Anne. *Adoption in a Color-Blind Society*. Lanham, MD: Rowman & Littlefield, 2007.

Rains Winslow, Rachel. *The Best Possible Immigrants: International Adoption and the American Family*. Philadelphia: University of Pennsylvania Press, 2017.

Rymph, Catherine E. *Raising Government Children: A History of Foster Care and the American Welfare State*. Chapel Hill: University of North Carolina Press, 2018.

Traver, Amy. "Adopting China: American China Adoptive Parents' Development of Transnational Ties to China." *International Journal of Sociology of the Family* 36, no. 2 (Autumn 2010): 93–115.

———. "(Ap)parent Boundaries: Parents' Boundary Work at Cultural Events for Families with Children Adopted from China." *Sociological Focus* 40, no. 2 (May 2007): 221–41.

Tyler May, Elaine. *Homeward Bound: American Families in the Cold War Era*. New York: Basic Books, 1988.

Yngvesson, Barbara. *Belonging in an Adopted World: Race, Identity and Transnational Adoption*. Chicago: Chicago University Press, 2010.

CHAPTER 1

The Intimate Politics of Race and Globalization

LAURA BRIGGS

In 2018 and 2019 the world watched as Donald Trump's administration in the US separated asylum seekers from their children. Far from encountering the orderly legal process required by US and international law, they found terror and chaos. It was produced as a spectacle, with some in Trump's political base actively cheering. As Republican Party operative Rick Wilson told a reporter:

> Their core supporters want anybody who's darker than a latte deported. They're not happy about immigration of any kind. They don't believe in the asylum process. They want to take and separate these families as a matter of deterrence and as a sort of theater of cruelty.[1]

In other words, they wanted the images of breastfeeding babies torn from their mothers' arms on television, wanted the sounds of wailing children who lost their parents on the radio waves. It strummed grotesque strings of pleasure for white nationalists.

The whole event provided an opportunity to take stock of where we are politically, and not just in the US. Trump has supporters everywhere and is both following and producing waves of extreme right-wing ethnic nationalism from Turkey to Sweden, Hungary to Austria, Britain to South Korea. The

---

1. Price, "Trump's Base Wants to Deport."

right in the US has intellectual debts reaching back decades into the European New Right, and of course the fantasy of a white ethnostate is anything but original; the Nazis got there first.[2] Anti-immigrant politics have spread transnationally, and while Australia's island concentration camps for migrants or Algeria's policy of abandoning immigrants in the Sahara without water, including pregnant women and children, were arguably crueler, these were done without fanfare or much international media. Routine practices in US immigrant detention of rape and beatings, disappearing people's belongings, and threatening or placing their citizen children in foster care or adoptions, are done behind closed doors.[3] They are not, in short, telegenic spectacles to whip up the venom of those who violently hate immigrants.

A funny thing happened in 2020 and 2021, however. The Trump administration moved the whole spectacle offstage—and the Joe Biden administration kept its policies in place. Trump and then Biden simply excluded virtually all those seeking to exercise their right to petition for asylum under US and international law. A "Remain in Mexico" policy put asylum seekers in squalid tent cities in Mexico to await their hearings, many never held. Then, with the COVID-19 pandemic, Trump got his "wall": his administration began using an obscure portion of the public health code, Title 42, to expel all asylum seekers without the "credible fear" interview to which they were entitled. With Biden in office, new tent cities were built on the Mexican side of the border. The one thing that changed was that the Biden administration made an exception to the Title 42 expulsions for unaccompanied minors, essentially encouraging parents to send their children across the border alone. It was a new round of child separations, but without the drama. Not surprisingly, children held on military bases were quickly reported to be encountering abusive and cruel conditions.[4]

While there are many things to say about this "theater of cruelty" and its subsequent replacement with the expulsion, here I am interested in what enabled this spectacle *and* its quieter version—that is, mainstream, ordinary foster care and adoption. Adoption and foster care generally begin with taking someone's children—almost always a single mother's. Once in the US, immigrant children taken at the border were quickly routed to existing foster homes and placement agencies. That is, a horrifying immigration policy

2. For a short history of the intellectual milieu of the white nationalist right in the US, see Stern, *Proud Boys and the White Ethnostate.*

3. Crea et al., "Unaccompanied Immigrant Children"; Hinnant, "Walk or Die"; Cave, "Timeline of Despair"; Kriel, "ICE Guards 'Systematically' Sexually Assault Detainees."

4. Gutierrez and Angulo, "As VP Harris Visits Mexico City"; Rose and Neuman, "Biden Administration Is Fighting in Court"; Flores and Aleaziz, "Immigrant Children Were Burned."

designed to deter asylum seekers relied explicitly on the existing foster and adoption infrastructure in the US. The policy's defenders were quick to point this out—that parents lose their children each day in the US; parents go to prison and their children go to foster care. While this argument collapsed a distinction that may matter—claiming the legal right to asylum is not the same thing as going to prison after being adjudicated for a crime—there is something important to attend to here, a kinship between these practices that is worth unearthing. I am not suggesting that all the ways that parents lose their children to foster care and adoption are the same as the Trumpian theater: far from it. But the case for the abolition of foster care on the grounds of its racism can count this argument in its favor as well: the aftermath of mass incarceration in foster care is hard to separate from immigrant and refugee detention camps.

In this chapter, I argue that there are at least two traditions from which the border policy, and adoption and foster care more broadly, derives. One is a humanitarian history in which parents willingly relinquish their children to protect them from harm or to promote their well-being. The period of the rise of European fascism in the 1930s and '40s gives us these humanitarian roots, when children were sent away from Spain and Germany to protect them from Francoism and Nazism, particularly Basque and Jewish children, to be fostered during the war in places that were safer for them. The second tradition is older, with origins in slavery in the Americas and US Indian policy, of separating children from parents to break resistance and to build wealth, as when children were torn from their mothers on slavery's auction block in the New World. The separation of children from tribal nations in Canada, Australia, and the US and the legacies of slavery and child separation were contested and debated through the transnational abolitionist movements and Indian policy reform movements in the Americas from the nineteenth century through the twentieth.[5] In the US, the long arc of these political movements was crystalized as reform of child-taking in the Indian Child Welfare Act of 1978 and the National Association of Black Social Workers statement on where Black children belong of 1972. Both traditions are nodded to in the 1948 Convention on Genocide, which identifies one of the elements of the crime of genocide as "forcibly transferring children of the group to another group." This law was referencing a history that was well known in 1948—recalling the hiding (and baptizing) of Jewish children during the war, as well as the more than 11,000

---

5. See Jacobs, *White Mother to a Dark Race*; Jacobs, *Generation Removed*; Briggs, *Somebody's Children*; Briggs, *Taking Children*.

Jewish children who were rounded up by the French police at the urging of the Gestapo and sent to the camp at Drancy, where only 300 survived.[6]

As the border separation of children from parents in 2018 and 2019 makes painfully evident, there is not always a bright line between the hostile, weaponized tactic of tearing children from parents and the humanitarian history. These currents have flowed apart and then together again, with the violence and cruelty of the former sometimes trying to disguise itself as the latter. In Europe and the Americas, the political history of the nation has alternated between a racial nationalism, associated with fascism and other hard-right formations, and a civic nationalism, which while often racist nevertheless imagines the nation as composed of different racial groups.[7] The history of child separation follows these broad contours, where an overt racial definition of the state allows for the genocidal separation of children, and a civic nationalism often demands a fig leaf to cover its racism, and so requires that racialized child separation look humanitarian. In what follows, this chapter begins with the paradigmatic case of producing child separation that was essentially genocidal as humanitarianism: the US Indian policy designed to "kill the Indian to save the man"—ending the nineteenth-century wars against Native people west of the Mississippi by taking their children. It then turns not to slavery's auction block but to the mid-twentieth-century reckoning with it in the US civil rights movement, sometimes called the Second Reconstruction.[8] Finally, in a nod to contemporary struggles over transnational adoption policy and the Hague Convention, it turns briefly to US evangelical Christians and the fight over adoption from Uganda. Again and again, I argue, we see the lines between caring for children by separating them from their families and child separation as a tactic of terror blur.

----

6. Roiphe, "Holocaust's Children." One Nazi legal theorist, Heinrich Krieger, provided a memo detailing US federal Indian law and Jim Crow for a National Socialist meeting on the Nuremberg laws that set out the special limitations on Jews, including stripping them of citizenship. Krieger published extensively on US race law, mostly in Germany. In one article in English, he argued that the best way to understand reservation policy (including reservations founded as camps for prisoners of war), the denial of US citizenship to American Indians (until 1924), the denial of the right to vote in elections (still not won by the time Krieger wrote in the 1930s), and the whole contradictory character of Indian law was to see it as a species of race law: "The proper nature of the tribal Indians' status is that of a racial group placed under a special police power of the United States." Whether this was the only or best understanding of Indian law, it is clear that boarding schools *could* be understood as a special instance of race laws under federal military power. See Blackhawk, "Federal Indian Law as Paradigm"; Krieger, "Principles of the Indian Law."

7. Stern, *Proud Boys and the White Ethnostate.*

8. Woodward and McFeely, *Strange Career of Jim Crow.*

Native Child Separation

Beginning in the late 1870s, separating Indigenous children from their families and communities was foundational to US federal policy to "civilize" Native peoples, to teach these children English, and to extinguish traditional religions, tribal organization, and ways of life. While it certainly was not the first time children were separated from their parents as part of a genocidal impulse in the midst of warfare, it remains one of the most paradigmatic. And because unlike Canada and Australia, the US never had a truth-and-reconciliation process in relation to this child-taking, it remains incumbent on historians to hold up this story and on all of us to remember what it means.

On July 20, 1867, during a pause in the US's nineteenth-century Indian Wars, Congress established the Indian Peace Commission to negotiate with Plains tribal nations that were warring with the US, to secure frontier settlements and land for agriculture, mining, and mineral rights, and to allow for the building of the railroads. The Peace Commission met in St. Louis, Missouri, on August 6, 1867, and traveled throughout the contested lands, from Missouri to the Dakotas to California. The commissioners argued that lasting peace was contingent on separating Indians regarded as "hostile" from those regarded as friendly, removing all Indigenous peoples to reservations away from the routes of US westward expansion, and providing for their maintenance.[9]

The official report of the Commission to the President of the United States, dated January 7, 1868, described numerous social and legal injustices to Native peoples and repeated violations of numerous treaties, including settlement on their land, acts of corruption by local agents, including overt starvation in Indigenous communities, and the culpability of Congress in failing to fulfill its legal obligations given by treaty. Commission members charged that employees of the railroad were shooting Indigenous people down "in wonton cruelty."

The purpose of detailing these depredations by white settlers was to inaugurate a new policy: of civilizing Native peoples in order to take their lands, build new settlements, and expand agriculture, railroads, and mining.[10] The Commission said that beyond the dishonesty, massacres, and unkindness of whites, the problem was also "the tribal or clannish organization" of Native people, and their failure to speak English. Thus, the Commission proposed the following plan:

---

9. Taylor et al., "Report to the President."
10. For an exemplary recent historical account, see Karuka, *Empire's Tracks*.

Agriculture and manufactures should be introduced among them as rapidly as possible; schools should be established which children should be required to attend; their barbarous dialects should be blotted out and the English language substituted. [. . .] The object of greatest solicitude should be to break down the prejudices of tribe among the Indians; to blot out the boundary lines which divide them into distinct nations, and fuse them into one homogeneous mass. Uniformity of language will do this—nothing else will.[11]

The proposal of the Peace Commission, in short, was to shift Native economies to those that would integrate well with the US and require a much smaller land base (and one that could be held by individuals, rather than tribes, making it easier for white settlers to buy or take the land), through boarding school education. This was, ultimately, exactly what happened because of the Dawes Act and boarding school policy. It is estimated that the land base of Indian country was depleted from 138 million acres of treaty land in 1887, when the Dawes Act was implemented, to a mere 48 million acres when allotment was finally halted in 1934, of which 20 million of the remaining acres were desert or semidesert.[12]

The shift from warfare to schools that could exterminate "barbarous dialects" and teach children to farm, however, was not fully taken up for nearly another decade, until after open warfare between the Sioux (or Dakota/Lakota) and the US Cavalry flared again in a dispute over mining in the Black Hills, sacred to the Lakota, in a war that included the defeat of the 7th Cavalry at the Battle of Little Bighorn ("Custer's last stand"). It is this context that makes clear that whatever veneer of humanitarianism may have covered the founding of boarding schools, it was not education but the usefulness of children in persuading Indigenous people to end their warring to defend what was negotiated by treaty. In 1877 Ulysses S. Grant annexed the Black Hills, after a military "surge" and great loss of life on both sides, including the culmination of an effort to starve Native peoples through the slaughter of buffalo and to demoralize them through assaults on women and children. Various chiefs of the Sioux federation sought peace, including Red Cloud (Oglala) and Spotted Tail (Sicangu), though the Sioux never ceded the Black Hills (even when the US carved presidents' faces in them and renamed one the Mount Rushmore National Monument).[13]

It was also the circulation of US War Department personnel from what was essentially that generation's Guantanamo Bay prison camp to running the

---

11. Prucha, *Documents of United States Indian Policy*, 107.
12. Canby, *American Indian Law in a Nutshell*.
13. Olson, *Red Cloud and the Sioux Problem*; Miller, *Ghost Dance*.

boarding school that can help us understand that it was the weaponization of child-taking that led to the boarding school policy. When it became clear that final military victory would remain elusive, the US federal government opened boarding schools. In 1878 the War Department ordered Lieutenant Richard Pratt to the Dakota Territory to begin the work of Indian education, specifically contacting "friendly" chiefs Red Cloud and Spotted Tail and, in its words, taking children as "hostages for the good behavior of their people."[14] Pratt was chosen because of his experience commanding a Black Cavalry regiment in Oklahoma ("Buffalo soldiers") and his experiments in the education and discipline of Native prisoners from the Red Hills War at Fort Marion in St. Augustine, Florida, and at the school for Black students, the Hampton Institute. The Fort Marion prisoners were considered singularly uncivilized and hostile, and Pratt had succeeded by mixing tribes, having Native peoples of different tribal nations guard and discipline each other, cutting their hair, teaching them English, compelling them to clean and cook, instituting military drills and tribunals (in which some prisoners sent others to the dungeon), and forcing prisoners to attend church. He also participated in torturing and killing some of them.[15] In 1879, while still on active duty, he opened the Carlisle Indian School, using many of these same practices and taking Dakota children far away to Pennsylvania and teaching them English, farming, and housework, while cutting their hair and confining their bodies in tight, Victorian-era clothing. Children were prevented from returning home during the summer months. Pratt relied on military-style drills, corporal punishment, and capture and incarceration of runaways to enforce his educational methods. Epidemics of cholera, influenza, and tuberculosis devastated children's numbers there, and many were buried in a cemetery on the grounds. His goal, Pratt said, was assimilation, eliminating children's "Indian-ness" as an alternative to warfare and extermination.[16]

Following what Anglo-Americans saw as the success of Pratt and the War Department, Christian missionaries and civil society "Friends of the Indian" groups began opening larger numbers of boarding schools in the 1880s to "civilize" Indigenous peoples. In 1881 Congress declared school attendance for Native children compulsory and authorized the Indian Bureau to deny benefits guaranteed by treaty right if children failed to attend; they were to "withhold rations, clothing, and other articles from those parents who resisted

---

14. Witmer, *Indian Industrial School*, 31.
15. Pratt, *Battlefield and Classroom*.
16. Mauro, *Art of Americanization*.

sending their children to school."[17] Native boarding schools spread through the West and Midwest. "Before and after" photos were popular throughout the US to show the process of "civilizing" Native children. Boarding school photos circulated like trophies among whites. As American Indian studies scholar K. Tsianina Lomawaima writes, "The famous 'before and after' pictures of Carlisle students are as much a part of American iconography as the images of Custer's Last Stand. 'Savages' shed buckskin, feathers, robes, and moccasins; long black hair was shorn or bobbed or twisted into identical, 'manageable' styles; pinafores, stiff starched collars, stockings, and black oxfords signified the 'new woman.'"[18]

The process of separating Native children from their parents was often violent and involved children as young as five or six. One witness, writing in 1930, reported on conditions on the Navajo (Diné) reservation:

> In the fall the government stockmen, farmers, and other employees go out into the back country with trucks and bring in the children to school [. . .] the wild Navajos, far back in the mountains, hide their children at the sound of a truck. So stockmen, Indian police, and other mounted men are sent ahead to round them up. The children are caught, often roped like cattle, and taken away from their parents, many times never to return. [. . .] I have heard too many stories of cowboys running down children and bringing them hogtied to town to think it is all an accident. [. . .] They are transferred from school to school, given white people's names, forbidden to speak their own tongue, and when sent to distant schools are not taken home for three years."

Some, especially children who ran away, would be taken across the country and did not return until they were sixteen or eighteen.[19]

Tribes, and occasionally even white lawyers and courts, were shocked by the violence of the Pratt system of Indian education and the removal of Indian children. In 1899 a federal district court granted a writ of habeas corpus to an Iowa tribe that demanded the return of a Native child from a boarding school, suggesting an alternative trajectory that might have ended boarding schools much sooner had it been followed. It found that tribes had to consent to the removal of a child.[20]

---

17. Theodore Fischbacher, *A Study of the Role of the Federal Government in the Education of the American Indian,* cited in Adams, "Fundamental Considerations."

18. Lomawaima, "Domesticity in the Federal Indian Schools."

19. Coolidge, "'Kid Catching' on the Navajo Reservation," 18–21.

20. In re Lelah-Puc-Ka-Chee.

Nevertheless, federal agents and missionaries ignored this court order and continued to promote compulsory off-reservation boarding schools, in some places until the late 1970s, arguing that it was essential to the civilizing process.[21] Although the details varied depending on who was in control of the Bureau of Indian Affairs, few Native children attended day schools or lived at home. Living on the reservation, especially with their parents, meant that children would revert to "savagery" by night and retain Indigenous languages, undoing the good work of the school's civilizing mission by day.[22] Visits home were also seen to impede the assimilation process and were discouraged as a matter of policy.[23] Instead, children across the country were "farmed out" in the summers, boys working as ranch hands and farm laborers, girls doing domestic labor.[24]

Scholars agree that the regimens at boarding schools were brutal. Children were punished, often beaten, for speaking Indigenous languages; dress was carefully monitored and checked by staff.[25] Some scholars have suggested that sexual abuse of both girls and boys was rife in boarding schools; an investigation into sexual abuse in boarding schools in Canada in the 1970s resulted in 3,400 complaints of such abuse. No similar investigation took place in the US, although some have argued that any full inquiry into the crimes in US Indian boarding schools would find not only starvation but also medical experimentation, involuntary sterilization of girls, and physical punishment that amounted to torture.[26] A recent survey of boarding school attendees found that nearly 30 percent reported being sexually abused there.[27]

Yet there was one official inquiry into boarding schools in the US. Throughout the 1920s Indian policy reform advocates ran ever more vociferous campaigns about the horrors of Indian policy, including ongoing land theft, detribalization, and the suppression of Native culture, language, and religious practices, and insisting that child separation and boarding school policies were a keystone of all these other processes. As a result of this public pressure, Hubert Work, the Secretary of the Interior, commissioned an independent report by the Institute for Government Research aiming to prove that the public campaign was rank exaggeration. The 1928 report, *The Problem of*

21. "Historic School Victory."

22. *Annual Report of the Commissioner of Indian Affairs*, 1880, cited in Adams, "Fundamental Considerations," 13.

23. Child, "Runaway Boys, Resistant Girls."

24. Archuleta, Child, and Lomawaima, *Away from Home*.

25. Archuleta et al., *Away from Home*.

26. Smith, *Conquest*.

27. Evans-Campbell et al., "Indian Boarding School Experience."

Indian Administration (better known as the Meriam Report, for its author), suggested that things were, if anything, worse than the press accounts had had it, with special reference to boarding schools. It described children living in overcrowded dormitories, without even adequate toilet facilities at times, subsisting on a vastly inadequate diet, subject to terrible health conditions, ill-clad. Boarding schools "operated below any reasonable standard of health and decency," as Lewis Meriam wrote. Children suffered high rates of illness and death and were subject to a curriculum of little value; the report noted continued high rates of illiteracy. They had virtually no leisure time and were forced to do manual labor to support the school (in apparent violation of child labor laws, the report noted). It urgently recommended that children be returned to their parents and communities. "The continued policy of removing Indian children from the home and placing them for years in boarding schools largely disintegrates the family and interferes with developing normal family life."[28]

The report's effect was electric. President Herbert Hoover immediately and publicly increased the allocation to boarding schools for food and clothing for children. Within a few years, a leader of the reform campaign, John Collier, was heading up the Bureau of Indian Affairs and introduced significant changes designed to recognize tribal organization and Native religion and culture, halt the reduction of the land base of Indian country, and close boarding schools in favor of day schools.[29]

The effects of boarding schools on children and Native communities were devastating. Mortality rates among children were very high. Those children who did return had often forgotten their native language and sometimes had no language in common with their parents. As one agent with the Indian Service, Dane Coolidge, noted, "Back in the hogans of their people the returned school[children] are quite unfitted for their life. [. . .] They start in all over again to learn to spin and weave and handle their sheep and goats."[30] Many attribute high rates of violence, family dysfunction, alcoholism, and drug abuse among some Native communities to the legacies of the boarding school experience and to the fact that for years, many Indian children were raised away from their parents. One scholar wrote, "I have attended several Native wellness workshops in which participants are asked to draw a family tree that shows the generation in their family in which violence, substance abuse, and

---

28. See, for example, Collier, "America's Treatment of Her Indians"; Collier, "American Congo"; Philp, *John Collier's Crusade for Indian Reform*; Institute for Government Research, *Problem of Indian Administration,* 348, 15.

29. Philp, *John Collier's Crusade for Indian Reform.*

30. Coolidge, "'Kid Catching' on the Navajo Reservation."

other related problems develop. Almost invariably, these problems began with the generation that first went to boarding school."[31] In the 1970s the American Psychiatric Association published an influential editorial that called boarding schools "a hazard to mental health."[32] In 1977 psychiatrist Joseph Westermeyer testified before Congress that Native families were in "crisis" as a result of the "ravages" of boarding schools and other familial separations, citing alcoholism and suicide attempts by parents who had lost their children.[33]

The legacy of boarding schools is not past; it lives in people who are currently alive and among us. Although day schools became more common in the 1930s, and boarding schools were largely phased out in the 1970s, the harm of being separated from parents at a young age continues into the present. In 1974 a survey by the Association of American Indian Affairs found one in three Native children separated from their parents, either in boarding school, foster care, or adoptions.[34] That number had risen by 1987, when another survey found even higher rates of children separated from their Native parents.[35] Scholars, mental health professionals, and activists may debate the proportions in which this is a legacy of policy—the habit of and deeply ingrained belief in separating Native children from parents—or of familial pain in the aftermath of the trauma of the boarding school experience. Regardless, it is amply clear that Indian families continue to suffer because of federal policy that separated children from parents, even many generations later.

When children who had been separated at early ages from their parents grew into adults, they often passed their trauma to their own children. In 2006 mental health professionals who surveyed nearly 500 Native American adults and youth found not only that the boarding school attendees in the group had much-elevated rates of suicide attempts, alcoholism, and drug abuse, but that children raised by boarding school attendees "are significantly more likely to have a general anxiety disorder, experience posttraumatic stress disorder symptoms, and have suicidal thoughts in their lifetime compared to others."[36]

Child Refugees and Humanitarianism

If US American Indian policy gives us the paradigmatic case of child-taking as a kind of warfare, it is the rise of European fascism that gives us the vision

---

31. Smith, *Conquest*, 44.

32. Besier, "Hazard to Mental Health."

33. US Congress, Senate, Select Committee on Indian Affairs.

34. Myers, *They Are Young Once*, 92–93.

35. Plantz, *Indian Child Welfare*.

36. Evans-Campbell et al., "Indian Boarding School Experience."

of the international migration of children without their parents as humanitarians. Indeed, we could say that the very idea of transnational adoption was born out of relief programs in and after World War II. The Kindertransport of mostly Jewish refugee children from Nazi-controlled areas to Britain and the evacuation of Basque children from fascist Spain were two of the best-known efforts. The Kindertransport floundered in the face of anti-Semitism, however, and the US refused these child refugees, calling them communists and job stealers, while Britain accepted them only on the condition that their visas stipulated that they would return to their home countries after the war. These and other child-evacuation efforts—including from London during the Blitz— were initiated by private agencies, who petitioned governments for visas and, in the US, lobbied Congress to change restrictive immigration laws to allow freer international movement of children.[37]

After 1945, however, these efforts were mostly organized by state actors and were centered in the US. Between 1945 and 1950 President Harry Truman brought 1,300 children from Hungary, mostly, but also from Poland, Germany, and Czechoslovakia to protect them from the Soviet army.[38] Anticommunism was also the ideology behind Operation Pedro Pan (Peter Pan to its critics), which authorized a Miami priest, Monsignor Bryan Walsh, to bring more than 14,000 children from Castro's Cuba from 1960 to 1962, to be fostered in families and wherever room could be found for them—military barracks, refugee camps, monasteries, and homes for troubled children. While the effort was long portrayed as simple humanitarianism, with a Freedom of Information search, historian Maria de los Angeles Torres found what Walsh's critics long suspected: it was part of a CIA effort to protect the children of the anti-Castro underground resistance by creating a mass exodus of children in which they could hide. From Guatemala, the CIA's propaganda organ, Radio Swan, created rumors that the government would "nationalize" children, while others circulated fears that they would be killed and turned into tinned meat. That Cuban parents were so afraid of Castro that they would send their children to relatives or even strangers in Miami also, not incidentally, made terrific anti-communist propaganda for the press.[39]

In the 1950s evangelical Christians—in the person of Harry Holt most prominently, but through a network of conservative churches—began a humanitarian program in South Korea, a Christian alternative to the scourge of communism. The Holts avoided the invasive "home study" process by sim-

---

37. Forbes and Weiss, "Unaccompanied Refugee Children"; Wyman, *Paper Walls*, 97–98.

38. See Forbes and Weiss, "Unaccompanied Refugee Children."

39. Torres, *Lost Apple*; Forbes and Weiss, "Unaccompanied Refugee Children"; Briggs, *Somebody's Children*.

ply selecting parents based on their Christian beliefs and church attendance. Others, secular figures and liberal mainline Christians, followed suit in China and Vietnam, bringing "Amerasian" children from the liaisons (and rapes) that occurred between US soldiers and civilians during World War II and then the Vietnam War. Holt and his compatriots made headlines for their adoption efforts, ultimately persuading Congress to pass enabling legislation, ease visa restrictions from Asia, and pressure more established international organizations to make transnational adoption simpler. Ultimately, the Holt family established their own organization to, as historian Arissa Oh put it, "save the children of Korea." While the Holt operation was private and sometimes exceeded what Congress or the State Department wanted, it was in many ways as clearly in harmony with US anticommunism as Monsignor Walsh's was in relationship to Cuba. It also, from the 1950s to the present, solved a significant problem for South Korea's government: how to grow the economy without building a welfare state, without providing for the children of single mothers. Over the subsequent decades, the Holt family effort became Holt International, and war refugees and Amerasian children became children that couldn't be cared for by their families—usually single mothers—often working in factories and otherwise contributing to Korea's "development" efforts.[40]

Native American and Black American Children: Communities in Rebellion

As with so much else in the US, racially minoritized populations within the country had a complex relationship to US foreign policy. On the one hand, as Kim Park Nelson among others has suggested, children brought to the US as refugees, or through private adoptions, have had to fit themselves into existing racial formations—including those from Asia, Latin America, and, in more recent times, Africa.[41] On the other hand, those groups who one way or another are or have become native to North America—Indigenous people on the one hand and the Black American descendants of slaves on the other—have troubled histories with adoption. In some ways, these were the communities most intimately connected to the shift from the widespread movement of children having something to do with refugees to the ways adoption began

---

40. Oh, *To Save the Children*; Kim, *Adopted Territory*; Park Nelson, *Invisible Asians*; Hübinette, *Comforting an Orphaned Nation*; Dorow, *Transnational Adoption*; Evans, *Lost Daughters of China*; Yngvesson, *Belonging in an Adopted World*; Johnson, *Wanting a Daughter, Needing a Son*.

41. Park Nelson, *Invisible Asians*.

to traffic with something even darker—a response to political rebellion in a deeply paranoid, dualistic Cold War world of communists and anticommunists. Black and Native communities were among the first to raise the alarm that families and communities were losing their children to punish them for political activism at a time when political rebellion was quickly tied to communism.

We all know the number produced by the Association of American Indian Affairs in the 1970s to demand greater legal protections for Native communities and families: that, at that time, one in three Native American children were in out-of-home care. One thing that became clear from that group's investigations into children who were sometimes taken from reservations—without any color of law—is that involvement with Indigenous sovereignty movements, particularly the American Indian Movement, put people at risk for losing their children.[42] It was a conspicuous echo of the use of boarding schools a century and a half earlier to effect the final end to the nineteenth-century Indian Wars on the North American continent. Taking people's children and attempting to strip them of their languages and traditional ways of life is a remarkably effective way of stopping rebellions.

The other thing that put people at risk was when single mothers got welfare—the Aid to Families with Dependent Children program that was the largest government program providing support for children from the 1930s to the 1990s. When activists insisted that women in Native communities were entitled to access to these programs, state governments and social workers saw this as effectively ending claims to self-government and sovereignty for tribal nations with respect to children. And so with welfare came state governments' right to take children—which they did, in massive numbers, ignoring the orders of tribal courts about children's placement. In 1978 the Association of American Indian Affairs succeeded in passing the Indian Child Welfare Act, which was supposed to return control of child placement to tribal courts. But that measure has been under constant assault in one way or another ever since—whether from social workers who argue that alcoholism, meth, or crack cocaine are such public health crises in Native communities that kids must be placed off the reservation or, alternately, by the conservative Goldwater Institute trying to wrest control of lucrative Indian gaming from tribal nations through a sideways attack on Native sovereignty, by going after their control of their children.[43]

---

42. Unger, *Destruction of American Indian Families.*

43. Briggs, *Somebody's Children*; Jacobs, *Generation Removed*; Cohen, "Indian Affairs, Adoption, and Race."

Black communities in the US in some ways fared even worse, and for some of the same causes—single mothers receiving welfare and political rebellion. In the 1950s and '60s, in the context of the civil rights movement, the racist right tried to turn the tables on the upstanding church folk who were the movement's public face by insisting on the sexual immorality of the majority of Black folks. Throughout this period, at a regional and local level, shaming unmarried mothers was a tactic of white segregationists. Children became a crucial issue in the movement, one of the front lines of civil rights. After 1954 and the *Brown v. Board of Education* decision and Emmett Till's murder in 1955, children were the public face of the desegregation of public spaces. In 1963 it was the Children's Crusade in Birmingham that cost high-profile white supremacist Bull Connor of Birmingham his job, as their courage in facing down his fire hoses and dogs was splashed across every newspaper in the country.[44]

White segregationists fought back by suggesting that their mothers were immoral, sexually loose women. From 1958 to 1964 in Mississippi, the legislature tried to pass mandatory sterilization laws for Black women who had "bastard" children. As lawyers and the incipient welfare rights movement pressed on the de facto exclusion of Black, Native, and Puerto Rican women from AFDC programs, welfare officials played cat and mouse with these new clients, trying to catch them with a man in the house by surprising them late at night and stationing someone at the back door or window, searching for men's underwear or shaving things, getting the scoop from gossipy neighbors. If they found evidence of heterosexual sex, they would argue that the children had a "substitute father" who should pay for their support and throw the woman and children off welfare. The more Black Americans in the South fought for civil rights, the more officials cut benefits to working-class women and children; between 1957 and 1967 the city of Birmingham decreased its total yearly expenditures on welfare from $31,000 to a mere $12,000.[45]

Throughout the 1940s and 1950s, progressives and conservatives clashed over whether giving cash benefits to impoverished people kept women and children alive or were a wasteful exercise in taxing and squandering money that simply contributed to immorality and wastefulness among those who received benefits. In the context of desegregation and rising Black unemployment (as defense jobs vanished with the end of the Second World War, and plants and other businesses were asked to lay people off to make way for returning soldiers—explicitly, women, but often Black American men

---

44. De Schweinitz, *If We Could Change the World.*
45. Kelley, *Race Rebels,* 95; Solinger, *Beggars and Choosers.*

were fired, too, for good measure), welfare was often weaponized as a tool to fight Black communities in rebellion. All over the South and the North, Black women lost benefits for failing to keep a "suitable home" or for having "illegitimate" children. In Louisiana in 1960, the legislature cut off thousands of children as part of a "segregation package" of legislation designed to punish the Black community for the radical act of sending four little girls to two white first grades in New Orleans. Governor Jimmie Davis called unmarried mothers "prostitutes"; hundreds were urged to "voluntarily" relinquish their children now that they had no way to feed them. The National Urban League responded with "Operation Feed the Babies," which became an international effort to raise money to help mothers pay for rent and clothing, while Black churches cooked meals and distributed thousands of pounds of food to help families keep body and soul together through the crisis.[46]

The culmination of these processes happened in 1961, when Congress authorized funding for the program known as ADC–Foster Care, which provided welfare funds for states to take the children of welfare mothers and put them in foster care. In the first year of the program alone, 150,000 southern children were placed in out-of-home care.[47] In subsequent years, ADC and foster care were transformed from a system that ignored Black children to one that acted vigorously to take them in the name of protecting them from the consequences of poverty. Although the Urban League fought vigorously for welfare payments that would keep children in their homes instead, the Eisenhower administration insisted that it was a "states rights" issue in which they could not intervene.[48]

It's worth noting, also, that the ADC–Foster Care program was what the much-maligned 1972 National Association of Black Social Workers statement was about: trying to find a tactic that protected Black unmarried mothers from losing their children. Black children were rarely being placed for adoption voluntarily; this was a fight about what became of children who were taken, sometimes maliciously, by welfare officials who found the state of Black communities' housing, poverty, and morals wanting. By claiming that Black children belonged in Black families, the NABSW was trying to shine a light

---

46. Lindhorst and Leighninger, "Ending Welfare as We Know It"; Bell, *Aid to Dependent Children.*

47. Altstein and McRoy, *Does Family Preservation Serve?*, 6–7; Schene, "Past, Present and Future Roles." This pattern was not limited to the South; in New York City, for example, the percentage of Black and Puerto Rican children (vs. white children) also soared after 1960. See Grant, *Politicization of Foster Care,* 31.

48. Lawrence-Webb, "African American Children"; Lindhorst and Leighninger, "Ending Welfare as We Know It"; Bell, *Aid to Dependent Children*; Brissett-Chapman and Isaacs-Shockley, *Children in Social Peril.*

on the positive resources of Black families: the ability to provide their children the wherewithal to survive and find psychic wholeness in a culture that often hated them. When white families adopted Black children, they took the cost of raising them off the hands of the state and vastly expanded the child welfare system's ability to take them in the first place. This was, and remains, the crucial issue in all fights about adoption policy, domestic and foreign: there is not and never has been a fixed number of children who are simply out there, "available" for adoption, and any time you make adoption easy, you also make it easy for birth families to lose their children.

The Hague Convention and Uganda

For example, consider the current state of transnational adoption. It seems fair to say that most of the people involved in negotiating and ratifying the Hague Convention on Intercountry Adoption believed that creating an orderly legal process for transnational adoption would result in an increase in the numbers of adoptees, much as had occurred with the ratification of the Convention on the Rights of the Child decades earlier. But the opposite has happened: the number of transnational adoptions has decreased dramatically and steadily.[49] While researchers disagree about the causes, based on my and others' research, I would argue that the strongest case is this: because the Hague Convention created a legal process that insisted on a degree of due process for birth parents, it stopped a lot of adoption agencies in their tracks. It became steadily more difficult to move children whose relinquishment status was unclear into transnational adoptions.[50] In Guatemala it provided a mechanism through which human rights groups could demand justice for birth parents who had been saying for decades that their children had been kidnapped and provided false birth certificates to get them out of the country.[51] While many have said that Guatemala was a notoriously bad actor, well known in international human rights circles for its illegal adoptions (which were documented in the Guatemalan press beginning in the 1990s, despite international press claims that the first case was discovered in 2008), the international decline in

49. Sarah Park Dahlen, "The Foreign Adopted Children's Act (FACE)," preserves the original posting and analysis of the Families for Orphans Act from Ethica in 2009, from their now defunct, excellent site.

50. Selman, "Global Decline of Intercountry Adoption"; Smolin, "Child Laundering and the Hague Convention"; Loibl, "Child Trafficking for Adoption Purposes."

51. See Lopez, "Dangerous Rumors"; Colindres and Morales, "Guatemala: Babies for Sale"; and, for example, Lásker, "¿Rodil, traficante?"; "Abogado Rubén Darío Ventura"; Najarro, "Guerra"; Avilés, "Desde Guatemala, red internacional."

adoptions suggests that this story was more typical than many had wanted to believe. The sharp decline in numbers following the ratification of the Hague Convention suggests that the globe-girdling system of transnational adoption relied on a certain amount of chaos and illegality, clandestine payoffs, and somewhat or violently coercive methods to get children into the system.

The US is a disproportionate player in this system because of size—it is the largest receiving country in intercountry adoption by raw numbers, although others have higher per capita rates—so it makes sense to pay particular attention to the US history. It was also an outlier in terms of acceding to the convention, waiting a long fourteen years between signing and fully adopting it, from 1994 to 2008, a lag resulting in no small part from Guatemala's troubles in coming into compliance. Guatemala was a small country in size but an outsized contributor to the population of transnational adoptees in the US. Even in the first five years after the US and Guatemala joined the community of nations within the Hague Convention boundaries, it still seemed possible to predict that transnational adoption would recover. While rates of transnational adoption were declining, the new mechanisms to ensure that there were meaningful protections for birth families that enabled them to plausibly contest adoptions based in exploitation or even kidnapping seemed limited in scope. If we believed the system was fundamentally sound, then adoption rates should recover. More cynically, we could say that growing global economic inequalities and shrinking state welfare systems seemed to predict that transnational adoption rates would stabilize at some lower, but persistent rate. Instead, transnational adoption has continued its steady decline globally, across all or nearly all receiving countries.[52]

At the same time, though, the likelihood that those adoptions are from African nations has expanded exponentially, confounding those, especially in the US, who predicted that transnational adoption would never extend to Black children because of the legacies of slavery and the ways it relied on Blackness as a marker of those who could not be the legal kin of those who enslaved them—even as we know how often they were in fact kin of their enslavers.[53] As we know, slavery was not just a US American problem, or even an Americas problem; it is also part of the history of Europe, of Holland, Germany, France, Portugal, Spain, Great Britain, and many others whose wealth

---

52. Selman, "Global Decline of Intercountry Adoption"; Smolin, "Child Laundering and the Hague Convention."

53. In "Private Race Preferences in Family Formation" and "Where Do Black Children Belong?," Bartholet argues that the preference to adopt transnationally was always a preference to adopt a child who was not Black. On enslavement and kinship, see, for example, Hartman, *Lose Your Mother*; Spillers, "Mama's Baby, Papa's Maybe."

was acquired through slavery—or slaving—in their colonies. I have to say that I was never inclined to the view that Black kids could not become adoptable, because it seemed to me that it sprang from the imagination that transnational adoption was largely governed by the inclinations and preferences of individual families, consumer-driven, rather than primarily organized by the state-to-state agreements and adoption agencies that direct the desires of individuals and couples who want to adopt. And from that perspective, it is official ideologies—liberal notions of human rights, for example—that operate institutional "feelings," not the officially archaic ideas, mostly from the English and US American worlds, of racial separation, regardless of how much they may matter to individuals.

So transnational adoption has expanded abruptly to African countries, particularly through the work and missions of evangelical Christians, including those who claim an "adoption gospel" that puts adoption at the center of their theology. For these believers, the biblical injunction to care for "orphans" (though not so much the "widows" always mentioned as the first half of that mandate) and the metaphor of the apostle Paul in claiming that the followers of Jesus are a people "adopted" by God mean that contemporary Christians should raise adopted children. Working primarily through religious networks, they have established orphanages that funnel children into international adoptions and have often treated international agreements and legalities as "red tape" or just as obstacles to carrying out religious obligations—which may mean neglecting the fine points of ensuring that their mothers or other kin have in fact relinquished them. They focus particularly on the "fatherless," children being raised by single mothers, as part of a larger set of beliefs about the weakness of women and the necessity of patriarchs.[54]

As a result, we are seeing the same dreary pattern from Latin America and Asian nations enacted in African regions: vast amounts of money (30,000 euros, 50,000 USD) chasing so-called orphans, followed by the shocked discovery that children have been involuntarily separated from their families, disappeared, kidnapped. For example, in 2017 a group called European Adoption Consultants—a US group that got their start in 1991 placing children from Russia—was found to have placed two children from Uganda whose mothers were tricked, through church networks, into relinquishing children they believed would be getting an education in the US. Adoptive parents were told that they were living in an orphanage after their single mothers neglected and abused them, though God's Mercy orphanage seems to have been built for the agency, after it found adopters who would pay significant amounts of

54. Joyce, *Child Catchers*.

money to intermediaries for the children, including a law firm that processed the guardianship order and government officials. Journalists suggested that there was evidence of others.[55]

THIS HISTORY—taking children from Native communities warring with the US; from US Black communities where mothers received welfare in the context of desegregation and the civil rights struggle; from impoverished communities in places like Guatemala, Russia, and India—laid the groundwork for the Trump administration's effort to prevent people from applying for refugee status by taking their children and for the ways the Biden administration has first encouraged children to cross as "unaccompanied minors" and subsequently looked the other way as three separate whistleblowers have come forward with allegations of cruel treatment of children in detention. The idea that impoverished and powerless people lose their children is one that those in the US—and perhaps elsewhere—have become tragically inured to. The older system, of taking refugee children whose parents *have voluntarily relinquished them,* is no longer the norm. Thus it is that the involuntarily relinquished children of those seeking refugee status can simply enter the mainstream of the US foster and adoption program.

Bibliography

"Abogado Rubén Darío Ventura fue capturado por supuesta participación en robo de niños." *La Hora,* January 11, 1995.

Adams, David Wallace. "Fundamental Considerations: The Deep Meaning of Native American Schooling, 1880–1900." *Harvard Educational Review* 58, no. 1 (1988): 1–29.

Altstein, Howard, and Ruth G. McRoy. *Does Family Preservation Serve a Child's Best Interests?* Washington, DC: Georgetown University Press, 2002.

Archuleta, Margaret, Brenda Child, and K. Tsianina Lomawaima. *Away from Home: American Indian Boarding School Experiences, 1879–2000.* Phoenix, AZ: Heard Museum, 2000. Distributed by Museum of New Mexico Press.

Avilés, Jaime. "Desde Guatemala, red internacional de tráfico de niños." *La Jornada,* September 22, 1997.

Bartholet, Elizabeth. "Private Race Preferences in Family Formation." *Yale Law Journal* 107, no. 7 (1998): 2351–56.

---

55. Kaye and Drash, "Kids for Sale." There was a Ugandan response—which critics say was authored by the "traffickers"—that says that the adoptions were perfectly legitimate, and mothers took their children back after getting tired of being accused of "selling" their children; Malaba, "Uganda: Adoption Saga."

———. "Where Do Black Children Belong? The Politics of Race Matching in Adoption." *University of Pennsylvania Law Review* 139, no. 5 (1991): 1163–1256.

Beiser, Morton. "A Hazard to Mental Health: Indian Boarding Schools." *American Journal of Psychiatry* 131, no. 3 (1974): 305–6.

Bell, Winifred. *Aid to Dependent Children*. New York: Columbia University Press, 1965.

Blackhawk, Maggie. "Federal Indian Law as Paradigm within Public Law." *Harvard Law Review* 132, no. 7 (May 2019): 1791–1877.

Briggs, Laura. *Somebody's Children: The Politics of Transracial and Transnational Adoption*. Durham, NC: Duke University Press, 2012.

———. *Taking Children: A History of American Terror*. Oakland: University of California Press, 2020.

Brissett-Chapman, Sheryl, and Mareasa Issacs-Shockley. *Children in Social Peril: A Community Vision for Preserving Family Care of African American Children and Youths*. Washington, DC: Child Welfare League of America, 1997.

Canby, William, Jr. *American Indian Law in a Nutshell*. St. Paul, MN: West Academic, 2014.

Cave, Damien. "A Timeline of Despair in Australia's Offshore Detention Centers." *New York Times,* June 26, 2019. https://www.nytimes.com/2019/06/26/world/australia/australia-manus-suicide.html.

Child, Brenda. "Runaway Boys, Resistant Girls: Rebellion at Flandreau and Haskell, 1900–1940." *Journal of American Indian Education* 35, no. 3 (1996): 49–57.

Cohen, Andrew. "Indian Affairs, Adoption, and Race: The Baby Veronica Case Comes to Washington." *The Atlantic*, April 12, 2013. https://www.theatlantic.com/national/archive/2013/04/indian-affairs-adoption-and-race-the-baby-veronica-case-comes-to-washington/274758/.

Colindres, F., and C. Morales. "Guatemala: Babies for Sale." *World Press Review* (from *La Crónica*), May 1994.

Collier, John. "America's Treatment of Her Indians." *Current History* (August 1923): 771–78.

———. "American Congo." *Survey*, August 1923.

Coolidge, Dane. "'Kid Catching' on the Navajo Reservation: 1930." In *The Destruction of American Indian Families*, edited by Steven Unger, 18–22. New York: Association on American Indian Affairs, 1977.

Crea, Thomas M., Anayeli Lopez, Theresa Taylor, and Dawnya Underwood. "Unaccompanied Immigrant Children in Long Term Foster Care: Identifying Needs and Best Practices from a Child Welfare Perspective." *Children and Youth Services Review,* no. 92 (September 1, 2018): 56–64.

Dahlen, Sarah Park. "The Foreign Adopted Children's Act (FACE) and Families for Orphans Act." *Musings on Korean Diaspora, Children's Literature, and Adoption* (blog), July 27, 2009. https://readingspark.wordpress.com/2009/07/27/the-foreign-adopted-childrens-act-face-and-families-for-orphans-act/.

De Schweinitz, Rebecca. *If We Could Change the World: Young People and America's Long Struggle for Racial Equality*. Chapel Hill: University of North Carolina Press, 2011.

Dorow, Sara K. *Transnational Adoption: A Cultural Economy of Race, Gender, and Kinship*. New York: New York University Press, 2006.

Evans, Karin. *The Lost Daughters of China: Adopted Girls, Their Journey to America, and the Search for a Missing Past*. New York: TarcherPerigee, 2008.

Evans-Campbell, Teresa, Karina L. Walters, Cynthia R. Pearson, and Christopher D. Campbell. "Indian Boarding School Experience, Substance Use, and Mental Health among Urban Two-Spirit American Indian/Alaska Natives." *The American Journal of Drug and Alcohol Abuse* 38, no. 5 (2012): 421–27.

Flores, Adolfo, and Hamed Aleaziz. "Immigrant Children Were Burned with Scalding Water and Threatened at an Emergency Shelter, a Whistleblower Said." *BuzzFeed News,* September 8, 2021. https://www.buzzfeednews.com/article/adolfoflores/fort-bliss-immigrant-children-shelter-whistleblower.

Forbes, Susan S., and Patricia Fagan Weiss. "Unaccompanied Refugee Children: The Evolution of U.S. Policies." *Migration News,* no. 3 (1985): 3–36.

Grant, L. Trevor. *The Politicization of Foster Care in New York City.* Jamaica, NY: Yacos, 1996.

Gutierrez, Gabe, and Erika Angulo. "As VP Harris Visits Mexico City, a Migrant Tent Camp Grows in Border Town." *NBC News,* June 8, 2021. https://www.nbcnews.com/news/latino/vp-harris-visits-mexico-city-migrant-tent-camp-grows-border-town-rcna11145.

Hartman, Saidiya. *Lose Your Mother: A Journey along the Atlantic Slave Route.* New York: Farrar, Straus and Giroux, 2008.

Hinnant, Lori. "Walk or Die: Algeria Strands 13,000 Migrants in the Sahara." *AP NEWS,* April 20, 2021. https://apnews.com/article/deserts-niger-africa-international-news-algeria-9ca5592217aa4acd836b9ee091ebfc20.

"Historic School Victory." *Indian Family Defense: A Bulletin of the Association on American Indian Affairs, Inc.* 1976.

Hübinette, Tobias. *Comforting an Orphaned Nation.* Seoul: Jimoondang, 2006.

In re Lelah-Puc-Ka-Chee. 98 F. 429. Northern District Iowa, 1899.

Institute for Government Research and Lewis Meriam. *The Problem of Indian Administration.* Johnson Reprint, 1928.

Jacobs, Margaret. *A Generation Removed: Fostering and Adoption of Indigenous Children in the Postwar World.* Lincoln: University of Nebraska Press, 2014.

———. *White Mother to a Dark Race: Settler Colonialism, Materialism, and the Removal of Indigenous Children in the American West and Australia, 1880–1940.* Lincoln: University of Nebraska Press, 2009.

Johnson, Kay Ann. *Wanting a Daughter, Needing a Son: Abandonment, Adoption, and Orphanage Care in China.* Edited and with an introduction by Amy Klatzkin. St. Paul, MN: Yeong & Yeong, 2004.

Joyce, Kathryn. *The Child Catchers: Rescue, Trafficking, and the New Gospel of Adoption.* New York: Public Affairs, 2013.

Karuka, Manu. *Empire's Tracks: Indigenous Nations, Chinese Workers, and the Transcontinental Railroad.* Oakland: University of California Press, 2019.

Kaye, Randi, and Wayne Drash. "Kids for Sale: 'My mom was tricked.'" *CNN,* October 14, 2017. https://edition.cnn.com/2017/10/12/health/uganda-adoptions-investigation-ac360/index.html.

Kelley, Robin D. G. *Race Rebels: Culture, Politics, and the Black Working Class.* New York: Free Press, 1996.

Kim, Eleana J. *Adopted Territory: Transnational Korean Adoptees and the Politics of Belonging.* Durham, NC: Duke University Press, 2010.

Krieger, Heinrich. "Principles of the Indian Law and the Act of June 18, 1934." *George Washington Law Review,* no. 3 (1935): 279–308.

Kriel, Lomi. "ICE Guards 'Systematically' Sexually Assault Detainees in an El Paso Detention Center, Lawyers Say." *ProPublica,* August 14, 2020. https://www.propublica.org/article/ice-guards-systematically-sexually-assault-detainees-in-an-el-paso-detention-center-lawyers-say?token=hrbLbJIMK_Aw_DSS2U-2OEkFSkO-mHm-.

Lásker, Sebastián. "¿Rodil, Traficante?" *Prensa Libre / Archivo de Recortajes CIRMA / 31.4 Niñez.* 1994.

Lawrence-Webb, Claudia. "African American Children in the Modern Child Welfare System: A Legacy of the Flemming Rule." In *Serving African American Children: Child Welfare Perspectives,* edited by Sondra Jackson and Sheryl Brissett-Chapman, 9–30. New York: Transaction, 1998.

Lindhorst, Taryn, and Leslie Leighninger. "'Ending Welfare as We Know It' in 1960: Louisiana's Suitable Home Law." *Social Service Review* 77, no. 4 (December 1, 2003): 564–84.

Loibl, Elvira. "Child Trafficking for Adoption Purposes: A Criminological Analysis of the Illegal Adoption Market." In *The Palgrave International Handbook of Human Trafficking,* edited by John Winterdyk and Jackie Jones, 401–17. Cham: Springer International, 2020.

Lomawaima, K. Tsianina. "Domesticity in the Federal Indian Schools: The Power of Authority over Mind and Body." *American Ethnologist* 20, no. 2 (1993): 227–40.

Lopez, Laura. "Dangerous Rumors." *Time,* April 18, 1994.

Malaba, Tom. "Uganda: Adoption Saga—Americans Forced to Return Ugandan Children." *AllAfrica,* August 20, 2018. https://allafrica.com/stories/201808200176.html.

Mauro, Hayes Peter. *The Art of Americanization at the Carlisle Indian School.* Albuquerque: University of New Mexico Press, 2011.

Miller, David Humphreys. *Ghost Dance.* New York: Duell, Sloan and Pearce, 1959.

Myers, Joseph A. *They Are Young Once but Indian Forever: A Summary and Analysis of Investigative Hearings on Indian Child Welfare, April 1980.* Oakland, CA: American Indian Lawyer Training Program, 1981.

Najarro, Oneida. "Guerra: la casa-cuna patrocinada por Rodil Peralta está legalizada." *Siglo 21,* May 2, 1994.

Oh, Arissa. *To Save the Children of Korea: The Cold War Origins of International Adoption.* Stanford, CA: Stanford University Press, 2015.

Olson, James C. *Red Cloud and the Sioux Problem.* Lincoln: University of Nebraska Press, 1965.

Park, "The Foreign Adopted Children's Act (FACE)," https://readingspark.wordpress.com/2009/07/27/the-foreign-adopted-childrens-act-face-and-families-for-orphans-act/.

Park Nelson, Kim. *Invisible Asians: Korean American Adoptees, Asian American Experiences, and Racial Exceptionalism.* New Brunswick, NJ: Rutgers University Press, 2016.

Philp, Kenneth R. *John Collier's Crusade for Indian Reform, 1920–1954.* Tucson: University of Arizona Press, 1977.

Plantz, Margaret. *Indian Child Welfare: A Status Report: Final Report of the Survey of Indian Child Welfare and Implementation of the Indian Child Welfare Act and Section 428 of the Adoption Assistance and Child Welfare Act of 1980.* Washington, DC: US Department of the Interior, 1988.

Pratt, Richard Henry. *Battlefield and Classroom: Four Decades with the American Indian, 1867–1904.* Oklahoma City: University of Oklahoma Press, 2003.

Price, Greg. "Trump's Base Wants to Deport 'Anybody Darker than a Latte,' a Leading Republican Strategist Claims." *Newsweek,* July 11, 2018.

Prucha, Francis Paul, ed. *Documents of United States Indian Policy.* Lincoln: University of Nebraska Press, 1990.

Roiphe, Anne. "Holocaust's Children, One by One by One." *New York Times,* February 7, 1997.

Rose, Joel, and Scott Neuman. "The Biden Administration Is Fighting in Court to Keep a Trump-Era Immigration Policy." *NPR,* September 20, 2021. https://www.npr.org/2021/09/20/1038918197/the-biden-administration-is-fighting-in-court-to-keep-a-trump-era-immigration-po.

Schene, Patricia A. "Past, Present, and Future Roles of Child Protective Services." *The Future of Children* 8, no. 1 (1998): 23–38.

Selman, Peter. "The Global Decline of Intercountry Adoption: What Lies Ahead?" *Social Policy and Society* 11, no. 3 (July 2012): 381–97.

Smith, Andrea. *Conquest: Sexual Violence and American Indian Genocide.* Cambridge, MA: South End, 2005.

Smolin, David M. "Child Laundering and the Hague Convention on Intercountry Adoption: The Future and Past of Intercountry Adoption." *University of Louisville Law Review* 48, no. 3 (2009–10): 441–98.

Solinger, Rickie. *Beggars and Choosers: How the Politics of Choice Shapes Adoption, Abortion, and Welfare in the United States.* New York: Hill and Wang, 2002.

Spillers, Hortense. "Mama's Baby, Papa's Maybe: An American Grammar Book." *diacritics* 17, no. 2 (1987): 65–81.

Stern, Alexandra Minna. *Proud Boys and the White Ethnostate: How the Alt-Right Is Warping the American Imagination.* Boston, MA: Beacon, 2019.

Taylor, N. G., J. B. Henderson, W. T. Sherman, and W. S. Harney. "Report to the President by the Indian Peace Commission." *Annual Report of the Commissioner of Indian Affairs for the Year 1868.* Washington, DC: Government Printing Office, 1868.

Torres, Maria de los Angeles. *The Lost Apple: Operation Pedro Pan, Cuban Children in the U.S., and the Promise of a Better Future.* Boston, MA: Beacon, 2004.

Unger, Steven, ed. *The Destruction of American Indian Families.* New York: Association on American Indian Affairs, 1977.

US Congress, Senate, Select Committee on Indian Affairs. "Indian Child Welfare Statistical Survey, July 1976, Appendix G." Indian Child Welfare Act of 1977: Hearing, on S. 1214, To Establish Standards for the Placement of Indian Children in Foster or Adoptive Homes, To Prevent the Breakup of Indian Families, and For Other Purposes. 95th Congress, 1st sess., August 4, 1977. Washington, DC: US Government Printing Office, 1977.

Witmer, Linda. *The Indian Industrial School: Carlisle, Pennsylvania 1879–1918.* Carlisle, PA: Cumberland County Historical Society, 1993.

Woodward, C. Vann, and William S. McFeely. *The Strange Career of Jim Crow.* Oxford: Oxford University Press, 2002.

Wyman, David S. *Paper Walls: America and the Refugee Crisis, 1938–1941.* Amherst: University of Massachusetts Press, 1968.

Yngvesson, Barbara. *Belonging in an Adopted World: Race, Identity, and Transnational Adoption.* Chicago: University of Chicago Press, 2010.

CHAPTER 2

US Adoption and Fostering of Immigrants' Children

A Mirror on Whose Rights Matter

PAMELA ANNE QUIROZ

The year 2016 marked a thirty-five-year low in transnational adoptions by US parents to 5,648 children adopted from different countries, and 2019 marked the year that 5,400 Latino children were separated from their families.[1] The decline in transnational adoptions has occurred for a variety of reasons that include the implementation of the Hague Treaty designed to minimize illicit adoption practices. Parallel to these changes, we have seen a shift in US immigration policy, with citizen and immigrant children separated from their [detained or deported] parents and placed in the child welfare system. In our current political climate, where children are being forcibly separated from their parents, the risks for Latino children (and their families) are substantial, as deportation and detention provide a new means of satisfying the desire for children in a diminishing transnational adoption market.[2] Drawing from an online domestic Latino adoption forum and interviews with foster and adoptive parents in 2015, this chapter examines the intersection of adoption and implementation of immigration policy to explore an issue salient in transnational adoption—the exploitation of children and families. Narratives of foster and adoptive parents convey whose rights matter in this moral dilemma as

---

1. US Department of State, "Annual Report on Intercountry Adoption Narrative" (2016).

2. On the changing and declining adoption demographics, see the appendix by Peter Selman in this volume.

biological parents are transformed into "temporary caretakers," "criminals," and "unworthy aliens."

Currently, enforcement of US immigration policy results in family separation and the placement of children in detention centers or the child welfare system. And despite laws that prohibit families from adopting children of migrants, investigative reporters recently found information revealing the adoption of migrant children.[3] These revelations by the press are not the first hint of illicit adoption activities involving Latino children of "mixed" status or undocumented families. In 2011 the Applied Research Center conducted a study, *Shattered Families,* that revealed the adoption of thousands of children of undocumented immigrants whose parents were detained or deported. This reality, added to the substantial changes in transnational adoption policies and immigration implementation practices, suggests a connection between these events and the increase of Latino children in foster care systems in the past decade.[4] As the Trump administration pursued its version of addressing immigration, it seemed certain this would have become a significant problem for "mixed" status and immigrant Latino families. These activities offer a new mirror on human rights and the tensions between family-building through adoption and the processes through which adoptive families are formed. By featuring a current aspect of domestic adoption that stems from detention and deportation of (overwhelmingly) Latino parents, I examine the complex nature of adoptive parenting that is too often elided—how building family occurs because of the loss of family. In many situations if not most cases, loss does not refer to the death of biological parents, since most children adopted domestically and transnationally have at least one biological parent living. Instead, "loss" results from a variety of separations, including placement of children into orphanages by biological parents who are unable to care for them or abandonment. We have even found nefarious practices by adoption mediators who persuade or deceive biological parents into relinquishing their children and even kidnapping children to send them to other countries.[5] While most of these practices have been associated with transnational adoption, in the US loss of family currently occurs through traumatic and forcible separation of children from their biological (but undocumented) parents.

Such incremental changes in US adoption policy involve the US finally ratifying and implementing the Hague Convention Treaty on Intercountry Adoption in 2008 which was created to protect all participants from illicit

---

3. Burke and Mendoza, "Deported Parents May Lose Kids."

4. Wessler, *Shattered Families.*

5. Rotabi, "Fraud in Intercountry Adoption."

activities and abuse in the transnational adoption process. The US had signed the Treaty in 1993; however, it did not ratify and implement it until 2008. Prior to ratification, most attempts of sending countries to restrict transnational adoptions met with resistance on the part of US adoption advocates who argued that preventing transnational adoption would only exacerbate the plight of poor children.[6] Between 1989 and 2004 the US was the largest receiving country of children from other countries as US citizens engaged in adopting hundreds of thousands of children. In 2005 these numbers began to diminish significantly as implementation of the Hague Treaty resulted in seriously reducing the number of US adoptions from other countries.

As an adoptive parent, I was approached in 2013 by one of four Chicago agencies trying to place Latino children with foster and adoptive parents. I later asked to interview participants to understand their perspectives on parenting citizen-children (children born in the US but also having at least one parent who is undocumented) who ended up in the Illinois child welfare system. Only a small number of participants responded (fourteen). Trying to achieve an understanding of adoptive and foster parents' views of Latino children, I looked to the Latino Domestic Adoption forum (2012–14) and performed an online ethnography of parent participation in fostering and adopting citizen-children and immigrant children of Latino immigrants.

Following a brief review of US adoption history, and a look at the current intersection of adoption and immigration, I present analysis of Latino adoption forum threads and describe foster, prospective, and adoptive parents' views of immigrant and citizen-children and their biological parents. Similar to US transnational adoptive parents online, these parents characterize the situations that bring citizen and immigrant children to them as "right" and as "destiny," ignoring the profound impact of physical, legal, and social relocation on adoptees and their biological families. These practices highlight the dilemmas raised by the United Nation's Convention on the Rights of the Child (1993), which guarantees each child the right to be raised in a family, have their basic needs met, and retain their identity. Though the US signed the treaty in 1993, it did not ratify and implement it until 2008. Such practices also point to the creation of a new market for US adoptive parents, a market that meets the litmus test of faith-based adoptive parents and prospective parents with the best of intentions, providing a child a home while satisfying their desire to become parents.

---

6. See Bartholet, "International Adoption."

US Adoption History

There are two periods in the US when formal adoptions increased substantially. The first occurred between 1853 and 1929 when more than 200,000 orphans and homeless children were relocated via "Orphan Trains" from East Coast cities to the Midwest and West Coast. A substantial number of these children were not orphans at all but children who were immigrant and poor. The results were mixed for the children. Many were adopted, others remained foster children, and some were treated as indentured servants or field hands.[7] Critics have portrayed this child welfare movement as a means of addressing the influx of immigrants from Ireland and Eastern and Southern Europe (largely Roman Catholic populations) and overcrowding in eastern cities. One objective of this movement was an effort to resocialize immigrant children who we now accept as "white" but who at that time were not regarded as white or proper Americans (children of Italians, Germans, Poles, and Irish).

One example of the nonwhite status of children from Eastern Europe and Ireland is Linda Gordon's historical analysis of forty Irish orphans sent from New York City to two small mining communities in Arizona, Clifton and Morenci, to live with Mexican families.[8] White families in the small mining communities vehemently responded to the adoption of white children by Mexicans, and ultimately vigilantes forcibly removed the children from their Mexican homes and placed them with white families. The US courts, including the US Supreme Court, sanctioned the actions of the vigilantes by leaving the children in the white homes. Gordon's account further demonstrates the shifting nature of racial categories with the case of the Irish orphans, as these children were unacceptable in the east because of their ethnicity but were racially reclassified as white in Arizona. White children needed to be rescued. This incident personifies the attitudes of early twentieth-century America toward "race-mixing" in general, and Mexicans specifically, as cross-cultural placements occurred in a direction unthinkable to the dominant population. Much in the same way that so-called miscegenation was regarded as subverting the "natural" social and political order, interracial and cross-cultural adoption was also reviled by the vast majority of the dominant population at the time. The narrative of rescue is found throughout US adoption history as transnational adoptive parents (and responses to adoptive families) often voice the notion that they have rescued a child from poverty, orphanages, or abandonment by their birth parents. Though modified, such a story resonates to the current conflicts regarding the best interests of citizen-children as we see the transfer

---

7. O'Connor, *Orphan Trains*; River, *Orphan Train Movement*.
8. Gordon, *Great Arizona Orphan Abduction*.

of parental rights from immigrant Mexicans to foster and adoptive parents, most of whom are white, and who regard themselves as rescuing these children from morally unfit parents.

Adoptions of Korean children in the 1950s through the 1970s placed thousands of "mixed race" children (children of Korean women and American soldiers from the Korean War), illegitimate children, and mentally and physically disabled children, and "Operation Babylift" placed more than 3,000 Vietnamese children in US households in the 1970s. However, it was in the late 1980s through 2004 that a substantial increase in the numbers of transnational adoptions by US citizens from multiple countries occurred. Since 1989 more than 300,000 children from other countries have been adopted by US parents, who are predominantly white, college educated, and middle class. These adoptions peaked in 2004, when more than 22,000 children were adopted to the US, predominantly from China, Russia, Guatemala, and South Korea. For a variety of reasons, these numbers have been dramatically reduced in recent years, and 2017 marks a thirty-five-year low in transnational adoptions of 4,059.[9] The latest figure is the lowest since 1981, when there were 4,868 transnational adoptions.

Several people have written about the marketplace of adoption and how changes in demographics and adoption policies shift adoptive parents' attention to new locations and opportunities.[10] For example, between 2003 and 2010 more than 35,000 children were adopted from African countries, most of these adopted from Ethiopia (22,282). During this same period, adoptions from China decreased by 70 percent, and adoptions from Russia had decreased by 34 percent prior to Russia's termination of US adoptions in 2012.[11] By 2016 we had seen a 72 percent decrease in transnational adoptions. Though the numbers of adoptions have changed, Chuck Johnson, chief executive of the National Council for Adoption, argues for the continued interest in adoption by Americans.[12] Given this viewpoint, shared by other adoption advocates, recent events in the US raise new concerns about the tensions between family-building and human rights, as Latino families are literally being separated through deportation and detention, and children placed into foster care and thus made available for adoption. This latest chapter in the history of US adoption underscores the role of power, exploitation, the political factors involved in family-building through adoption, and adoptive parents' role in these processes.

---

9. US Department of State, "Annual Report on Intercountry Adoption" (2018).

10. Freundlich, *Market Forces in Adoption*; Smolin, "Child Laundering"; Quiroz, *Adoption in a Colorblind Society*; Raleigh, *Selling Transracial Adoption*.

11. Selman, "Rise and Fall of Intercountry Adoption."

12. "As Numbers of Adoptions Drop."

US Immigration Policy: From Obama's 400,000 to Trump's "Build a (Spiked) Wall" and Cages

The Obama administration's deportation and detainment of more than 400,000 undocumented persons resulted in a group of children, predominantly Latino, being impacted by foster care and adoption. In 2011 the Applied Research Center (ARC, now called Race Forward) found more than 5,000 Latino children in foster care or adopted because their parents had been detained or deported. The ARC projected that unless the immigration enforcement and child welfare systems worked to articulate their processes, another 15,000 children would be in this situation within the next five years. Though no studies comparable to the ARC's have since been done, other data on the number of US Latino children with parents who have been deported provides indirect support for the ARC's projections. In 2014 Immigration and Customs Enforcement carried out more than 72,000 deportations of parents who said they had US-born children, and estimates from various research institutes and state and government agencies suggest that parents of the four million US citizen-children are among the hundreds of thousands of undocumented immigrants expelled each year.[13] In California it is estimated that more than 10,000 parents of US citizen-children are detained each year and that half of these detainees have no criminal history or record.[14] The state of Texas deports more unauthorized persons than any other state in the US, more than twice that of California and almost ten times that of Illinois (22,041 last year alone).[15] Though Mexicans are about 60 percent of the undocumented population in the US, in 2010 Mexicans accounted for 83 percent of the detained, 73 percent of those forcibly removed, and 77 percent of voluntary departures (those who either anticipate being deported and therefore leave voluntarily before this happens, and those who simply choose to return to Mexico because they never intended to stay or because they see themselves as binational).[16]

With the election of Donald Trump, we have seen even harsher approaches to implementing immigration policies such as increased separation of children from parents (immigrant children and citizen-children with undocumented parents), placement of children in cages, and proposals of such draconian measures as shooting migrants in the legs. The ACLU reports that the total number of immigrant children separated from their parents since July 2017

---

13. Dreby, "How Today's Immigration Enforcement Policies"; "Deportation of a Parent"; "U.S. Citizen Children Impacted"; Golash-Boza, *Deported*.

14. Nicholson, "'I Still Need You.'"

15. "U.S. Deportation Outcomes by Charge, 2017."

16. Dreby, "How Today's Immigration Enforcement Policies"; Golash-Boza, *Deported*.

is more than 5,400. It seems fair to assume that the projections reported in the ARC study have been realized. Despite federal court decisions mandating the reunification of children with families, tracking these children is nearly impossible. These separations were larger than the number previously assumed, and it is unclear whether they have continued.

Despite the legal, moral, and logistical implications of these separations, the reality is that children are being placed in foster care and adoption.[17] What remains unclear is the extent to which this occurs or to what extent US couples interested in adoption are now looking to this newly created "market." Because adoption continues to be an activity engaged in by predominantly white couples, multiple issues emerge. And what will happen once these issues do? Given the increase in the number of Latino children in foster care, I wanted to understand the process and perspectives of those who seek to foster/parent immigrant and citizen-children.[18] This chapter shows how prospective and adoptive US parents view the families whose children they are interested in making their own.

Adoption Parent Networks and Forums

My former research and some updates serve as the backdrop for understanding the implications of immigration policy and fostering and adoption of Latino children. Prior research on private adoption agencies in the largest online adoption directory (the Open Adoption Directory, also known as the DMOZ) presented a picture of two- and three-tiered adoption programs with placement of children depending on their racial/ethnic identities, and criteria and costs of adoption based on program placement.[19] Placement of Latino and Asian infants suggested a type of honorary white status for members of these groups, as these children were placed with and priced the same as white ethnic children, except in the Southwest, where "fully Hispanic" infants occupied a middle tier with looser restrictions for adoption, lower costs (relative to adopting a half-white/half-Hispanic child), and fewer criteria to be met by adoptive parents. Black American and "biracial" babies, defined by virtually every website as children with any Black American heritage (reminiscent of the one-drop rule), were placed into separate programs with substantially different costs, criteria, and wait times, and the minimal wait time for "Caucasian" children (nine months to four years) served as the maximum

17. Rodrigo, "Migrant Children May Be Adopted."
18. Wessler, *Shattered Families.*
19. Quiroz, *Adoption in a Colorblind Society.*

wait time for Black American and "biracial" children (one month to nine months). Websites also assured prospective parents that Black American and "biracial" children were "healthy" and not "drug addicted." Some did not and instead signaled, however inadvertently, that something might be wrong with Black American children by their guidelines and the way they described the "Black American and Biracial Program." For example, the Evangelical Child and Family Agency stated in its guidelines for adoption that "childlessness" or infertility was required for "healthy newborn Caucasian, Asian or Latino adoption" but not for all others (that is, Black American). Similar to other agencies, ECFA separated its infants into five programs: Healthy Newborn Adoption, Special Needs, Black American Infants, Intercountry Adoption, and Agency-Assisted Adoption. One agency simply combined a sales pitch with its program listings: "For healthy white infants this fee is twelve percent of the family's previous year's income—$3,000 minimum to $8,000 maximum. Black American children—no fee. Special needs children—as low as $300. Can be $0 with board approval." These ways of juxtaposing and advertising [and pricing] children reflect the racial hierarchy of our society (see table 2.1).

TABLE 2.1. Pricing Adoption according to Race (Open Adoption Directory, 2006)

PROGRAM TYPE	COST	RESTRICTIONS	WAIT TIME
Caucasian (37–48%)	$20,000–$50,000	No more than 1 child in home; parents no more than 50 years of age	9 months to 4 years
"Fully Hispanic" (7–13%)	$16,000–$28,000	Same as Caucasian (except in the Southwest)	Same as Caucasian (except in the Southwest)
Asian (3–13%)	$16,000–$30,000	Same as Caucasian	Same as Caucasian
Black American (0–5%)	$0–$10,000	Unlimited number of children in home; parents no more than 60 years of age	1 to 9 months

n = 96 agencies

Another aspect of adoption I examined is parent preferences. The existence of online adoptive parent networks allowed me to view prospective parents' preference ordering of racial/ethnic children. These networks were essentially websites where adoptive couples would advertise themselves to birth mothers for selection. Descriptions conformed very much to that of an ad used to attract potential birth mothers: couples listed their hobbies and religion and described their jobs and home in ways designed to promote selection by the birth mother. These advertisements (always accompanied by photos of the couple and the house) also included their preferences for the type of child they would accept. The size of each network averaged around 300 participants. In 2007 prospective parents demonstrated clear preferences by race, with virtually no parents willing to adopt Black American or "biracial" children and comparatively few willing to adopt a "fully Hispanic" or "fully Asian" child. Though responses may be unique to the participants in these networks, there is research on Asian adoptees that characterizes a substantial degree of alienation and personal dissonance as a result of how race was handled by their adoptive families.[20] All I do know is that in these networks, at that time, very few adoptive parents listed "fully Hispanic" or "fully Asian" children, and no one was willing to accept Black American or "biracial" children. Again, these were relatively small samples of 300 couples, and it was within a racial preference ordering, so that may have made the difference.

A comparison of one of these networks in 2006 and 2016 shows modest but significant changes in acceptance of racially different children by predominantly white ethnic prospective parents.[21] This is consistent with data from other studies and the adoption market to which US parents turn when countries limit or abandon transnational adoption. Parents who in 2016 were willing to cross the racial divide by adopting children from other racial/ethnic groups were still less than half of all parents for each ethnic category (less than 50 percent). However, the percentage of those parents who were willing to adopt racially/ethnically different children had increased. It was the changes toward adoption of Latino children to which I draw attention given current events involving immigration and what is happening to so many Latino families (see table 2.2).

Adoption statistics have changed over the years. When my book was published in 2007, fewer children from foster care were adopted, and typically by relatives. Domestic transracial adoptions were a very small proportion of private adoptions (3 to 4 percent). What remains consistent is the difference in costs between adopting from foster care, private and transnational adoption, programs for different groups of children, and projections of an increasing number of Latino children in foster care. Drawn to the stories of Latino children who were entering foster care and adoption, my read of *Shattered Families,* the changing transnational adoption landscape, and my personal experience of being solicited to foster a Latino child, I returned to the internet to explore a domestic Latino adoption forum (2012–14) and conducted

---

20. Kim, *Adopted Territory*; Tuan and Shiao, *Choosing Ethnicity, Negotiating Race*; Park Nelson, *Invisible Asians*; McGinnis et al., *Beyond Culture Camp.*

21. See my analysis at https://adoptionnetwork.com/.

TABLE 2.2. Adoptive Parent Racial/Ethnic Preferences of Child
(AdoptionNetwork.com)

RACIAL/ETHNIC PREFERENCE	2006	2016*
White	49%	98%
Hispanic	5%	28%
Asian	13%	37%
Black American	0%	11%
White/Hispanic	27%	76%
White/Asian	15%	63%
White/African American	1%	32%
Any Child	0%	11%

* Percentages for 2006 reflect shares of the total number of 350 requests for children because there was no preference ordering available for more than one category of child at that time. In 2016 parents were allowed to provide preference orderings; thus, the sum of the percentages for 2016 exceeds 100% because parents were allowed to select more than one preference.

interviews with a small convenience sample of adoptive/foster parents to see how participants engaged in this process.

Adoption Forums

Adoption forums present online spaces where adoptive parents can express a shared sense of community. In these virtual spaces, participants engage in unscripted discussions that they generate (threads) and that extend across time (hours, days, and weeks). Credibility of interpretation of analysis relies on detail of the analytic process, time engaged in gathering data, the research-er's positioning of themselves in the study, interpretation of data in relation to other studies, and careful explanation of the data's limitations with respect to the questions it raises.

Forum threads on the intersection of immigration, fostering, and adoption initially contained an average of 200 posts (per week). After acquiring approval to "lurk" in the forum, I observed threads intermittently throughout the first year as I informally followed participants' interactions. However, I conducted formal analysis of threads for a two-week period during each of six months in the second year, and messages in this forum eventually grew from an average of 200 to 700 posts a week by the end of 2014. Individual posts ranged from one or two lines to half a page (ten to fifteen lines). The actual number of participants engaged in any given interaction is significantly smaller than the number of posts. Like most conversations that occur offline, certain topics generated greater involvement by a subset of participants. Many participants engaged in the forum for extended durations, others for brief times; very few engaged only once. I downloaded the entire set of messages in the threads and analyzed interactions using discursive analysis of patterns found in written text.

Language is a particular focus because terminology and language use can evoke positive or negative attitudes toward groups. For example, in my prior research I found that language used for race-based programs was not merely a neutral descriptor; it operated to mark children (most often Black American children) as the "Other." Additionally, program labels were juxtaposed in racially evocative ways. When descriptors like "healthy" are used to describe one type of child but not another, a flag is implicitly raised in the minds of adoptive parents regarding the programs that lack this descriptor. In 2004 some programs were explicit and stated "no crack babies" when describing Black American programs.

Terms can soften harsher images of persons or generate and confirm stereotypes and responses to those images, such as the current study, where adoptive/foster parents legitimate their rights to the child by criminalizing the child's biological or "birth" parents and minimizing the biological parents' status as parents. Thus, the communicative power of language and adoption discourse perpetuates myths about parents and even entire communities and allows identities to be constructed and maintained. Within the past three years, we have witnessed how such communication feeds into a larger political narrative in the US, particularly with respect to our southern border, the Wall, and an increase in views of Mexican immigrants as criminals and job stealers. Indeed, in their study on Latinos and health, Vargas and colleagues found that when Latinos were mistakenly identified as Mexican, they described greater incidents of prejudice and discrimination.[22] Needless to say, Mexicans described more health problems than other Latinos did.

Foster and Adoptive Parent Interviews

While I collected online data, I also interviewed fourteen foster and adoptive parents. Four Chicago agencies were trying to place Latino children with foster parents through adoption, and I had been solicited by one of these agencies as a potential foster parent to Latino children. Although the agencies

---

22. Vargas et al. "Latino or Mexicano?"

explicitly sought to place children with Spanish-speaking Latino families, ten of my interviews were with white ethnic parents (only one of whom spoke Spanish) and four Latino parents. Four of the parents were adoptive, and the rest were foster parents. Each of the interviews occurred with the adoptive or foster mother and consisted of open-ended questions about the process of becoming a foster or adoptive parent to a child whose parent(s) were detained or deported. I also asked how participants viewed the situation that brought children to them. Interviews averaged forty minutes, and though these interviews are limited in how they can inform us about this phenomenon, primarily because of the limited number and self-selection of participants, the responses of parents who were interviewed differed from online expressions of how they approached fostering and adoption, offering different perspectives about the process and the children for whom they cared.

As Emily Noonan's analysis of Guatemalan adoption forums points out, participants' narratives about adoption do not occur in a vacuum.[23] Rather, they are grounded in prior experiences, understandings of identity, and awareness about the social status of different groups in society. Forum interactions in the current study present foster, adoptive, and prospective parents of immigrant and citizen-children, creating identities and justifying appropriation in adoption. The following analysis focuses on these participants' views of the children they foster or want to adopt and their parents. They also provide insights into the processes that allow them to benefit from the system that oppresses the families from whom they acquire their children.

The Power of Appropriation in Adoption

Discussions about fostering and adopting citizen and immigrant children were explicit and spontaneous in forums as prospective parents asked about the logistics, legal challenges, and possible conflicts with "illegal" parents. Often foster or adoptive parents shared information about their own or friends' experiences. A small sample of such thread titles include "Illegal immigrant bio [biological] parents," "Adopting illegal children," "Illegal aliens? Foster care and adoption," "Bio parent illegal," "Adopting an illegal immigrant," "Experiences with the undocumented," "Deportation of Bios [biological parents] while children are in foster care." Many of these discussions revolved around seeking information and sharing personal experience; however, significant attention was also given to how adoptive/foster parents could secure

---

23. Noonan, "Adoption and the Guatemalan Journey."

their rights. Because discursive analysis assumes that language use has social consequences, and because language regarding immigration is a contentious issue, it is notable that the term *illegal* was used instead of *undocumented* or *unauthorized*.

> One of my friends who is a foster mom is dealing with this. [. . .] The mom is an American but the dad is an illegal immigrant. [. . .] The kids got removed from the mom and now the dad is coming for a visit. He has kept in contact with the case workers but this is his first visit. The kids have been in care since the end of May. How would his rights be affected by him being illegal? (Seeking)

> He has all the rights as any legal citizen. If he should be deported or re country, it will not stop RU [reuniting]from happening. Believe me, we are up to our eyeballs in this mess. According to some of the international conferences regarding children's rights, (forget which ones exactly), the children are also considered dual citizens of the US and biological dad's country. Therefore, should dad want to, he could get his home country's consulate involved, which could have some pull. Unless Biological dad is unfit to raise the children, honestly, there is nothing the illegal status will affect. (Diane)

> Here is a link to a story here in Portland Oregon that I have been following that is along the same lines. I am disgusted with the state's decision to send the US born child to Mexico. (Mommy)

> We had friends who were trying to adopt a little boy in Oklahoma a couple of years ago. They had him for over six months, then his BF (biological father), an illegal immigrant, showed up and with the court's backing took him back to Mexico. They [?] felt that the BF was not a fit parent but that he had family in Mexico and they [?] decided that there was no legal standing to keep the baby in the US since his birth mom had terminated her rights. My friends were devastated, but there was nothing they could do except pray that he would be loved by BF's [birth father] family. (Alice)

Accompanying language regarding biological and "illegal" parents is a sense of indignation on the part of participants and avoidance in addressing the broader social and economic realities of children and their families.

> I'm in Denver and we had a newborn drug addicted girl whose mother wouldn't work her plan and her dad is an illegal alien. We were told by the

first caseworker that he wouldn't get her because he's illegal. [. . .] NOT TRUE. The case was transferred to the Spanish speaking division and everything changed. I will avoid the Spanish division as long as I can (long long story about another child). Luckily the only reason cases go there is if the parents do not speak English. DHS (Department of Human Service) does not care about alien status for parents. They do not report to immigration and our daughter now lives with her dad. He speaks no English, we speak no Spanish, but we are lucky enough get her every weekend. (Colorado)

One of my friends, is currently going through something similar. The Biological dad was deported. A home study was completed in Mexico for the grandma. The kid had lived with my friend on and off for years (failed RU) (reunited). My friend said the home study in Mexico was a joke. The kid doesn't even know his grandmother. CPS told her the kid was illegal anyway and costing the state money. Nice. She was pretty broken up about it. (peaceforall)

Interwoven with these perspectives were narratives that resonate to prior studies about adoptive mothers' instant connections to their adopted/foster children.[24] Foster and adoptive parents in forums describe their instinctive connection to the child they parent (or wish to parent), even before meeting him or her. These discussions revealed the distancing of foster and adoptive parents from the situations in which citizen and immigrant children were located, and often divorced children from their biological families. Adoptive/ foster parents frequently laid claim to "destiny," stating their conviction that the desired child was meant to be theirs or would soon be legitimately theirs once they received the Transfer of Parental Rights. Such constructions help validate rights to a child and mitigate personal dissonance about the circumstances under which we become parents. The following post provides information. However, it also implies support and encouragement for termination of [biological] parental rights and minimal acknowledgment of birth parents while revealing the variation in judges' timelines regarding decisions to terminate parental rights.

I don't know if it varies from state to state but we are in Missouri and had our permanency hearing the last part of October when the judge gave the orders for TPR (termination of parental rights) to be filed. Our regular Juvenile Officer was on maternity leave and just came back this week. She has

---

24. Anagnost, "Scenes of Misrecognition."

told us that the actual TPR petition will be filed by the middle of January. At that point, the petition has to be served to all those involved in the case. The biological parents have a certain amount of time to appeal the termination. We have been told that we could have a TPR hearing within several months after filing. We have a new judge in our county and he is moving TPR's rather quickly. If the parents contest, whether they're in jail or not, it can slow things down. In Missouri, incarceration is not a valid reason to terminate rights. [. . .] It is my understanding that after the TPR hearing, the biological parents may still contest it for up to thirty days. Our county has heard contested TPR's past the thirty day-period, however, most counties also will look for a relative placement once the child is free for adoption. If no suitable relative placement can be found, foster parents usually have the first option to adopt the child, if the "team" is in agreement. Hope this helps. Hang in there. It can be a long process. Our case worker has a friend who filed last year to adopt their foster child and on the last day of the appeal time frame, the Biological Dad decided to appeal it, from jail. It has taken eleven months to go through. But keep your chin up. I know for us, it will be worth it once our little girl is finally ours! God knows your child's destiny and he knows where your child needs to be in order for His will to be accomplished in his/her life! (Cali)

What is not understood or addressed by participants is how the child welfare and immigration enforcement systems fail to articulate to one another. Often biological parents who are detained are sent to detention centers distant from their families. Biological parents may lack appropriate information and opportunities to maintain parental rights (for example, they are often not notified of hearings they must attend to maintain parental rights, or they may be unable to attend these hearings even when they do know about them).[25] Additionally, data are difficult to compile, as child welfare systems and immigration enforcement do not typically document cases of families who enter their systems in this way, and opportunities to examine the conditions of those in detention centers are minimal.

The constructions of online participants involved juxtaposing a narrative of biological families as undeserving, immoral, or even dangerous with narratives of adoptive parents that focused on rights, salvation, and legality. But unlike the features of transnational adoption, where nominal efforts are made to relay ethnoracial awareness and the significance of cultural maintenance, no discussions about cultural literacy or obligations to culture emerged. Addi-

---

25. Wessler, *Shattered Families*.

tionally, no discussion emerged online about the trauma of children, and no mention was made of the trauma of their parents.

Family-Building / Family Dissolution

Adoption is truly an act of love and faith, but it is also an act of power and loss. Power is not always recognized, and loss is not always located in some distant past or vague set of memories. In the aftermath of Haiti's massive earthquake in 2010, ten American missionaries were jailed after attempting to smuggle thirty-three Haitian children who were not orphans (children whose parents were deceased) into the Dominican Republic without seeking proper paperwork or permission from the Haitian government. Their purpose was to place these children for adoption with US families, having persuaded their parents they would be helping their children have a better life. Such stories are common for parents and children from many countries, including Ethiopia, Guatemala, and Nepal. As UNICEF has pointed out, many children who are adopted are not orphans, and many parents who relinquish their children often believe they are participating in educational opportunities as opposed to permanent legal separation.[26] In short, parents may not know or willingly engage in relinquishing their children. This is clearly the situation for children whose parents have been detained or deported.

More than four million Latino children face the possibility of having a parent deported, and literally hundreds of thousands of children have had this experience.[27] Under President Trump's administration, priorities for deportation vastly expanded, and it is therefore possible that more children had this experience. These children suffer economically, emotionally, and physically, and many are forced into different family situations.[28] We have heard this story before; however, it has not been situated as having its origins within the US.

There have been attempts to align work between the child welfare and immigration enforcement systems, to encourage ICE officials to consider parental responsibilities when enforcing immigration law, and to place children with relatives or Latino families when parent(s) are detained. However, participants in adoption forums, social workers, immigration lawyers, children of deported parents, and adoptive and foster parents suggest a number

---

26. UNICEF. "UNICEF's Position."

27. "U.S. Citizen Children Impacted"; Wessler, *Shattered Families*; Foley, "Deportation Separated Thousands"; DePillis, "U.S. Has Deported."

28. Dreby, "How Today's Immigration Enforcement Policies"; "Deportation of a Parent"; "U.S. Citizen Children Impacted."

of ways the system fails these children and their families as it results in creating new ones.

Changes in available children have always created new markets and shifted adoptive parent interest to different groups of children. As we see the increased willingness of white ethnic parents to foster/adopt Latino children, it is easy to wonder what impact detention, deportation, and separation of families might have for prospective parents looking to adopt, particularly in a shrinking transnational adoption market. Whereas the majority of transnational and private adoptions cost more than $30,000, foster care adoptions are typically free or at minimal cost or subsidized. This is the type of adoption that occurs through detention and deportation. It may serve the interests of prospective parents, but it does little to reduce the trauma for children whose first families are torn apart. Until we alter current immigration policies, we need to provide foster/adoptive parents a more nuanced and reflective understanding of the emotional, cultural, and health-related costs of parenting these children. Foster/adoptive parents need mandatory workshops that address the conditions of power and privilege in the formation of family, as those who adopt and those who are adopted occupy radically different cultural, economic, social, and racial spaces. More importantly, we must ask whether the appropriate response is to separate families and place children in foster care and process them as adoptees. The moral and ethical answer to this question seems obvious.

We now have evidence from research on adult adoptees that the outcomes of adoption are often experienced and viewed disparately by adoptees and their adoptive parents, as many parents are not prepared to address the complexities of parenting across racial groups, and it is the children who pay the price. However, it is also their biological families who are literally erased from their lives along with their identities. This is particularly true of "mixed race" families (for example, white parents and children from other racial groups).[29] According to critics, adoption is a neocolonial practice that reflects one's status in the globalized capitalist system. Poor families and their children are part of a system of "stratified reproduction" where some groups are empowered to reproduce, foster, and adopt, while other groups are disempowered, impoverished, and forced to provide the children who are adopted.[30]

29. Tuan and Shiao, *Choosing Ethnicity, Negotiating Race*; Samuels, "Being Raised by White People"; Quiroz, "Adoptive Parents Raising Neoethnics"; Hübinette, "Post Racial Utopianism"; Leinaweaver, *Adoptive Migration*.

30. Briggs, *Somebody's Children*; Briggs, *How All Politics Became Reproductive Politics*; Eng, "Transnational Adoption and Queer Diasporas"; Hübinette, "Post Racial Utopianism"; Noonan, "Adoption and the Guatemalan Journey"; Fonseca, "Traditional Influences in the Social Production."

Subsequent to the ARC study, most of our current evidence about the impact of detention and deportation on adoption and fostering of citizen-children is anecdotal and qualitative, in part because it is difficult to acquire funding for studies and to obtain access to such data. Nor are data systematically maintained by these key systems. It has been speculated by researchers and professionals in the child welfare system that expanded deportations will increase the number of citizen-children who enter the foster care and adoption process, exacerbate their mental health needs, and negatively affect their well-being. Nor do attempts to coordinate the immigration enforcement and child welfare systems guarantee a positive judicial outcome, as courts can decide that simply being an undocumented parent requires the child to be placed elsewhere. Even if immigration policy were to shift, planned tax cuts could result in spending reductions in child welfare systems, further burdening systems that are already underfunded, as demanding caseloads may reduce opportunities to address the special needs of citizen-children in those systems.

Conclusion

In the nineteenth-century scenario of Mexican adoption of Irish children, antipathy toward Mexicans reinforced social boundaries as US courts sanctioned the actions of white vigilantes who perceived themselves to be rescuing children from inappropriate parents. In the twenty-first century, we appear to be doing the same thing, as white adoptive parents in this forum narrate themselves as "rescuing" children (again, from Mexican parents). The simultaneous vilification of the children's biological parents as criminal, immoral, and unworthy serves to alleviate the guilt and personal dissonance of adoptive parents as they participate in the process of appropriation.

The real and not too subtle conditions of power can be seen in the traumatic separation of biological families and subsequent formation of "new" families. And though minor in comparison to the issue of appropriation, the images and views of these families, as presented by adoptive/foster and prospective parents online, make it difficult to expect maintenance of cultural contacts appropriate for these children. Clearly, forum participants may not represent the adoptive parent population of Latino children; nor is the full range of attitudes and cultural views systematically captured here. At best, we have a window on the practices of adoption and fostering of Latino immigrant and citizen-children by some US parents. Still, it is important to note who gets to direct the discourse in these discussions as they present us with opportunities to examine human rights and whose rights matter. It is incumbent on adoptive parents to ask how we protect human rights and balance our needs with the well-being and rights of others. The more serious and difficult question is whether we want to become part of this highly questionable and immoral process in order to become parents.

We should keep in mind that the data were gathered in a pre-Trump era of measures taken to discourage immigration. Since 2016 we've seen children as young as a few months literally taken from their parents and young children placed in cages. Others are taken into the black hole of "detention," while many are placed in the child welfare system. Just how many children enter this world we do not know for certain, but it is likely that the projections of the ARC did not take into account a Trump presidency.

The intersection of current immigration policies and the adoptive parent market continues to illustrate, in bold relief, the power of appropriation by cultures of privilege. Even though I am Latina, as an adoptive parent I cannot remove myself from the conundrum of becoming a parent through my position of privilege and my sons' (and their parents') position of disempowerment. I therefore bear responsibility, as I am part of this reality. While I have reasoned that as a woman of color whose experiences and career sensitize me to inequalities, I am at least aware of and reflexive about these realities, but I know this argument is self-serving. Despite the current nationalist rhetoric, adoption is directly linked to the neoliberal environment that stimulates it. Much in the way that other aspects of life have been subjected to commodification and consumption, adoption in the US has now become part of the migration of goods, services, and people in our new global reality. As a nation we need to be aware of the multitude of consequences of such policies; and as a population of persons longing to build families, adoptive parents must avoid knowingly participating in processes that benefit us at the expense of others.

Whenever I give a talk on this topic, I tell the story about having once attended a workshop where an adoptive couple was sincerely thanking a young Mexican American birth mother for the "gift" she was giving to them, at which point she became visibly upset, and with tears in her eyes angrily responded, "Never misunderstand or believe that I am doing anything *for you. I love my son. You* are the gift I am giving to my son." That was more than sixteen years ago, but I have never forgotten that moment. And as I struggle to be worthy of my sons' and their mothers' struggles, sacrifices and loss, I am ever hopeful about the liminal space my children occupy between loss and opportunity, pain and love, and I engage reflexively to become a worthy "gift" to them. As the years pass, I also hope to become part of the solutions required to ensure that one family not be dissolved to form another.

Bibliography

Anagnost, Ann. "Scenes of Misrecognition: Maternal Citizenship in the Age of Transnational Adoption." *Positions* 8, no. 2 (2000): 389–421.

"As Numbers of Adoptions Drop, Many US Agencies Face Strains." *Boston Globe,* April 30, 2017. https://www.bostonglobe.com/news/nation/2017/04/30/number-adoptions-drops-many-agencies-face-strains/TxGI6mq1QaqyS92GlR5kcM/story.html.

Bartholet, Elizabeth. "International Adoption: A Way Forward." *New York Law School Law Review* 55, no. 3 (2010/2011): 687–700.

Briggs, Laura. *How All Politics Became Reproductive Politics: From Welfare Reform to Foreclosure to Trump.* Berkeley: University of California Press, 2017.

———. *Somebody's Children: The Politics of Transracial and Transnational Adoption.* Durham, NC: Duke University Press, 2012.

Burke, Garance, and Martha Mendoza. "AP Investigation: Deported Parents May Lose Kids to Adoption." *AP News,* October 9, 2018. https://apnews.com/article/immigration-us-news-ap-top-news-international-news-arrests-97b06cede0c149c492bf25a48cb6c26f.

DePillis, Lydia. "The U.S. Has Deported More Than Half a Million Parents since 2009: Here's What Happens to Their Kids." *Washington Post,* September 21, 2015. https://www.washingtonpost.com/news/wonk/wp/2015/09/21/this-is-what-would-happen-to-the-children-of-11-million-illegal-immigrants-if-president-trump-deported-them/.

"Deportation of a Parent Can Have Significant and Long-Lasting Harmful Effects on Child Well-Being, as a Pair of Reports from MPI and the Urban Institute Detail." *Migration Policy Institute,* September 21, 2015. https://www.migrationpolicy.org/news/deportation-parent-can-have-significant-and-long-lasting-harmful-effects-child-well-being-pair.

Dreby, Joanna. "How Today's Immigration Enforcement Policies Impact Children, Families, and Communities: A View from the Ground." *Center for American Progress,* August 20, 2012. https://www.americanprogress.org/issues/immigration/reports/2012/08/20/27082/how-todays-immigration-enforcement-policies-impact-children-families-and-communities/.

Eng, David L. "Transnational Adoption and Queer Diasporas." *Social Text* 3, no. 76 (2003): 1–37.

Foley, Elise. "Deportation Separated Thousands of U.S.-Born Children from Parents In 2013." *Huffington Post,* June 25, 2014. https://www.huffingtonpost.com/2014/06/25/parents-deportation_n_5531552.html.

Fonseca, Claudia. "Traditional Influences in the Social Production of Adoptable Children: The Case of Brazil." *International Journal of Sociology and Social Policy* 26, no. 3/4 (2006): 154–71.

Freundlich, Margaret. *The Market Forces in Adoption.* Washington, DC: Child Welfare League of America / Evan B. Donaldson Adoption Institute, 2000.

Golash-Boza, Tanya Maria. *Deported: Immigrant Policing, Disposable Labor and Global Capitalism.* New York: New York University Press, 2015.

Gordon, Linda. *The Great Arizona Orphan Abduction.* Cambridge, MA: Harvard University Press, 1999.

Hübinette, Tobias. "Post Racial Utopianism, White Color-Blindness and 'the Elephant in the Room': Racial Issues for Transnational Adoptees of Color." In *Intercountry Adoption: Policies, Practices and Outcomes,* edited by Judith L. Gibbons and Karen Smith Rotabi, 221–32. Surrey, England: Ashgate, 2012.

Kim, Eleana J. *Adopted Territory: Transnational Korean Adoptees and the Politics of Belonging.* Durham, NC: Duke University Press, 2010.

Leinaweaver, Jessica B. *Adoptive Migration: Raising Latinos in Spain.* Durham, NC: Duke University Press, 2013.

McGinnis, Hollee, Susan Livingston Smith, Scott D. Ryan, and Jeanne A. Howard. *Beyond Culture Camp: Promoting Healthy Identity Formation in Adoption.* New York: Evan B. Donaldson Adoption Institute, 2009.

Nicholson, Lucy. "'I Still Need You': Detention and Deportation of Californian Parents." Human Rights Watch, May 15, 2017. https://www.hrw.org/report/2017/05/15/i-still-need-you/detention-and-deportation-californian-parents#.

Noonan, Emily J. "Adoption and the Guatemalan Journey to American Parenthood." *Childhood* 13, no. 3 (2007): 301–18.

Park Nelson, Kim. *Invisible Asians: Korean American Adoptees, Asian American Experiences, and Racial Exceptionalism.* Rutgers, NJ: Rutgers University Press, 2016.

O'Connor, Stephen. *Orphan Trains: The Story of Charles Loring Brace and the Children He Saved and Failed.* Chicago: University of Chicago Press, 2004.

Quiroz, Pamela Anne. *Adoption in a Color-Blind Society.* Lanham, MD: Rowman & Littlefield, 2007.

———. "Adoptive Parents Raising Neoethnics." In *Families as They Really Are,* edited by Barbara Risman and Virginia Rutter, 464–78. New York: Norton, 2015.

Raleigh, Elizabeth. *Selling Transracial Adoption: Families, Markets and the Color Line.* Philadelphia: Temple University Press, 2017.

River, Charles. *The Orphan Train Movement: The History of the Program That Relocated Homeless Children across America.* CreateSpace, 2016.

Rodrigo, Chris. "AP: Migrant Children May Be Adopted after Parents Are Deported." *The Hill,* October 9, 2018. https://thehill.com/policy/international/americas/410653-ap-migrant-children-may-be-adopted-after-parents-are-deported.

Rotabi, Karen. "Fraud in Intercountry Adoption: Child Sales and Abduction in Vietnam, Cambodia, and Guatemala." In *Intercountry Adoption: Policies, Practices and Outcomes,* edited by Judith Gibbons and Karen Rotabi, 67–76. New York: Routledge, 2015.

Samuels, Gina. "Being Raised by White People: Navigating Racial Difference among Adopted Multiracial Adults." *Journal of Marriage and Family* 71, no. 1 (2009): 80–94.

Selman, Peter. "The Rise and Fall of Intercountry Adoption in the 21st Century: Global Trends From 2001 to 2010." *International Social Work* 52, no. 5 (2015): 575–94.

Smolin, David. 2005. "Child Laundering: How the Intercountry Adoption System Legitimizes and Incentivizes the Practices of Buying, Trafficking, Kidnapping, and Stealing Children." *bepress Legal Repository.* Retrieved December 5, 2016. https://law.bepress.com/expresso/eps/749/.

Tuan, Mia, and Jiannbin Lee Shiao. *Choosing Ethnicity, Negotiating Race: Korean Adoptees in America.* New York: Russell Sage Foundation, 2011.

UNICEF. "UNICEF's Position on Intercountry Adoption." Released October 5, 2007. http://www.hcch.net.

"U.S. Citizen Children Impacted by Immigration Enforcement." *American Immigration Council,* June 24, 2021. https://www.americanimmigrationcouncil.org/research/us-citizen-children-impacted-immigration-enforcement.

US Department of State. Bureau of Consular Affairs. "Annual Report on Intercountry Adoptions Narrative." 2016. https://travel.state.gov/content/dam/NEWadoptionassets/pdfs/AnnualReportonIntercountryAdoptions6.8.17.pdf.

US Department of State. Bureau of Consular Affairs. "Annual Report on Intercountry Adoption." 2018. https://travel.state.gov/content/dam/NEWadoptionassets/pdfs/Tab%201%20Annual%20Report%20on%20Intercountry%20Adoptions.pdf.

"U.S. Deportation Outcomes by Charge, 2017. Completed Cases in Immigration Courts." Retrieved September 12, 2017. https://trac.syr.edu/phptools/immigration/court_backlog/deport_outcome_charge.php.

Vargas, Edward D., Nadia Winston, John Garcia, and Gabriel Sanchez. "Latino or Mexicano? The Relationship between Socially Assigned Race and Experiences with Discrimination." *Sociology of Race and Ethnicity* 2, no. 4 (2016): 498–515.

Wessler, Seth Freed. *Shattered Families: The Perilous Intersection of Immigration Enforcement and the Child Welfare System.* New York: Applied Research Center, 2011. https://www.immigrationresearch.org/report/other/shattered-families-perilous-intersection-immigration-enforcement-and-child-welfare-syst.

CHAPTER 3

"Natural Born Aliens"

Transnational Adoptees and US Citizenship

ELEANA J. KIM AND KIM PARK NELSON

In April 2016 Korean American adoptee Amie Kim was interviewed on Minnesota Public Radio to discuss her undocumented status. Adopted to Minnesota in the late 1970s at the age of two, Kim was never naturalized by her parents. Unbeknownst to her, her green card expired when she turned eighteen years old, leaving her undocumented. She described how she inadvertently committed a felony by voting in the 1992 presidential election at the age of eighteen.[1] Although Kim said she planned to apply for US citizenship, she went on to say, "I actually feel like my current status as not exactly a Korean citizen and not exactly a US citizen—it actually fits my identity and how I feel about myself."[2]

Although one cannot be, as Kim puts it, "not exactly" a citizen of a country—one either does or does not have citizenship—Kim's description illuminates the connection between legal citizenship and cultural citizenship, or the experience of cultural belonging. This sense of being a liminal cultural subject, neither fully Korean nor fully American, is one that has been widely shared among Korean adoptees but is more typically expressed from the security of knowing that one has legal citizenship somewhere.[3] When the security

---

1. Under the Child Citizenship Act of 2000, adoptees like Kim, who voted under the impression that they were eligible citizens, are granted automatic clemency.

2. Xaykaothao, "For Adopted Kids."

3. Park Nelson, *Invisible Asians*; Kim, *Adopted Territory*.

of legal citizenship is taken away, however, the problems of existing in an in-between, liminal, or hybrid cultural identity may be compounded by a feeling of "humiliation or unfairness," as Kim expressed toward the close of the interview:

> I'm trying to think of the words that fit the best. But when I'm going through all this work and spending all this money to be able to stay legally in this country, that I haven't known any other country—I don't know if the feeling is humiliation or unfairness. But it seems a little surreal to have grown up with the mindset that I had—white family, white suburb, white state—and then find myself as an adult here, you know, forty years old, and standing in line and having to prove myself to be able to stay in this country. It's—it's, it's just not right.[4]

Kim described herself as someone who had already been psychologically displaced and physically transported from Korea into a "flag-toting, Republican, patriot" family. Now she experiences another displacement, "standing in line and having to prove myself." The "surreal" feeling of unfairness, in combination with Kim's "white family, white suburb, white state" mindset, evokes an image of an American (unjustly) marginalized by being made to stand in a line that is presumably composed of nonwhite, nonsuburban (not middle-class) noncitizens: that is, members of categories that she (a forty-year-old adult) cannot believe she is now a part of.

Although Kim can't be considered representative of all adoptees, her ambivalent expressions of non/belonging and (white) privilege are, we argue, reflective of the ambiguous politics of adoptee citizenship. Foreign-born adoptees' presence in the US has been historically, legally, and socially based on exceptions and immigration privilege—adoptees have long been viewed as *non-immigrant immigrants* whose legal and cultural citizenship are considered to be, like transracial adoptive kinship itself, (as-if) natural-born and (almost) white.[5] We use the term *immigration privilege* to describe the ways in which, as children, Korean and other transnational adoptees have been granted priority for entry into and acceptance by the US. This privilege, however, has depended on the rights conferred by US legislators upon their (white) US-citizen adoptive parents. Thus, the entitlement some adoptees feel to both legal and cultural citizenship is related to their adoptive parents' racialized privilege as a predominantly white group of US citizens.

---

4. Xaykaothao, "For Adopted Kids."
5. Kim, *Adopted Territory*.

In our examination of adoptee immigration privilege, we ask: If adoptees' entry into the US and their citizenship are based on their familial relationships to their US-born adoptive parents, does this mean that adoptees should not be considered immigrants? What cultural assumptions about adoptee belonging are embedded in the legal categories that have governed transnational adoption to the US? Further, if it is the case that, as Devon W. Carbado argues, naturalization is not simply a "formal process that produces American citizenship but [also] a social process that produces American racial identities," then how has the ambiguous immigrant status of Korean transnational adoptees also entailed a process of racial naturalization?[6] As members of families that generally identify as white, raised in white-majority neighborhoods or towns, transnational transracial adoptees are often assimilated into both the family and their related racial and cultural identities of whiteness.

For Asian American adoptees, their assimilation into white families has been embedded in a racialized dialectic that sociologist Mia Tuan termed "forever foreigner, honorary white," which is further complicated by their adoption into white families.[7] Psychologist Rich Lee dubs this the "transracial adoption paradox," in which "adoptees are racial/ethnic minorities in society, but they are perceived and treated by others, and sometimes themselves, as if they are members of the majority culture (that is, racially White and ethnically European) due to adoption into a White family."[8] Adoptees, to use Tuan's terms, are honorary whites among family and friends but often cast as forever foreigners outside the home. Whiteness is further normalized through the ideology of colorblind love, which frames the nonwhite child as almost white, and guarantees their cultural and social inclusion by implicitly equating whiteness with being American.[9]

In the remainder of this essay, we examine US federal immigration policies governing entry, immigration, and citizenship for transnational adoptees since the 1950s. We identify ways in which these laws have reproduced a gap between kinship and citizenship that has both legal and cultural ramifications. We also discuss ways in which these laws have sharply distinguished adoptees as non-immigrant immigrants from other kinds of immigrants. This distinction has become particularly complicated since the passage of the Immigration and Nationality Act of 1965 (also known as the Hart–Celler Act), which eliminated national-origin quotas for immigration and paved the way for major demographic shifts evident in US society today. Because Asian Ameri-

---

6. Carbado, "Racial Naturalization," 637.

7. Tuan, *Forever Foreigners and Honorary Whites.*

8. Lee, "Transracial Adoption Paradox," 711.

9. Park Nelson, *Invisible Asians.*

cans have a long history of being racially "extraterritorialized," or assumed to be from elsewhere and not representative of American identity, the gap between kinship and citizenship has been experienced as acutely painful.[10] And in light of dominant narratives of familial belonging and immigrant privilege in transnational adoption, the idea that adoptees must be "naturalized" contradicts the very ethos of "colorblind" love that has long informed the practice of transracial, transnational adoption to the US.

Given the upsurge in anti-immigration policies and the normalization of racist xenophobia during the Trump presidency (2016–20), transnational transracial American adoptees, along with many other immigrants, have experienced more frequent and intense persecution based on their racial appearance. In combination with widely publicized cases of transnational adoptees being deported to their countries of birth, these developments have inspired national campaigns led by Korean and other transnational adoptee activists to raise awareness about adoptees who lack citizenship. This has steered some to renounce or disidentify as (nonwhite) immigrants to shore up the privilege rooted in white familial belonging that guaranteed their immigration privilege as children. However, other adoptees, in some instances for the first time, are actively identifying *as* immigrants, and *with* other immigrants.

The interview with Amie Kim was occasioned by the introduction of Senate Bill 2275 by US Senator Amy Klobuchar of Minnesota. The 2016 Adoptee Citizenship Act (ACA), if passed, would have granted citizenship to adoptees like Kim, who were not covered by the Child Citizenship Act of 2000 (CCA) because they were older than eighteen at the time of the CCA's enactment in February 2001. The adoptees most likely to be affected by the bill were those who had committed felonies and, even if they had served their time, would be subject to detention and deportation. As we discuss below, deportations of adoptees had been taking place since the mid-1990s, but a shift in adoptee sentiment and attitudes regarding deportations and citizenship became noticeable during the 2016 presidential race, and particularly after Trump's victory. The anti-immigrant sentiment stoked by Trump created a more threatening climate than in the past. One indication of the new degree of fear and anxiety under the Trump administration is the fact that, in 2017, Holt International Children's Services, the largest international adoption agency in the US, contacted adoptees whom they had placed to encourage them to confirm their citizenship paperwork. They further advised all transnational

---

10. Carbado, "Racial Naturalization," 638.

adoptees to attain a Certificate of Citizenship, even those who already had naturalization documentation.[11]

This essay is the result of a transdisciplinary collaboration that entailed multiple research methods. As scholars of transnational Korean adoption and adoptee networks, we first noted the emergence of transnational adoptee advocacy projects around Korean adoptee deportee cases in the early 2010s. Adult Korean adoptees had by that time established a strong global network of adoptee organizations and mobilized NGO support for adoptees in South Korea (including some deportees).[12] Many Korean adoptees in the US took the initiative to raise awareness about this issue to help adoptees under imminent threat of deportation. Transnational adoptees from many different sending countries are affected by the laws governing international adoption, and advocacy projects have evolved to support all those who are affected. We refer in this essay to both Korean American adoptees and transnational American adoptees more generally. Our goal is to illuminate the complicated and contradictory history of American immigration policy with respect to transnational adoption, and to ascertain the effects of these changing policies on the discourses and practices of transnational adoption. Our archive therefore includes legislative documents related to adoptee entry and naturalization, news coverage related to adoptee immigration legislation, and information on recent court cases related to the deportation of transnational adoptees. As we witnessed changes in adoptee activism and advocacy in response to the increasing normalization of racism and xenophobia after the 2016 presidential election, we expanded our archive to include interviews with adoptees who are active in the US adoptee citizenship movement. Park Nelson also conducted participant observation in November 2018 and March 2019 with members of Adoptees for Justice (A4J), an adoptee citizenship advocacy group.

Creation of the "Natural Born Alien"

The title of this essay, "Natural Born Aliens," draws attention to the original ambiguity of transracial adoptees' immigration status under US law. The term derives from Senate Bill 2312 ("An Act for the Relief of Certain Korean War

---

11. Cox, "Why All Adoptees Need." There is a higher likelihood under the more progressive Biden administration for legislative action that could secure citizenship for transnational adoptees who lack it. Yet we underscore that the history of anti-immigrant sentiment at the federal level has been pervasive throughout US history and has not been restricted to conservative administrations.

12. Kim, *Adopted Territory*.

Orphans"), which was introduced to the Senate on June 24, 1955. It was introduced to the House of Representatives two days later, and by July 30 it had
been unanimously passed by both houses. Less than two weeks later, it was
signed into law by President Dwight D. Eisenhower as Private Law 48-275.
Congress and the White House expedited this law to allow two US citizens,
Harry and Bertha Holt, to adopt six children from war-torn South Korea.
The Refugee Relief Act of 1953, which governed international adoption at the
time (mostly applying to postwar Korea), permitted a maximum of two children per American family. The bill's author, Senator Richard Neuberger of the
Holts' home state of Oregon, stated in his address to the Senate that Harry
Holt had traveled to Korea on a calling from God and had "eight small children from the ravaged and tormented country of Korea" that he wanted to
"bring to the security and comfort of America."[13] Because the bill was written
specifically to address the needs of the six additional children, they are identified individually using their new, adoptive names: "Joseph Han Holt, Mary
Chae Holt, Helen Chan Holt, Paul Kim Holt, Betty Rhee Holt, and Nathanial
Chae Holt[, who] shall be held and considered to be the natural-born alien
children of Harry and Bertha Holt, citizens of the United States." Rather than
coming to the US as refugee children as they would have under the Refugee
Relief Act, Congress and the president permitted them to enter as "natural-
born alien children" of "citizens of the United States," introducing a novel legal
category that rewrote biological procreation but never erased the children's
"alien" origins.

Transnational adoption to the US began after World War II as a humanitarian effort to resettle displaced children from Britain, Japan, Germany, Greece,
and Italy. At the same time, many so-called GI babies, some of them "mixed
race," were being adopted into American homes. Whereas transnational adoption programs at the time were all considered temporary measures to provide
for children in nations recovering from war, this changed in the aftermath of
the Korean War. Rather than tapering off following the cessation of hostili-
ties, the number of adoptions increased rapidly—particularly after the Holts
established the Holt Adoption Agency, in 1956.[14] In 1961 the Immigration and
Nationality Act of 1952 was amended to include intercountry adoption as a
permanent category in US immigration law; before this, children from Asia
could only enter the country under the terms of temporary "refugee" acts.
Each of these acts was temporarily extended by Congress, which generated

---

13. "Mr. and Mrs. Harry Holt, of Creswell, Oreg., and Eight Korean War Orphans," 84
Cong. Rec. S12,223 (daily ed. Jul. 30, 1955) (statement of Sen. Neuberger).

14. For more on the reasons for this see Kim, "My Folder Is Not a Person," and Kim,
Adopted Territory.

extreme urgency for US organizations involved in overseas adoption to get visas approved for as many children as possible before the acts expired. After concerted lobbying efforts by the Holts, their adoptive parent allies, and other agencies involved with intercountry adoptions, Public Law 87-301 was passed in 1961 to create the "orphan visa" as a permanent instrument with the sole purpose of allowing foreign children to enter the US for adoption. Note that when this special visa designation was approved, federal Asian exclusion laws had been repealed, but tight quota restrictions effectively barred most individuals of Asian nationality from immigration until the 1965 immigration reform; transnational adoption from Korea and other Asian nations was a legal exception to Asian exclusion policies between 1953 and 1965.[15]

Whereas Private Law 48-275 had created the "natural-born alien" category to allow the children adopted by Holt to enter the US, Public Law 87-301 replaced the term *natural-born alien children* with *eligible orphans*. Children who qualified as "eligible orphans" were those younger than fourteen years of age whose parents had died or who had been relinquished by at least one birth parent. Through adoption, these children were "reunited" with American citizens as "immediate relatives." Different relationships and processes that had been lumped together into the oxymoronic "natural-born alien children" were now disarticulated, so that children first had to be legally cut off from existing parents, that is, orphaned in their countries of origin. American citizens could then apply for the "Petition to Classify Orphan as an Immediate Relative" (using the Orphan Visa I-600 to qualify for an Immediate Relative, "IR" visa, one of many orphan visas that have existed since 1961), thereby aligning the child with a nonquota visa provision for immediate relatives, namely spouses and children of US citizens, codified in the Immigration and Nationality Act of 1952 (INA).

The "Proxy Battles"

The terms of the 1961 amendment of the INA were hotly debated between 1958 and 1960, with much of the disagreement centered on a conflict between Harry Holt and the newly legitimated professional social work establishment regarding the practice of "proxy adoptions."[16] The issue of adoptees' citizenship was not central to these debates. Instead, the debate was framed in terms of the legal principle of "the best interests of the child" and on efforts to align

---

15. On national quotas and Asian exclusion, see Ngai, *Impossible Subjects*.

16. See Oh, *To Save the Children*; Winslow, *Best Possible Immigrants*; Choi, "Protection Against Good Intentions."

international adoption procedures with both the restrictions on entry into the US set by the 1952 INA and the standards set by state welfare agencies for selecting adoptive parents and ensuring "child-centered adoption" that had become the norm in domestic adoptions (and which followed the protocol of race matching).[17]

Many social workers considered Holt's practice of obtaining power of attorney from prospective parents in order to serve as their "proxy" in South Korean courts dangerous for the children. Proxy adoptions were finalized before parents and children had met and without the six-month trial period that was overseen by a professional social worker, and which was typically mandated in domestic adoptions. Social workers argued that children from foreign countries, who faced additional challenges in terms of language, cultural adjustment, and racial difference, would be vulnerable to abuse, neglect, or abandonment without proper oversight. Opposition to proxy adoption was spearheaded by Susan T. Pettiss, assistant director of the International Social Service–American Branch (ISS-AB), which had facilitated adoptions from Korea since the Korean War. The Holts and their supporters presented proxy adoption as a necessary expedient given the dire circumstances faced by "mixed race" orphans in South Korea, whom they described as being maladapted to survive in Korea because of their racial difference. The Holts rallied their adoptive parent clients and supporters to rail publicly against the bureaucratic processes that the ISS-AB insisted on, arguing that red tape put children's lives in danger.

The proxy battle was nominally won by ISS and professional social workers, in that the 1961 legislation explicitly states that children adopted from overseas must be "observed" by the adopting petitioner and spouse "prior to or during the adoption proceedings." This was considered the end for proxy adoptions and a victory for professional social workers like Pettiss. However, proxy adoptions continued in all but name; South Korean children were delivered "sight-unseen" to parents who readopted them in their home states.[18] Because the adoptions were not considered finalized under US law, these were technically not proxy adoptions, even though the legal guardianship of the child had been transferred to the adoption agency. This interpretation of the legal role played by state-licensed adoption agencies allowed most American parents to adopt without traveling to Korea, a practice that continued for decades until South Korea disallowed it in 2012.[19]

---

17. For more on regulatory authority over transnational adoption, see Choi, "Protection Against Good Intentions"; and Winslow, *Best Possible Immigrants*.

18. Oh, *To Save the Children*, 150.

19. Park Nelson, *Invisible Asians*.

Under the amended 1961 INA, a child would be legally relinquished by their biological parents and rendered a "paper orphan" in the sending country; the foreign adoption agency would send information about the child to the state-licensed American adoption agency in the US, which would then "refer" the child to prospective parents who had been approved, meaning that they had passed a criminal background check and home study in compliance with state laws. The adopting parents would then file a petition with the INS for this "eligible orphan" to be recognized as an "immediate relative," who could be granted an orphan visa. The child would enter the US as a legal permanent resident, but the adoption would not be finalized for at least six months or up to one year, in keeping with state child welfare laws. At that point, a new birth certificate would be issued showing the child as the "natural born" offspring of the adopting parents. Two years later, the child would be eligible to apply for US citizenship. Thus, a child who entered the US under an orphan visa and whose adoption was finalized in the US would have to wait at least two and a half years before being naturalized.

Under the 1961 legislation, a foreign-born adopted child's legal status shifted across federal immigration categories of "eligible orphan," "immediate relative," "legal permanent resident," and, if naturalized, "US citizen." Until the passage of the Child Citizenship Act of 2000, these shifting statuses were disconnected from the adoption process, which falls under state jurisdiction. Distinct processes generated different paperwork—entry visas for immigration, green cards for legal permanent residence, birth certificates to show legal parentage, and naturalization certificates for citizenship. Within this patchwork of state family law and federal immigration law, it was possible for a child to be legally adopted by a US citizen (and recognized as such by a state court), hold a birth certificate naming the American parents as his or her natural parents, and yet not be a US citizen. Conversely, a child could enter the country under an orphan visa, and even be naturalized, without their adoption being finalized. In this way, the institutionalization of transracial adoption by the 1961 amendment replicated the original gap between kinship and citizenship that had been peculiar to the "natural-born alien children" adopted by Holt in 1955.

The 1977 Amendment

By the 1970s adoptive parents were seeking legislative solutions to close this gap, which had both bureaucratic and social implications. Attempting to reduce the burden on parents, US lawmakers began to question the underlying assumptions written into the 1961 INA amendment. Letters entered into congressional testimony in 1977 to change the law suggested that the legally mandated two-year wait between the adoption and the application for citizenship caused hardship for parents when they registered their children for school and also intensified the adopted children's sense of difference from their peers and other members of their adoptive families.[20] Additionally, parents were unhappy with the limit of two orphan visa petitions per family. Some parents resorted to nonpreference visas to circumvent these restrictions, and such cases were facilitated by sympathetic officials at the INS and State Department, though both the two-year waiting period and the two-child visa limit were legacies of previous legislation and had been intended as checks against child adoption fraud. The two-year naturalization waiting period was designed to allow illegal adoptions to be reversed if needed, such that children could be returned to their birth countries, where they would have retained citizenship. The two-child limit placed an automatic check on child traffickers and on anyone else seeking to adopt large numbers of children.

Throughout the congressional hearing, adoptive parent and adoption agency testimony emphasized the undue hardship placed on adopters; ultimately, the exigencies of protecting the best interests of the child and maintaining safeguards against fraud were abandoned. As a result, the INA was amended in 1978 to remove both of the contested requirements, allowing parents to file for naturalization immediately and to apply for an unlimited number of orphan visas, despite testimony from the INS and the Department of State that revealed a pattern of limited oversight and reliance on the paperwork generated by foreign courts and adoption agencies, whose primary interest, at least in Korea, was in moving as many children as possible.[21] Legal scholar Richard Carlson summarized the situation:

> Despite the interdependence of the foreign relinquishment, United States immigration, and state adoption processes, each is governed by entirely separate bodies of law. State adoption laws are generally quite highly developed, yet devoid of any specific recognition or acknowledgement of transnational adoption. Federal lawmakers and regulators, on the other hand, have developed a body of immigration law which addresses transnational adoption specifically, but which focuses primarily on the immigration aspects. The foreign law regulating relinquishment may be based on totally different con-

---

20. *Alien Adopted Children: Hearings Before the House Subcomm. on Immigration, Citizenship, and International Law, Committee on the Judiciary*, 95th Cong. (1977).

21. Sarri, Baik, and Bombyk, "Goal Displacement and Dependency"; McKee, "Monetary Flows and the Movements of Children."

cepts than those embodied in United States common law. As a result, the law and process of transnational adoption remains disjointed. Most transnational adoptions succeed despite the lack of forthright law, but the failure of lawmakers to provide a clear process creates unnecessary risks and uncertainties.[22]

Given the "disjointed" character of the complex legal and administrative processes of transnational adoption, state courts and immigration officials largely deferred to the expertise of state-licensed adoption agencies. Indeed, private adoption agencies (there are no public agencies at the state or federal levels that facilitate international adoptions to the US) have been the primary and most powerful actors coordinating among the various systems and requirements of foreign governments and US state and federal bureaucracies. The lack of oversight permitted problematic outcomes, the unethical contours of which have only become more obvious over the past two decades. With the thousands of Korean and other transnational adoptees searching for their documents, many of those adopted during the 1960s, 1970s, and 1980s have discovered that fraudulent and falsified documentation is so common as to be considered the norm.[23] Inaccuracies and outright falsifications were rubber-stamped and replicated transnationally by US adoption agencies and ultimately became part of adoptees' personal and familial biographies.[24] Yet today's concerns over the ethics of transnational adoptions are not new; the practices of adoption agencies, particularly in Latin American countries, were explicitly discussed during the 1977 congressional hearing. The Holt Adoption Agency also came under scrutiny in the mid-1970s from international social workers who criticized the expansion of its placement operations into European countries, during a period in which the military government of South Korea was actively promoting the export of children.[25] Whereas the 1961 amendment made adoption a permanent feature of US immigration law and prohibited proxy adoptions as a measure of protection for children from fraudulent or hasty adoptions, the 1977 amendment removed some of the few remaining regulations because they were seen as burdensome to adoptive parents. Both the 1961 and 1977 amendments framed the problem of international adoption in terms of the interests and concerns of adoptive parents and adoption agencies to bring children expeditiously into American homes.

---

22. Carlson, "Transnational Adoption of Children," 320.
23. Park Nelson, "International Adoption."
24. Kim, "My Folder Is Not a Person."
25. Byma, "Overseas Adoptions."

In sum, rather than creating new legal frameworks to address the unique-
ness of transnational as well as transracial adoption, the 1961 and 1977 amendments to the INA replicated the paradox of the (Asian) "natural-born alien
child" of white, US-citizen parents. These amendments instituted legal fictions
that upheld biological kinship as the basis for national and familial belonging yet stopped short of granting the natural-born alien child automatic US
citizenship. This dissonance between the citizenship status of adoptive parents
and that of their adopted children would become more socially and politically
charged by the early 1990s, as larger waves of refugees and undocumented
migrants from the Global South entered the US. As the experiences of Korean
and other transnational adoptees suggest, questions of legal and cultural citizenship became increasingly contested and racialized.

The Creation of the Adoptee Deportee and the Child Citizenship Act of 2000

It was not until the mid-1990s that changes in US immigration and deportation policies began to reveal the consequences of the gap between kinship and
citizenship for transnational adoptees. The Illegal Immigration Reform and
Immigrant Responsibility Act (IIRIRA), passed in 1996 in response to the 1993
bombing of the World Trade Center and the 1995 Oklahoma City bombing,
made it easier to deport immigrants convicted of crimes. While US immigration law has included the consideration of criminal behavior as far back
as the Immigration Act of 1891, which barred immigration by people with
criminal records, the IIRIRA placed increased importance on the removal of
immigrants with criminal records.[26] The act defined more crimes as deportable offenses and thereby rendered more people deportable. In addition, it
changed deportation law from a two-step process that first considered deport-
ability and then weighed the consequences of deportation to a one-step process, largely eliminating the second step that considered the circumstances
of the potential deportee. This change made it more difficult for judges to
exercise discretion and for individual deportations to be waived because of
specific circumstances.[27]

As legal scholar Nancy Morawetz writes in reference to the IIRIRA, "Congress has mandated the deportation of persons whose family members may all
reside in this country, who may have grown up here, who may be needed for

---

26. Gossett, "'[Take from Us Our] Wretched Refuse.'"
27. Morawetz, "Understanding the Impact."

emotional and financial support for minor children or elderly parents, or who may present other compelling equities that counsel against deportation."[28] With respect to transnational adoptees, she continues, "No one imagines that any of these children will engage in crimes, but crime is a statistical certainty with any group. For immigration law to treat [adoptees] as strangers because of [. . .] criminal convictions disrespects the fundamental commitment that [adoptive] parents [. . .] make to their foreign-born adopted children."[29] Morawetz also notes that the IIRIRA fundamentally shifted decades of US immigration policy from one that prioritized family unity to one that disregards it. Since the provisions of the IIRIRA make deportation applicable to more individuals and relief from deportation available to far fewer, the contexts and circumstances of each case, including the consequences of family separation, receive little or no consideration in deportation proceedings.

Between 1910 and 1980, the US had processed about 56,000 deportations because of criminal convictions. In 1999, as a consequence of the 1996 act, that total was surpassed in a single year, and in 2004 about 88,000 individuals were deported after having been convicted of a crime.[30] Since that time, the rate of criminal deportations has averaged about 150,000 per year.[31] With the huge uptick in deportation proceedings overall, and specifically for immigrants convicted of crimes or facing criminal charges, the twenty-year trend of increasing deportation now affects all classes of immigrants, including transnational adoptees.

It only took three years after the passage of the IIRIRA for the first adoptees to be deported. The cases of John Gaul III (deported to Thailand in 1999) and Joao Herbert (deported to Brazil in 2000 and murdered there in 2004) were widely reported at the time. In response to the specter of deportation, US adoptive parents (including one of the bill's main authors, US Representative William Delahunt, adoptive parent of a Vietnamese transnational adoptee) succeeded in passing the Child Citizenship Act of 2000 (CCA), which became effective on February 27, 2001.[32] The CCA conferred automatic citizenship on most future transnational adoptees (all those traveling on nonquota, immediate relative visas IR-3 and IR-4) and on those who had entered the US on orphan visas and who were under the age of eighteen on the date of the bill's enactment. Though the CCA was originally intended to confer citizenship on all transnational adoptees, the legislation was compromised by legislators'

28. Morawetz, "Understanding the Impact," 1938.
29. Morawetz, "Understanding the Impact," 1936.
30. Gossett, "'[Take from Us Our] Wretched Refuse.'"
31. Radford, "Key Findings about U.S. Immigrants."
32. Myers, "Creating (Un)equal Families."

anxiety about not appearing "tough on crime" in the case of any adult immigrant, transnational adoptees not excepted.[33]

The process by which the bill was deliberated and modified offers telling evidence that legislators, who were overwhelmingly supportive of transnational adoptions and the desires of Americans to adopt foreign-born children, considered adoptees to be all but biological offspring of their adoptive parents. Bill HR 2883, introduced in the House of Representatives by Lamar Smith (R-TX) in 1999, was designed to retroactively confer birthright citizenship on all "adopted orphans," as if they had been born in the US. In the eyes of the INS, however, foreign-born adopted children were immigrants who had to be naturalized in order to receive the benefits of citizenship. The agency considered the proposal to retroactively confer birthright citizenship problematic, not only because it would rewrite history and erase the foreign origins of the child, thereby potentially challenging the sovereignty of the sending nation, but also because such an action would "create the perception that adopted children who currently are subsequently naturalized don't enjoy the same rights and privileges as children born to US citizens."[34]

Smith's "Adopted Orphans Citizenship Act" was intended to close the gap between kinship and citizenship, and between family law and immigration law. It sought to apply the legal fiction of "natural-born" to nullify the "alien" origins of the adoptee. But the bill that was ultimately passed, the Child Citizenship Act of 2000, was a combination of Delahunt's bill (HR 3667) and Smith's bill.[35] Its significant change to the original Smith bill was to retain the naturalization requirement procedurally for adoptees whose adoptions had already been finalized rather than granting retroactive as-if-native-born citizenship. From the date the law was enacted, a foreign-born adoptee child would be granted privileged entry as a legal permanent resident (LPR) through the orphan visa. If the child's adoption had been finalized in the sending country, their US citizenship would be automatically granted (IR-3 visa). If the child's adoption had to be finalized in US courts, then they would continue to be an LPR until that time and would obtain citizenship at the time their adoption was finalized (IR-4 visa). By January 2004, after a few years of bureaucratic delay, US Citizenship and Immigration Services (the successor

---

33. Gossett, "'[Take from Us Our] Wretched Refuse.'"

34. *Adopted Orphans Citizenship Act and Anti-Atrocity Alien Deportation Act: Hearings on HR. 2883 and H.R. 3058 Before the Subcomm. on Immigration and Claims, Committee on the Judiciary,* 106th Congress (2000), 12.

35. Gossett, "'[Take from Us Our] Wretched Refuse.'"

agency to the Immigration and Naturalization Service) was automatically processing certificates of citizenship for adopted children entering on IR-3 visas.[36]

Thus, the gap between kinship and citizenship was narrowed but not entirely closed by the CCA, in large part because of INS objections. Smith's bill had attempted to import the biologistic rationale of state adoption laws into the reckoning of national belonging; if adoptees' parental origins were routinely rewritten at the state level through newly issued birth certificates that erased their biological histories, why couldn't federal law perform the same function in the geopolitical sphere by retroactively conferring citizenship to erase their foreign origins? This legal framing of adoptees as not only "as-if-genealogical" but also "as-if-native" reflected how transnational adoptees had been constructed as non-immigrants by their families and communities since the 1950s. For the INS, however, prioritizing the biological basis of citizenship would set a dangerous precedent by suggesting that naturalization was inferior to birthright citizenship. The agency argued strenuously against retroactive citizenship for this reason, also adding that because some foreign-born biological children of US-citizen parents did not automatically receive US citizenship, conferring it on adopted children could create inequality among children within the same family.[37] In other words, if some biological children of US citizens were immigrants under the law, then transnational adoptees also had to be immigrants. The final legislation resolved this issue by removing the naturalization requirements for foreign-born biological children of US citizens. The alienness of the adopted child as an immigrant was thus minimized by rendering them as equivalent as possible to children of US citizens born outside the US. In this way, the CCA maintained biological relatedness as the basis for adoptive kinship, such that adoptive kinship continues to be "as-if-natural-born."[38]

Rep. Delahunt addressed the issue of alienness in his remarks when the CCA came up for vote in the House:

> Mr. Speaker, today is truly a good day, a day that has been long in coming for adoptive parents like myself who feel deeply that their children who were born overseas have been treated differently, as if they were less American than are children who were born in the United States. For the law currently

---

36. *Adopted Orphans Citizenship Act and Anti-Atrocity Alien Deportation Act: Hearings.*

37. *Adopted Orphans Citizenship Act and Anti-Atrocity Alien Deportation Act: Hearings.*

38. The CCA did not, however, address the legal distinction between foreign-born biological children and foreign-born adopted children of *naturalized citizens*—the former automatically derive their US citizenship from their parents, regardless of cohabitation, but the latter do not. Some of these adopted children have also been deported because of felony convictions.

provides that our foreign-born sons and daughters are aliens. They do not have the benefits of citizenship when they arrive on our shores, come into our homes and fill up our lives with joy and love. No, we must petition for naturalization on their behalf, as if we, their parents, were not American citizens. That is unacceptable to Americans who have adopted and particularly for those who are considering adoption. [. . .] It is insulting to parents who have already overcome innumerable administrative obstacles to adopt our children and to bring them home. And more importantly, it is disrespectful to our children.[39]

The INS was clear in its congressional testimony that citizenship by naturalization and citizenship by birth must be equal under the law and used this as a justification for their opposition to granting birthright citizenship to adoptees. But Delahunt's speech suggests that, at least socially and culturally, there is a difference, one that encodes naturalization as inferior to birthright citizenship. For this reason, rather than being celebrated as a joyful rite of passage that makes adoptees into Americans, as is the case for other new Americans in a nation of immigrants (and as was frequently depicted in newspaper articles in the 1950s and 1960s), naturalization of adopted children is instead represented as an "insult" to adoptive parents. The fact that the foreign origins of overseas adoptees mark them (temporarily) as "aliens," and as categorically different from US-born children, is framed as "unacceptable," if not unjust.

Yet the CCA left unaddressed the more severe injustice—the deportation of adoptees whose parents failed to naturalize them before they turned eighteen. The bill had been introduced by Delahunt in part because of the IIRIRA and the deportation cases of Gaul and Herbert.[40] Yet supporters of the bill framed it primarily in terms of the "delay and expense" imposed on adoptive parents who had to remember to file for the child's naturalization before the age of eighteen, when they had "already gone through a costly and cumbersome adoption process."[41] Another reason cited by the bill's legislative supporters was that many parents were unaware that their transnationally adopted children did not already receive citizenship automatically.[42] Positioning transnational adoptees as victims of an unfair policy appealed to a commonsense understanding of transnational adoptees as as-if-native-born Americans, not immigrants. Bureaucratic backlogs were also part of the rationale, as the number of LPRs seeking naturalization had skyrocketed in the late 1990s. Some

---

39. *Adopted Orphans Citizenship Act and Anti-Atrocity Alien Deportation Act: Hearings.*
40. See Gossett, "'[Take from Us Our] Wretched Refuse.'"
41. *Adopted Orphans Citizenship Act and Anti-Atrocity Alien Deportation Act: Hearings,* 5.
42. Dorning, "Petty Acts Now Haunt Immigrants."

adoptive parents, like those of John Gaul III, failed to make their child's eighteenth birthday deadline because of INS delays, which could be as long as two years. The CCA left adoptees over eighteen years of age responsible for their own naturalization and contained language specifically excluding them.[43]

As discussed above, the CCA's exclusion of unnaturalized adoptees born before February 27, 1983, and those entering the US under non-orphan visas left an unknown number of adoptees legally vulnerable for deportation under IIRIRA, and the cases that have emerged since the passage of the CCA are a direct result of this gap. Particularly after 9/11, the intensification of surveillance, security, and documentation requirements has created more situations in which adoptees—who had driver's licenses and Social Security numbers and believed themselves to be US citizens—had to provide proof of citizenship, adoption, and/or naturalization when applying for college, filling out job applications, or getting married, or during encounters with the criminal justice system.

Adoptee Immigration Justice Advocacy: The Deportable Adoptee and the ACA

There are no reliable statistics available on the number of transnational adoptees who lack US citizenship, who have been deported, or who are at risk of removal or deportation. The information that is available about individual cases has been compiled by watchdog or advocacy groups and is largely derived from journalistic sources. For example, Pound Pup Legacy, an online watchdog group that tracks child abuse in adoption and foster care via media reports, as of this writing lists thirty-four cases of adoptees who have been or are subject to deportation. The adoptee advocacy and lobbying coalition Adoptees for Justice (A4J) includes six cases on their website involving adoptees from multiple birth nations and by their count, there are "at least fifty adoptees deported since 2000."[44] Through our informal tracking of newspaper accounts, we know of at least twenty-six.

In the past several years, high-profile cases of adoptee deportations have appeared in the mainstream media. These cases, like those of Russell Green and Adam Crapser, involve adult men who were born in Korea and adopted

43. See Romero, "Child Citizenship Act," for a comparison between the CCA and the unsuccessful Family Reunification Act of 2001, which would have granted citizenship to the undocumented parents of US-citizen children under the family unity principle.

44. Adoptees for Justice, accessed May 2, 2022, https://www.adopteesforjustice.org/impacted-adoptee-stories.

as children by white Americans. Following troubled adoption histories, they were caught up in the criminal justice system and, because they had never been naturalized, became subject to deportation. In the 2010s, in response to the growing problem (and heightened visibility) of adoptee deportation, transnational-adoptee-led organizations began forming to raise awareness of adoptee deportation and advocate for policy changes to provide citizenship for more or all of the US transnational adoptees who currently lack it. During the 2012 AdopSource campaign to oppose the deportation of Russell Green, we noted a significant shift in the lobbying and activism around the issue of adoptee citizenship—from adoptive-parent-led to adoptee-led.

AdopSource, a Minnesota-based organization, developed a campaign that included both adoptive parents and adoptees, most of them Korean adoptees (probably because of the high concentration of Korean adoptees in the state of Minnesota).[45] Although reports on American transnational adoptees in the deportation system had been appearing in the US media since the early 2000s, this was the first campaign to focus on preventing the deportation of an individual adoptee. AdopSource produced a PSA-style video message that circulated widely on social media platforms.[46] It focused on the psychological and physical abuse Green suffered as a child and connected that abuse to the failure of his American adoptive parents to secure his naturalization. The video presented members of several adoptive families telling Green's story; the narrators invoke our common humanity, stating, "We are all Russell Green." Whether "we" are white or Asian, adoptee or parent, the video encourages viewers to identify with Green as an American who has been wronged—first by his adoptive parents, and now by his country.

AdopSource underscored Green's Americanness, downplaying his immigrant status and his criminal record. Like earlier forms of adoptive-parent-led advocacy that upheld adoptees' immigration privilege, this message did not advocate for communities of new Americans and/or American communities of color, nor did it present a critique of deportation in general. Rather, it made a case that transnational adoptees should be treated not like other foreign-born populations but as "real Americans" who are being unjustly discriminated against precisely because they are being treated similarly (through deportation policies that are otherwise fair) to immigrant America. In the fall of 2012, Green's case came to an end when he was allowed to stay in the US not as an adopted child of an American citizen but as an asylee on the basis of his "mixed race" background and his health status.

---

45. Park Nelson, *Invisible Asians.*
46. "Russell Green / Adult Adoptee Deportation PSA."

In 2013, perhaps in response to visible publicity around pending deportation proceedings against Green, adoptive parent and US Senator Amy Klobuchar sponsored an amendment to the Border Security, Economic Opportunity, and Immigration Modernization Act. This amendment would have provided retroactive citizenship to transnational adoptees not covered by the Child Citizenship Act. The bill passed the Senate but was voted down in the House.[47] Klobuchar's bill was the first of several failed federal bills that attempted to address the problem of adoptees without citizenship; Klobuchar was also the sponsor of the first Senate version of the Adoptee Citizenship Act, introduced in 2015. Neither that version nor the one introduced to the House ever came up for a legislative vote.[48]

When the case of Korean adoptee Adam Crapser was widely reported in 2015, a more extensive movement for legislative solutions began to take shape.[49] Adopted in 1979 at three years of age, Crapser had two disrupted adoptions; neither set of parents applied for naturalization on his behalf. Crapser was processed for deportation because of a years-old felony conviction, after he applied for a green card in 2012. Largely in response to Crapser's case, the Adoptee Rights Campaign (ARC) formed within the National Korean American Service & Education Consortium (NAKASEC) to advocate for transnational "adoptees without citizenship." ARC focused on building public awareness about noncitizen adoptees, providing noncitizen adoptees with resources, and actively lobbying for the passage of the ACA (the 2015–16 version, the 2018 version, and the current 2021 version). ARC is notable for its composition: unlike previous activist groups seeking to improve immigration rules for overseas adoptees, which were made up primarily of adoptive parents, most of ARC's members are adult transnational adoptees. Ultimately, ARC's efforts to prevent the deportation of Crapser failed, and in November 2016 he was deported to South Korea, where he currently lives.

In 2018 ARC broke away from NAKASEC, and several core members of ARC left over an internal disagreement about alterations to the language of the ACA. These modifications created carve-outs that would exclude deported adoptees and/or adoptees with felony convictions from citizenship under the proposed legislation. At the time, ARC had been strongly advised by then chair of the Senate Judiciary Committee Chuck Grassley that the best strategy for passing the 2018 version of the ACA would be to distance the bill from any discussion of noncitizen adoptees with criminal convictions. Some ARC members believed the exclusion of adoptees with criminal convictions (as had

---

47. Bowman, "Senate Includes Foreign Adoptees."
48. Gossett, "'[Take from Us Our] Wretched Refuse.'"
49. Jones, "Adam Crapser's Bizarre Deportation Odyssey."

been the case when the 2000 CCA was being debated) would help the bill become law, given the little likelihood that a bill repatriating any immigrant deported under the IIRIRA would be approved by Republican members of Congress. Others, however, believed that failure to close all citizenship loopholes for adoptees would extend the current problem and would also constitute the abandonment of the very adoptees around whom ARC had formed (including Crapser).

Before its restructuring in 2019, ARC asserted on its website the position that adoptees are non-immigrants: "Children brought into the US at the request of their American parents or whose adoptions were facilitated by the federal government *are not immigrants* and should be treated the same as biological children who are born abroad to Americans" (emphasis in the original).[50] This view is consistent with adoptive parent activism around the CCA, which posited that citizenship should be inherited through a transnational adoptee's citizen parents rather than conferred through naturalization, as is the case for immigrants. ARC also stated that its position was to "oppose solutions that co-mingle US foreign adoption and standard immigration policies," suggesting that the organization does not see transnational adoptee citizenship as an immigrant justice issue commensurate with politically sensitive issues like DACA (Deferred Action for Childhood Arrivals), which was intensely debated before and after the 2016 presidential election.

In November 2018 a new transnational adoptee advocacy group formed. Calling themselves Adoptees for Justice, the founding members are all transnational adoptees, some of whom themselves lack US citizenship. Some members were formerly part of ARC, though most were members of other adoptee networking groups across the US. The group formed with the specific goal of securing citizenship for all transnational adoptees, not as a familial right but as immigration reform. Unlike previous organizations advocating for adoptees without US citizenship, A4J identifies closely with other immigrant rights groups seeking immigration justice, including those covered by DACA. In addition, A4J has more in common with immigration and human rights organizations than those involved in past movements. A4J organizes around the motto "Citizenship for All" and has pledged never to compromise on legislation providing citizenship for all transnational adoptees. Because of the causal relationship between criminal convictions and adoptee deportation, the group also recognizes that criminal justice reform needs to be a part of A4J's agenda.

---

50. Adoptee Rights Campaign. In 2019 ARC shifted their attention to focus solely on outreach. It helped form the National Alliance for Adoptee Equality (NAAE), an advocacy organization focused on legislative efforts to pass the 2021 Adoptee Citizenship Act (see Adoptee Rights Campaign).

The creation of A4J, and its ideological ties to immigrant advocacy groups, signals a new direction in transnational adoptee organizing: a shift from total disidentification with immigrant identity for transnational adoptees to total identification of adoptees as immigrants, as well as solidarity with other US immigrants and communities of color. Like ARC, A4J is also inclusive of all transnational adoptees without citizenship, and its membership includes adoptees from South Korea, Taiwan, Costa Rica, Brazil, and Vietnam. As of this writing, A4J is growing and actively organizing in Washington, DC, and around the US in support of their immigration justice policies.[51]

The orientation toward immigrant co-liberation and immigration justice in the early iteration of ARC and currently within A4J can be largely attributed to former ARC members and founding A4J members Becky Belcore and Taneka Jennings. Both are Korean American adoptees based in Chicago and working full-time in immigrant advocacy organizations. Belcore is currently co-director of NAKASEC, and Jennings is the deputy director of the HANA Center, which provides support services and advocacy for Korean American immigrants. Speaking of the time between the creation of ARC and the creation of A4J, Belcore reflected that "just very recently, there is more of an interest from adoptees in pairing the issue of adoptee justice with immigrant justice. [. . .] I had not really heard that before." She also noted the participation of transnational adoptee activists in a twenty-two-day DACA vigil in Washington, DC, that NAKASEC organized from August 15 to September 5, 2017.[52] Though NAKASEC had taken on adoptee citizenship advocacy when they decided to house ARC in 2015 (before Belcore was hired there), the engagement of adoptee activists in other immigrant advocacy work appears to be a reaction to the 2016 election. Jennings drew on this connection between adoptee citizenship and immigrant rights, commenting that "adoptees in this kind of climate that's so anti-immigrant, anti-people of color, anti-women, you know, that is really attacking so many parts of who we are, for anyone who was racialized [. . .] I think there's just a natural feeling of oppression in this kind of environment."[53] Adoptees like Jennings and Belcore are examining hegemonic hierarchies of race, migration, and belonging in order to critique the racist logics that frame adoptees as either racialized immigrants of color or almost-white non-immigrants who deserve exceptional privileges.

---

51. The group has about forty core members across many US states.
52. Becky Belcore, personal communication with Kim Park Nelson, September 24, 2018.
53. Taneka Jennings, personal communication with Kim Park Nelson, October 1, 2018.

Conclusion

In our examination of the history of US transnational adoptee immigration policy and efforts to revise it, we observed repeated attempts to fit adoptees into pre-existing immigration paradigms, into none of which they fit neatly. In a country where citizenship is based on the paradigms of *jus sanguinis* and *jus soli,* much of adoptee immigration law attempts to erase adoptee foreign identity to "naturalize" and normalize adoptee national belonging based on as-if-blood/as-if-natural connections to their adoptive families. We found a long history of adoptive parents effectively leveraging their racial and citizenship privilege to enact policies that extend their entitlements to their foreign-born children. Meanwhile, because of the disconnect between federal authority over immigration and state authority over family law, it appears that private adoption agencies have often been left with the role of steering (or not) adopters (but not adoptees) through both the adoption and the immigration processes—with varying degrees of success. While the effort to streamline a legal transformation of transnational adoptees into American citizens addresses some issues of national and culture belonging, it also creates additional blind spots.

Although adoptee deportations have taken place since at least the 1990s, adoptee advocacy and activism helped bring the cases of Russell Green and Adam Crapser into mainstream visibility. With the cultural normalization of white supremacy and heightened anti-immigration discourses during the Trump presidency, adoptee activism took on new urgency, but it also led to sometimes heated debate among adoptees over the (non)immigrant status of transnational adoptees. As of this writing, it is too soon to say whether nascent identifications among some adoptees with other immigrants will be lasting, and whether liberal discourses and legislative changes more sympathetic toward immigrants will affect these dynamics. We can assert, however, that the dominant view among adoptees and adoptive parents continues to be reflected by ARC activists who argue that they are owed exceptional treatment and greater access to citizenship protections than other immigrant groups based on their status as "as-if-natural-born" children of US-citizen parents. Given this fact, future efforts by adoptees and their advocates are likely to pursue outcomes that reinforce the immigration privilege adoptees have held since 1961.

In conclusion, we ask what rights and privileges transnational adoptees should be able to expect under US law. Instead of arguing for the creation of more exceptions for adoptee immigrants, we view the transnational adoptee population as a bellwether for immigration politics and policies to come. In other words, if after several generations of federal treatment as non-immigrant immigrants, transnational adoptees cannot be secure in their residence and citizenship in the US, then no immigrant can. Therefore, it is not the immigration status of transnational adoptees that needs protection but that of all immigrants to the US.

Bibliography

Adoptee Rights Campaign. Accessed September 6, 2019. https://adopteerightscampaign.org/.

Bowman, Michael. "Senate Includes Foreign Adoptees in US Immigration Reform Bill." *Voice of America,* June 19, 2013. https://www.voanews.com/a/senate-includes-foreign-adoptees-in-us-immigration-reform-bill/1684745.html.

Byma, Sydney. "Overseas Adoptions Threaten Development of Local Services." *Canadian Welfare* 50, no. 3 (1974): 7–11.

Carbado, Devon W. "Racial Naturalization." *American Quarterly* 57, no. 3 (2005): 633–58.

Carlson, Richard R. "Transnational Adoption of Children." *Tulsa Law Journal* 23, no. 3 (1988): 317–77.

Choi, Cathi. "Protection Against Good Intentions: The Catholic Role in the Campaign to Ban Proxy Adoption, 1956–1961." *Journal of Policy History* 31, no. 2 (2019): 242–72.

Cox, Susan. "Why All Adoptees Need a Certificate of Citizenship." *Holt International Blog.* February 8, 2017. www.holtinternational.org/blog/2017/02/why-all-adoptees-need-a-certificate-of-citizenship/. Page discontinued.

Dorning, Mike. "Petty Acts Now Haunt Immigrants; Deportations Soar Under 1996 Law." *Chicago Tribune,* February 20, 2000, section 1, page 1.

Gossett, DeLeith Duke. "'[Take from Us Our] Wretched Refuse': The Deportation of America's Adoptees." *University of Cincinnati Law Review* 85, no. 1 (2017): 33–89.

Jones, Maggie. "Adam Crapser's Bizarre Deportation Odyssey." *New York Times Magazine,* April 1, 2015. https://www.nytimes.com/2015/04/01/magazine/adam-crapsers-bizarre-deportation-odyssey.html.

Kim, Eleana. *Adopted Territory: Transnational Korean Adoptees and the Politics of Belonging.* Durham, NC: Duke University Press, 2010.

———. "My Folder Is Not a Person: Kinship Knowledge, Biopolitics, and the Adoption File." In *The Cambridge Handbook of Kinship,* edited by Sandra Bamford, 451–80. Cambridge: Cambridge University Press, 2019.

Lee, Rich M. "The Transracial Adoption Paradox: History, Research, and Counseling Implications of Cultural Socialization." *The Counseling Psychologist* 31, no. 6 (2003): 711–44.

McKee, Kimberly D. "Monetary Flows and the Movements of Children: The Transnational Adoption Industrial Complex." *Journal of Korean Studies* 21, no. 1 (2016): 137–78.

Morawetz, Nancy. "Understanding the Impact of the 1996 Deportation Laws and the Limited Scope of Proposed Reforms." *Harvard Law Review* 113, no. 8 (2000): 1936–62.

Myers, Kit. "Creating (Un)equal Families in the Child Citizenship Act of 2000." In *The Intercountry Adoption Debate: Dialogues Across Disciplines,* edited by Robert Ballard et al., 567–90. Newcastle upon Tyne: Cambridge Scholars, 2015.

Ngai, Mae M. *Impossible Subjects: Illegal Aliens and the Making of Modern America.* Princeton, NJ: Princeton University Press, 2004.

Oh, Arissa. *To Save the Children of Korea: The Cold War Origins of International Adoption.* Stanford, CA: Stanford University Press, 2015.

Park Nelson, Kim. "International Adoption: Intro: Will There Be a Golden Age for Korean Adoptees?" *POV: In the Matter of Cha Jung Hee,* Public Broadcasting System, September 14, 2010. http://archive.pov.org/chajunghee/international/6/.

———. *Invisible Asians: Korean American Adoptees, Asian American Experiences, and Racial Exceptionalism.* New Brunswick, NJ: Rutgers University Press, 2016.

Radford, Jynnah. "Key Findings about U.S. Immigrants." *Fact Tank: News in the Numbers,* Pew Research Center, June 17, 2019. https://www.pewresearch.org/fact-tank/2019/06/17/key-findings-about-u-s-immigrants/.

Romero, Victor C. "The Child Citizenship Act and the Family Reunification Act: Valuing the Citizen Child as Well as the Citizen Parent." *Florida Law Review* 55 (2003): 489–509.

"Russell Green / Adult Adoptee Deportation PSA" [Video]. *AdopSource,* January 8, 2012. Accessed September 6, 2019. https://www.youtube.com/watch?v=lWOOfxXzLlQ.

Sarri, Rosemary C., Yenoak Baik, and Marti Bombyk. "Goal Displacement and Dependency in South Korean–United States Intercountry Adoption." *Children and Youth Services Review* 20, nos. 1&2 (1998): 87–114.

Tuan, Mia. *Forever Foreigners and Honorary Whites: The Asian Ethnic Experience Today.* New Brunswick, NJ: Rutgers University Press, 1998.

Winslow, Rachel Rains. *The Best Possible Immigrants: International Adoption and the American Family.* Philadelphia: University of Pennsylvania Press, 2017.

Xaykaothao, Doualy. "For Adopted Kids, Having American Parents Doesn't Always Mean U.S. Citizenship." *MPR News,* April 12, 2016, video, 6:55–7:42. https://www.mprnews.org/story/2016/04/12/adult-adoptee-citizenship-bill.

CHAPTER 4

Cosmopolitan Families

Globalizing Americans' International Adoptions

AMY E. TRAVER

Analyses of Americans' international adoptions tend to center the concept of the nation. For example, Briggs situates international adoption within a nationalistic discourse that privileges (white) Western family constructions and postwar liberal interventionism.[1] Similarly, Dorow describes how international adoption helps shore up the American nation-state by engaging myths of national exceptionalism, benevolence, and open borders.[2] Yet, as a phenomenon that both relies on and transgresses the nation, international adoption is also a potential case study for an analysis of the contemporary tenets and tensions of cosmopolitanism. In this chapter, I draw on semistructured in-depth interviews with more than ninety Americans involved or interested in an adoption from China (herein referred to as American China adoptive parents) to understand whether, when, and how these parents perceive and frame international adoption as a cosmopolitan effort. In doing so, I hope to add empirical weight to the literature on "actually existing cosmopolitanisms,"[3] helping to propel the concept out of the domain of abstract theorizing and into the realm of everyday practice and empirical analysis.

---

1. Briggs, "Mother, Child, Race, Nation."
2. Dorow, *Transnational Adoption.*
3. Malcomson, "Varieties of Cosmopolitan Experience."

I begin the chapter with a review of relevant theoretical and methodological frameworks.[4] I then move into an exploration of the case at hand: American China adoptive parents' cosmopolitan orientations. Consistent with the theoretical goals of the chapter, I conclude with a summary of conceptually significant findings (the tools, transgressions, and tensions that ground American China adoptive parents' engagement with and deployment of cosmopolitan tropes) and proposed directions for future research.

Theoretical Framework

Cosmopolitanism is a concept of rich history and diverse application. Yet, as exemplified by the work of Nussbaum, it has traditionally been used to describe moral ideologies of and/or allegiances to the global community.[5] While rooted in the purportedly natural universality of humans as humans, applications of cosmopolitanism have long focused on the concept's relevance to human political life (political rights and citizenship) as well as the relationship between cosmopolitanism and particularities like the nation-state.[6]

In this chapter, I use *cosmopolitanism* to refer to the ways in which an actor's local experiences (their perspectives, sentiments, and actions) engage, reflect, and are potentially transformed by their consideration of global others and concerns. Grounded in the realities of our contemporary globalized world, this usage borrows heavily from Levy and Sznaider's definition of cosmopolitanism as "a process of 'internal globalization' through which global concerns become part of local experiences of an increasing number of people."[7]

Globalization has impacted the study and applicability of cosmopolitanism in three significant ways. First, through "the geographical expansion [. . .] of international trade," "the global networking of finance markets," and "the growing power of transnational corporations," advanced capitalism has undermined national boundaries and evidenced cosmopolitanism as a lived reality.[8] Second, the transnational institutions and social movements that have emerged with globalization have made visible a cosmopolitan civil society that

---

4. Beck, "Cosmopolitan Society and Its Enemies," 21.

5. Nussbaum, "Patriotism and Cosmopolitanism."

6. See, for example, Rée, "Cosmopolitanism and the Experience of Nationality"; Calhoun, "Class Consciousness of Frequent Travelers."

7. Levy and Sznaider, "Memory Unbound," 87.

8. Beck, "What Is Globalization?," 102.

both contains and exists beyond the nation-state.[9] Third, the rise of human rights frameworks, which Levy and Sznaider identify as prominent in/to conceptualizations of cosmopolitanism, have exposed the more universal ideals that run counter to existing intra- and international divisions.[10]

In other words, as a phenomenon "that intensifies connections, enhances possibilities for cultural translations, and deepens the consciousness of globality," globalization has helped demonstrate the relevance of cosmopolitanism to all aspects of social life—not just politics.[11] For example, in studies of social identity, culture, and association/affiliation, scholars now use cosmopolitanism to capture the movement toward shared knowledge, multiple attachment, and complex allegiances that define the "second age of modernity."[12]

Additionally, globalization has helped show how cosmopolitanism's universalism exists alongside of and often through the particular. For instance, in studies of the breadth and depth of global integration, scholars have identified instances of "rooted cosmopolitanism," wherein actors' local attachments mediate their felt connections to and actions toward global others.[13] In this research, cosmopolitanism is often associated with notions of openness, compatibility, multiplicity, and plurality and difference.[14] In fact, for many contemporary scholars of cosmopolitanism, it is the tensions between the global/local and the universal/particular, as well as the changes that such tensions inspire, that define cosmopolitanism today.[15]

Notably, contemporary international adoptions unfold in intersecting global and local contexts that encourage the complex particularities and boundary-blurring multiplicities that constitute the aforesaid definition and use of *cosmopolitanism*. Consistent with the focus of this volume, this reality is well evidenced in the structural and cultural conditions that give shape to international adoptive parents' engagement with their children's ethnic heritage. For instance, global human rights endeavors—like the Convention on the Rights of the Child, which was adopted by the United Nations General Assembly in 1989, and the Hague Convention on Protection of Children

---

9. Kaldor, "Cosmopolitanism and Organized Violence."

10. Levy and Sznaider, *Human Rights and Memory*; see also Beck, "What Is Globalization?"; Soysal, *Limits of Citizenship*.

11. Delanty, "Cosmopolitan Imagination," 38.

12. Beck, "Cosmopolitan Perspective." See, for example, Robbins, "Introduction Part I."

13. Appiah, "Cosmopolitanism." See, for example, Beck, *Cosmopolitan Vision*; Lamont and Aksartova, "Ordinary Cosmopolitanisms."

14. Delanty, "Cosmopolitan Imagination"; Lamont and Aksartova, "Ordinary Cosmopolitanisms"; Hollinger, *Postethnic America*; Cohen, "Rooted Cosmopolitanism"; Anderson, *Cosmopolitan Canopy*.

15. Delanty, "Cosmopolitan Imagination"; Beck, "Cosmopolitan Society and Its Enemies."

and Cooperation in Respect of Inter-Country Adoption, which was adopted by the Hague Conference on Private International Law in 1993—charge that internationally adopted children are entitled to ethnocultural continuity and community.[16] Similarly, in the US, internationally adopted Korean Americans, adoption scholars, and adoption agency representatives and social workers attest to the social-psychological value of internationally adopted children's connections to their ethnocultural heritage and nation of birth.[17] Yet how does an American international adoptive parent actualize a child's right to a specific ethnic identity/community and nation without marking that child as "'naturally' (belonging) to another (family) or place"?[18] Research indicates that they do so by personally identifying with the ethnocultural heritage of their child, transforming the (weighty) particularities of the child's ethnocultural identification into a shared (cosmopolitan) family project.[19]

Methodological Framework

At present, few scholars have applied the concept of cosmopolitanism to the study of American international adoptive parents.[20] One reason for this might be that the nation-state is such a visible unit of analysis in international adoption. For example, the acts of individual nation-states make international adoption necessary: a sending state's policies render children available for adoption (China's one-child policy or the relative absence of social welfare support in South Korea, to give just two examples), as do national reactions to war and poverty (decision-making in postwar Vietnam and postsocialist Russia). Likewise, the acts of individual nation-states—often prompted by state citizens' activism—make international adoption structurally possible: the agents of sending and receiving states sanction international adoptions, while

---

16. Rios-Kohn, "Intercountry Adoption."

17. See, for example, Huh and Reid, "Intercountry, Transracial Adoption and Ethnic Identity"; Yoon, "Intercountry Adoption"; Mohanty, Keokse, and Sales, "Family Cultural Socialization."

18. Yngvesson, "'Niña de Cualquier Color.'"

19. Traver, "Becoming a 'Chinese American' Parent"; Hollinger, *Postethnic America*.

20. Scholars' scant references to international adoptive parents' cosmopolitanisms tend to take one of two forms. The first focuses on parents' "thin" cosmopolitanisms, exploring international adoptive families that are created in/by a spirit of rescue (Dorow, *Transnational Adoption*) and/or aspirations of ethnonational/ethnocultural harmony (Anagnost, "Scenes of Misrecognition"; Dorow, "Racialized Choices"). The second equates parents' cosmopolitanisms with privilege and neocolonialism, noting how international adoptive families are built at the expense of the developing world (Yngvesson, "'Niña de Cualquier Color'").

the transfer of national citizenship marks *many* previously foreign *orphans* as officially adopted.[21]

Another reason for this could be that the international adoption discourse tends to rely heavily on the language of the nation. For example, studies of receiving nations reveal how themes of national exceptionalism and paternalism, as well as nationalistic models of family and caregiving, mediate the messages and actions of international adopters, adoption agency employees, and policymakers.[22] Likewise, research on sending nations indicates that state governments construct adoptees as a "national resource" at the same time that their citizens experience international adoption as a "national shame."[23]

Yet, because cosmopolitanism tends to work with and through the nation rather than against it, it is important that scholars of international adoption not be hindered by what Beck calls "methodological nationalism," that is, the assumption that the nation is "the power container of social processes" and that the national is "the key-order for studying major social, economic, and political processes."[24] Instead, scholars should strive to recognize those moments when participants perceive and frame international adoptive families as existing both because of and beyond the nation-state. Studies by Kim and Yngvesson, which reveal the deterritorialized identities of many international adoptees, evidence the power of this perspective.[25] By applying a new methodological framework to interviews with American China adoptive parents, I hope to better understand both the theoretical applicability of cosmopolitanism and the experiences of international adopters, more generally.

In 2005 I conducted semistructured in-depth interviews with ninety-one American adults involved or interested in an adoption from China. Interviewees were located via a snowball sampling technique initiated from a variety of starting points: friends and their acquaintances, calls for participants posted on adoption research sites or in adoption newsletters, and calls for participants distributed via adoption blogs, chat groups, and email discus-

---

21. Yngvesson, "'Niña de Cualquier Color.'" The word *many* is used to highlight the variability and tenuousness of citizenship claims in international adoption (see Kim and Park Nelson in this volume). Likewise, the word *orphans* is set in italics to signify that many of the children made available for international adoption are not, in fact, orphans.

22. Melosh, *Strangers and Kin*; Dorow, *Transnational Adoption*; Eng, "Transnational Adoption and Queer Diasporas"; Briggs, "Mother, Child, Race, Nation"; Dorow, *Transnational Adoption*.

23. Yngvesson, "'Niña de Cualquier Color'"; Dorow, "Racialized Choices"; Melosh, *Strangers and Kin*.

24. Robbins, "Introduction Part I"; Beck, "Cosmopolitan Society and Its Enemies," 21.

25. Kim, "Wedding Citizenship and Culture"; Yngvesson, "'Niña de Cualquier Color.'"

sion lists. Interviews lasted one to two hours, and all were tape recorded and transcribed.

In selecting the aforementioned starting points, I endeavored to capture the range of American China adoption experiences, constructing a sample that was not representative but reflective of existing scholarship in the relevant literature(s). To begin, I divided the sample into three groups of interviewees, each symbolizing a particular stage of adoption from China: preadoption, in the midst of an adoption or waiting, and postadoption. This spectrum of adoptive parents gives the project a sense of longitudinal time, which, in turn, permits exploration of Americans' adoptions from China as a process.

In addition, each spectral stage reflects the diversity of American parents who adopt from China: white, Black American, and Asian American parents are included in each group, and each group is also diversified by variables like parent gender, age, socioeconomic status, geographic location, and family form (adoptive or biological/adoptive families; single-parent, married, or divorced families). As unique cases nestled within the same phenomenon, these parent clusters serve a deliberately comparative function: they reveal variations in parents' beliefs/behaviors while exposing the potential mediating conditions of this variability.

I then read the interview transcripts through a process of open coding, applying the same conceptual categories or codes to all data at an analytical moment—today—that is admittedly different from the time of data collection and the initial period of data analysis.[26] At that time, Americans were debating the fixedness and fluidity of ethnocultural/racial identities, and my guiding framework reflected those concerns.[27] More recently, as the US grapples with simultaneous appeals to/for global partnership and (white) nationalism, the data called out for a new analysis. Thus, I made an effort to read the interview transcripts closely—as an observer employing a methodologically "cosmopolitan outlook"—for moments when nationally situated parent participants engage and deploy cosmopolitan tropes.[28] This act of rereading data is consistent with the work of Dorow and Swiffen, who, in their research on "U.S. parents of children adopted from China," illustrate how reinterpreting previously collected data through a "new set of questions" can provide additional insights into ongoing phenomena.[29]

---

26. Emerson, Fretz, and Shaw, *Writing Ethnographic Fieldnotes.*

27. For readers interested in more information on this framework, see Traver, "Becoming a 'Chinese American' Parent"; Traver, "Towards a Theory of *Fictive Kin Work.*"

28. See Beck and Sznaider, "Unpacking Cosmopolitanism for the Social Sciences."

29. Dorow and Swiffen, "Blood and Desire," 564.

Findings

In this section, project findings are organized according to the main themes that emerged during the most recent analysis. The first two themes relate to American China adoptive parents' embrace of a cosmopolitan orientation in the period leading up to and including their international adoption, revealing the role that global media and travel play in this embrace.[30] The second two themes highlight how American China adoptive parents use the language of cosmopolitanism to frame their actions and identifications in the period following an international adoption. While these themes help illuminate aspects of Americans' international adoption experiences, they also highlight the ways in which cosmopolitanism is constructed, experienced, and employed by the nationally situated.

Global Media

Volkman describes how American China adoptive parents frequently define themselves as "active citizens of the world" prior to their adoption.[31] For many, this identification stems from membership in transnational families or employment with multinational corporations. Kim, a white waiting parent, draws on both experiences as she describes her family's decision to adopt internationally:

> We have kind of an international family, and when you have family that is so far away you learn that [. . .] people might be different looking or like to eat different things but we are all also the same, when it comes down to it. And my husband has a lot of business that is international, so I think that makes the world very small to us, too. You know, everybody is connected.

Despite Kim's example, however, research indicates that most manifestations of cosmopolitanism today aren't a function of globe-spanning familial or professional networks. If this were the case, then cosmopolitanism would, by necessity, be an orientation reflected only by the globally mobile and/or elite. Instead, studies demonstrate that in constructing a "global public," global media have helped make the "boundaries of inclusion and exclusion" dynam-

---

30. For readers interested in American China adoptive parents' global consumer behaviors, see Traver, "Home(land) Décor."

31. Volkman, "Embodying Chinese Culture," 31.

ic.[32] In the field of international adoption research, Yngvesson indicates that global media have made the distant "familiar" to international adopters,[33] encouraging them to experience themselves as existing in "a single social space" with children around the world.[34]

Cartwright builds on this idea, exploring media's role in making visible and circulating the image of the global social "orphan": a child in need of care and protection "beyond what (the) home state could provide."[35] Reflecting on Arendt's distinction between a politics of compassion and a politics of pity, she argues that global media have led to a collapse in distance, which encourages potential adopters to experience and articulate a sense of proximal suffering with the world's orphan children.[36] Levy and Sznaider ground the theoretical tenets of this argument, noting how global media can inspire both a sense of moral obligation and a (re)action to the distant other.[37] Pamela, a white waiting parent, exemplifies this as she roots her decision to adopt internationally—and to parent, more generally—in her mediated awareness of children's suffering:

> We were going to Disney World and I saw a *USA Today* article while we were on the plane about the lost boys of the Sudan. Before that I'd been like, you know, "Parenthood, I can really do without this forever." But I read that article and suddenly needed to be a parent. So then I started researching adoption, and in China there is a huge need.

Significantly, in both Cartwright's analysis and Pamela's orientation/ experience, the global social orphan is a child of color, and the mechanism of obligatory assistance is the white family. In this way, racial difference seems to heighten both the felt need for, and the felt significance of, proximity: through global media, children marked as other are constructed and consumed as both familiar and potentially familial.

Equally notable, however, is that unlike many of their historical counterparts who adopted from Korea and Vietnam after viewing televised images of children orphaned by war, many American China adoptive parents frame

---

32. Delanty, "Cosmopolitan Imagination," 37.
33. Yngvesson, "'Niña de Cualquier Color,'" 181.
34. Beck, "What Is Globalization?," 29.
35. Cartwright, "Images of 'Waiting Children,'" 198.
36. See also Yngvesson, "'Niña de Cualquier Color.'" Of additional relevance is Ahmed, *Cultural Politics of Emotion*, which reveals the movement and cultural/structural power of emotions, particularly in relation to the nation.
37. Levy and Sznaider, "Memory Unbound."

international adoption not as an act of rescue but as a means to actualize the rights of another. Writing about the global agreements that arbitrate international adoption, Rios-Kohn describes how orphans are no longer depicted as victims in need of care; instead, they are portrayed as individuals robbed of the universal right to a name, identity, and family.[38] Connie, a white waiting parent, draws on rights-based notions as she defends her preferred method of family formation against accusations of paternalistic (inter)nationalism:

> I just try to stack it all up and say, "All in all, does a child not have a right to a family and to whatever resources, you know, seem fundamental?" I guess how I think about it, the child, the individual child, is much easier to think about than the borders of the countries.

Taken together, American China adoptive parents' statements indicate how global media have helped render and circulate images of children in need alongside cosmopolitan conceptions of global proximity and universal rights/responsibilities. In turn, these images and conceptions have had a direct impact on Americans' rooted journeys to and framings of international adoption.

Global Travel

While American China adoptive parents' motivations to adopt can reflect an already existing cosmopolitanism, the act of adopting internationally can also spur a cosmopolitan orientation among the previously unidentified. For some parents, it is the selection of a sending nation—and their efforts to learn about other countries and cultures along the way—that prompts this development. Demonstrating how cosmopolitanism can work with and through the construct of the nation, Vivian, a white waiting parent, states: "I've been reading so much about China and Chinese stuff. I feel like I have an entrée into the world."

---

38. Rios-Kohn, "Intercountry Adoption"; see also Yngvesson, "'Niña de Cualquier Color.'" As indicated in an earlier section of this chapter, both the Convention on the Rights of the Child, which was adopted by the United Nations General Assembly in 1989, and the Hague Convention on Protection of Children and Cooperation in Respect of Inter-Country Adoption, which was adopted by the Hague Conference on Private International Law in 1993, charge that internationally adopted children have a right to cultural continuity and community (Rios-Kohn, "Intercountry Adoption").

For other American China adoptive parents, it is the act of meeting new people while gathering and submitting their extensive adoption paperwork that encourages cosmopolitanism. AnnMarie, a white waiting parent, explains:

> The neatest thing about this whole process is all the people along the way who help you to become a family. That's the community, the global part of it. To adopt this child, I have met so many people, and I have had relationships with people I would have never expected to have had a relationship with.

Notably, while AnnMarie characterizes her new relationships as global, the bulk of the process that she references unfolds within the US. As a result, her comments are perhaps best read through the lens of Lamont and Aksartova, who see cosmopolitanism in actors' efforts to engage "broad principles of inclusion" in their negotiation of local differences and distances.[39] For American China adoptive parents, who, by virtue of Chinese adoption regulations, must complete their paperwork and travel in agency-organized groups of adopters, these "broad principles" include interactions across the vast religious, socioeconomic, and regional differences that divide Americans. Liana, a white waiting parent living in a large city on the East Coast of the US, describes how a collective adoptive parent identity emerged out of the online interactions of her diverse travel group:

> At first I thought, "We don't need to be friends." I heard that people bond on these trips (and I thought), "That's ridiculous, I can't see bonding with these people." I have to admit, I was real snobbish about, like, "What do I have in common with, you know, this woman from Kansas that's got three children already?" When people told me about these web groups, I really looked down [on them] because people weren't like me. But now I'm kind of addicted to it! Some of these women, they're so cutesy, they have quilt swap and recipe swap. I mean, I'm loving it because I feel connected to these women, and they are not like me.

Additionally, and reflective of Allen and Hamnett's work on globalization's "democratization" of travel, American China adoptive parents' adoption trip—as a trip—plays a large role in their burgeoning cosmopolitanism.[40] According to Volkman, these trips are historically unique: before the 1990s most Americans who become parents through international adoption met their children

---

39. Lamont and Aksartova, "Ordinary Cosmopolitanisms," 3.
40. Allen and Hamnett, A Shrinking World?, 184.

stateside.[41] John, a white father of a three-year-old girl, reveals how visiting China to complete his daughter's adoption impacted his perspective on the world:

> (Before traveling) I was wound up so tight, because this is the first time I had ever been out of the country, and I didn't know what to expect. But, you know, then you get back, and it hits you a couple of weeks later, "Man, I was just halfway across the world a couple of weeks ago." The world is such a smaller place now. I could get on a plane and go anywhere I want in just a few hours. It changes your life and your outlook, your viewpoint tremendously.

Building on this point, Catherine, a white mother of a two-year-old girl, outlines how adoption travel changed more than just her impression of global physical space; it also impacted her emotional connection to those she once perceived as different and distinct.

> The (2004 Asian) Tsunami hit me more than it would have before I adopted. Before I think I would have felt a little sense of, "Oh, well, that's somewhere else." And now, having adopted, you realize someone somewhere else is not that far, and that has been a wonderful aspect that has changed. We definitely feel more like global citizens now than we did before we adopted. Whatever that sense of "other" was, whether it was because of racism or lack of travel experience or a mixture of things, that's really shifted in a stealth way.

In other words, as with global media consumption, global travel seems to have a direct impact on American China adoptive parents' sense of themselves as proximal to a universe of once distant others. Significantly, these others include Americans and non-Americans, signaling the ways in which travel impacts and integrates the national and the global in diverse, complex ways.

Yet, American China adoptive parents' cosmopolitanisms are more than just a function of their global media consumption and travel; they are also intimately linked to their construction of family. Amending her comments above, Catherine reveals how, by simultaneously crossing the boundaries of nation and biology, she furthered her cosmopolitan orientation: "Also, by loving somebody who is not biologically related, I just feel like we really are all connected." Thus, the following two themes—global actions/connections and conceptions of belonging—take up the unique and central role of kinship in this development.

---

41. Volkman, "Embodying Chinese Culture."

Global Actions/Connections

American China adoptive parents' cosmopolitan orientations do not dissipate after their adoption. For many, the act of bearing witness to global inequalities—both directly, through travel, and indirectly, through media and their child's experiences—only compounds it. According to Melosh, Americans who adopt internationally often come into contact with previously unknown levels of deprivation and suffering.[42] Describing her new job with a global NGO, Beth, a white mother of a two-year-old girl, reveals how, in expanding her "circle of sympathy," international adoption compelled her to act more formally on behalf of children around the world:[43]

> You know, since bringing Meghan home I have, I don't know, I've been in so much pain over the fact that kids are in orphanages. I mean, obviously I knew that beforehand, but it didn't hit me the way it did until I had her. And so I've really been struggling and trying to figure out what to do.

Robbins writes that cosmopolitanism signifies a "willingness to consider the wellbeing of someone who does not belong to the same nation."[44] Bartholet's findings reflect this idea, evidencing how American international adopters become aware of children in crisis—and how frequently they respond with wide-ranging forms of support.[45] Becky, a white mother of a three-year-old boy, explains how their adoption prompted her husband to engage in global humanitarian work:

> Six months after he came home with Lee (their son) he went back and worked in an orphanage for three weeks. You see, he came in from China with Lee and he went into a terrible depression about life not being meaningful because, I mean, you go over there and the things that you see, and then when you come home you have to start fixing people's computers or whatever silly job you do. He really, really wanted to go back. Even now, he would get up and go to China in a minute. Then, when everybody heard about the (2004 Asian) Tsunami I said to him, "You know what, why don't you just go and do something there?" So he did that, and then he worked in Thailand.

---

42. Melosh, *Strangers and Kin*.
43. Levy and Sznaider, "Institutionalization of Cosmopolitan Morality," 155.
44. Robbins, "Introduction Part I," 6.
45. Bartholet, "International Adoption."

Notably, parents' "willingness to consider the wellbeing" of another also extends to those who may suffer because of international adoption: their children's birth parents. Acknowledging that all parents "belong to the same symbolic universe of reference," Ellen, a white mother of two girls under the age of seven, expresses a strong desire to bring comfort to her daughters' first families:[46]

> My heart just breaks thinking of my little girls' birth parents. Both of them had a little red envelope left with them with their birth date, and one had a little blessing written on it. We looked into running an ad in the local paper, I don't know if they [their birth parents] would ever see it, but to tell them that their babies have been adopted and are happy and healthy. Just to give them some sort of reassurance. I mean, what a horrible, what a void, for a parent. They don't ever get to know what happens to them.

Presently, in the US, adoptive parents are actively encouraged by social workers, family therapists, and adult adoptees to consider, refer to, and identify with their children's birth parents. Writing specifically about American parents who adopt from China, Dorow notes that birth parents assume a "shadowy presence" in the lives of adoptive families today: while not physically present, they are never far from the family's collective imagination.[47] Janet, a white mother of two girls under the age of ten, exemplifies this: "I talk about birth family a lot with my kids. We have birth family traditions we do, like between Mother's Day and Father's Day we plant a fir tree or a perennial every year for their birth parents."

Johanna, a white mother of a six-year-old girl, evidences the emotions that ground and stem from these shadows:

> At times it is overwhelming to have a little kid who is constantly talking about her Chinese mommy and daddy [. . .] but it's been a really important thing for us to really try to be open. I've had people say, "Doesn't it hurt you when she says that?" But it doesn't, because it's the reality and gosh, golly, I can't imagine what it would be like from her perspective.

Significantly, Johanna's sentiments also reveal the extent to which American China adoptive parents' cosmopolitanisms serve a distinctly local purpose: in making and sustaining globe-spanning connections with those made

---

46. Lamont and Aksartova, "Ordinary Cosmopolitanisms," 3.
47. Dorow, *Transnational Adoption*, 15.

visible or left behind by international adoption, parents transcend the American cultural trope of exclusive belonging to both unify and define their particular family form.[48]

Conceptions of Belonging

American China adoptive parents' felt connections to multiple nations and family units exemplify the spirit of multiplicity that defines cosmopolitanism today.[49] Virginia, the white mother of a twenty-month-old girl, reveals how China is more than her daughter's birth nation; it is also a nation with which her family identifies:

> When we first made the decision to adopt from China, not only did we feel this sense of joy that we were going to add to our family, but I know both of us sort of felt like, "Wow, we're, kind of, not adopting the country but opening up a relationship with the country." And for us that was very exciting.

Volkman describes how international adoptive families' efforts to engage a new national referent has increased exponentially with globalization.[50] For example, many international adoptive families now avail themselves of regular travel to, and state-sponsored homeland tours in, their child's first home. Yngvesson adds to this finding by describing the impacts of these regular border-crossings on adoptees and adoptive parents, alike.[51] Writing about his family's first return trip to China, Alan, the white father of seven-year-old Ting, brings these impacts to light:

> We walked the streets, breathed the air, and imagined what life would have been for Ting had she not been spirited across the Pacific five years ago. [. . .] It felt to all of us like going home. Considering that our family is now Chinese American, that should come as no surprise.[52]

Alan's reference to his family's new binational/bicultural identity reflects the cosmopolitan sentiment that "everybody matters—but they matter in their

---

48. See also Shiao, Tuan, and Rienzi, "Shifting the Spotlight."
49. Vertovec and Cohen, "Introduction."
50. Volkman, "Embodying Chinese Culture."
51. Yngvesson, "Going 'Home.'"
52. Morse, "Returning to China."

specificity."[53] Significantly, most American China adoptive parents today recognize and celebrate their children's ethnocultural heritage. Janet, again:

> Before the feeling was different, it was that you bring the kids back, you pretend that they are the same as you, and end of story. [. . .] But the child is going to feel different. I mean, the child *is* different [emphasis hers], so you might as well celebrate that difference and the diversity of the family.

But as both Alan and Janet indicate, many white American China adoptive parents see themselves as agents and subjects of their family's Chinese cultural socialization. In contrast to multiculturalism, which emphasizes rigorous notions of group belonging and culture, cosmopolitanism is less culturally essentialist, stressing the voluntary and fluid nature of ethnic identification and the dynamism of ethnocultural content and collectives.[54] Reflecting on her attendance at a Lunar New Year celebration, Beth confirms this theoretical insight:

> So I've been thinking about it, and it was really through this event that I realized that it's about, you know, experiencing this with her, not introducing her to her culture. Does that make sense? It's really about experiencing it with her and learning and growing myself. And that is just extremely powerful because it's not about obligation or duty; It's a wonderful gift.

Thus, many American China adoptive parents recognize that in embracing Chinese culture, their families are also actively constructing a new cultural form. For example, while David, a white father of a ten-year-old girl, defines his family as Chinese American, he adds the caveat: "You know, there are a number of different models of being Chinese American and we are going to be yet another one." Making a connection between international adoptive families' creative cultural constructions and the proliferation of global cultural forms today, Connie summarizes this point: "What's wrong with creating a hybrid culture? Don't those happen all over the place now?"

Kim shows how cultural hybridity is directly relevant to the experiences of adult Korean adoptees, who, upon returning to a welcoming South Korea, realize their liminality.[55] According to Hübinette, one common response to this realization is the embrace of a "third space," where "culture has no unity, purity or fixity, and where primordial notions of race and nation have been

---

53. Appiah, "Cosmopolitanism."
54. Vertovec and Cohen, "Introduction"; Hollinger, *Postethnic America*.
55. Kim, "Wedding Citizenship and Culture."

replaced by a floating and hybrid existence."[56] Margaret, a white waiting parent who worries about her future daughter's ability "to integrate all of the different pieces of herself into one confident, self-actualized young woman," finds comfort in that prospective hybridity. Making an almost explicit reference to cosmopolitanism, she speaks volumes about her daughter and her family: "You know, that's why I think she's really going to be more of, like, a global child than any one specific thing, also just because that's who we are."

Discussion and Conclusion

The definition of cosmopolitanism has expanded with globalization. While once used in reference to moral ideologies of and/or allegiances to the global human community, particularly in the realm of politics, it is now employed to capture experiences of human openness, compatibility, multiplicity, and plurality and difference. Similarly, while the concept's explicit claims to universalism were once challenged by such particularities as the nation-state, cosmopolitanism is now understood to work both with and through social actors' rooted experiences. As a result, the analytical relevance and application of cosmopolitanism has also expanded. More social scientists are using the concept in their empirical research, and more social actions/interactions are coming to be viewed as instances and examples of "actually existing cosmopolitanisms."[57]

Yet, at the time of this writing, few social scientists have applied cosmopolitanism to the case of international adoption—and those who have done so have limited their analyses to adoptees or critiqued the "thin" cosmopolitanism of adoptive parents. In an effort to add empirical weight to analyses of cosmopolitanism while countering and complementing the "methodological nationalism" of the international adoption literature, I coded transcripts of interviews with more than ninety Americans involved or interested in an adoption from China for the presence of cosmopolitan tropes.[58] In this chapter, I reviewed the results of that analysis, moving beyond evaluative assessments of the (im)practicality of cosmopolitanism as a concept and/or the (in)authenticity of international adopters' felt cosmopolitanisms to concentrate, instead, on the rich theoretical and experiential potential at the intersection of both fields.[59]

---

56. Hübinette, "Adopted Koreans and the Development of Identity," 23.
57. Malcomson, "Varieties of Cosmopolitan Experience."
58. Beck, "Cosmopolitan Society and Its Enemies."
59. See also Anagnost, "Scenes of Misrecognition."

Beginning with the mechanisms of preadoptive parents' early cosmopolitan orientations and ending with postadoptive parents' experiences of cultural hybridity, my analysis reveals that many American China adoptive parents engage, reflect on, and are transformed by the global in their family-building. For instance, evidence indicates that when American China adoptive parents decide to adopt and as they move through the adoption process, global media and travel serve to temper distinctions of difference and distance, helping put parents in felt and real proximity with others in the US and around the world. Guided by these tools, and cognizant of the rights-based frameworks and historically informed discourses that structure international adoption today, they come to recognize and embrace the permeability of national boundaries from rooted positions of stateside privilege and family-based interests. In doing so, they evidence a tension central to cosmopolitanism, that of the global and the local.

After their adoption, American China adoptive parents articulate a cosmopolitan orientation that is both made and mediated by the experiences and emotions of family. Reckoning with the suffering that surrounds international adoption and endeavoring to connect with their child's first family, ethnocultural community, and nation, they circulate expanding and expansive conceptions of kinship, allegiance, and identity while promoting new hybrid forms of belonging. In this way, they evidence another tension at the heart of cosmopolitanism—the pull between the universal and the particular.

Thus, American China adoptive parents' cosmopolitan orientations reflect the tools, transgressions, and tensions that ground more democratic applications of cosmopolitanism today. They also reveal opportunities for further theoretical development and consideration. For example, and as indicated, many white American China adoptive parents experience international adoption as an opening for new subnational and national referents and relationships. Such openness is "created out of the encounter of the local with the global," wherein local ideas about the cultural appropriateness and structural feasibility of openness mediate its global reach.[60] Given this, and the fact that it was predominantly white American parents who engaged and deployed cosmopolitan tropes in my research, it is essential that future research questions the extent to which parents' whiteness and Americanness shape their "expectations and beliefs about the availability of options and the appropriateness of exploration."[61]

---

60. Delanty, "Cosmopolitan Imagination," 27; Grotevant, "Toward a Process Model."

61. Grotevant, "Toward a Process Model," 215. See, for example, Hübinette and Arvanitakis, "Transracial Adoption, White Cosmopolitanism."

Additionally, given that my analysis revealed that American China adoptive mothers were most likely to engage and deploy cosmopolitan tropes, future research must also interrogate gender as a medium of/for cosmopolitan identification.[62] For example, could the use of cosmopolitan tropes be an extension of American China adoptive mothers' culturally specific "role identities" as mothers, or an effort to make visible and maintain a maternal relationship that has long been characterized in/by American culture as "unnatural" and "in need of continual support"?[63] Moving forward, it is important, both theoretically and empirically, to consider the cathectic and functional dimensions of this gendered finding.[64]

Likewise, as international adoption is an expensive endeavor, American China adoptive parents' cosmopolitanism is a classed project, wherein socioeconomic privilege helps structure the extent to which parents can and do employ the tools of boundless identification. In fact, classed desires might motivate American China adoptive parents' deployment of cosmopolitan tropes: a labored cosmopolitan identification could stem from parents' middle-class anxieties about the potential and productiveness of their children, and it could be consistent with an effort to actualize a (family's/parent's/child's) elite global subjecthood.[65] With these and other intersecting and local inequities in mind, new scholarship in this area should be mindful of the extent to which actors' existing structural positions mediate their cosmopolitan orientations and serve to simultaneously efface and reinforce existing social constructs and hierarchies.

Yet, alongside a critical study of the positionality and privilege of cosmopolitanism, scholars should also take note of, and seriously, the fact that many actors today do seek to act and feel beyond the nation-state. For instance, and as evidenced, American China adoptive parents' efforts to build a particular kinship unit actively depend on and integrate an expanding sense of universal human kinship and identification. International adoption researchers, specifically, may recognize these efforts as similar to—and even reflective of—international adoptees' struggles to claim a space between and beyond single nation-states and families.[66] Future research should explore international adopters' cosmopolitan orientations as a means of compassion for and

---

62. See also Shome, *Diana and Beyond*.

63. Howard, "Social Psychology of Identities," 371; Eng, "Transnational Adoption and Queer Diasporas."

64. See, for example, Traver, "Mothering Chineseness."

65. See also Anagnost, "Scenes of Misrecognition."

66. See, for example, Kim, "Wedding Citizenship and Culture"; Yngvesson, "'Niña de Cualquier Color.'"

connection to adoptees' feelings and experiences of liminality. Further, given that such feelings and experiences are emblematic of today's mobile global existence, more generally, additional research into the ways that international adoption—as a case and a social process—"decenter(s) our world" should also be pursued.[67]

Bibliography

Ahmed, Sara. *Cultural Politics of Emotion.* London: Routledge, 2004.

Allen, John, and Chris Hamnett, eds. *A Shrinking World? Global Unevenness and Inequality.* Oxford: Oxford University Press, 1995.

Anagnost, Ann. "Scenes of Misrecognition: Maternal Citizenship in the Age of Transnational Adoption." *Positions* 8, no. 2 (2000): 389–421.

Anderson, Elijah. *The Cosmopolitan Canopy: Race and Civility in Everyday Life.* New York: Norton, 2011.

Appiah, Kwame Anthony. "Cosmopolitanism: How to Be a Citizen of the World." Interview by Julian Brookes. *Mother Jones,* February 23, 2006. https://motherjones.com/politics/2006/02/cosmopolitanism-how-be-citizen-world.

Bartholet, Elizabeth. "International Adoption: Current Status and Future Prospects." *The Future of Children* 3, no. 1 (1993): 89–103.

Beck, Ulrich. "The Cosmopolitan Perspective: Sociology in the Second Age of Modernity." In *Conceiving Cosmopolitanism: Theory, Context, and Practice,* edited by Steven Vertovec and Robin Cohen, 61–85. Oxford: Oxford University Press, 2002.

———. "The Cosmopolitan Society and Its Enemies." *Theory, Culture, and Society* 18, no. 6 (2002): 17–44.

———. *The Cosmopolitan Vision.* Cambridge: Polity, 2006.

———. "What Is Globalization?" In *The Global Transformations Reader: An Introduction to the Globalization Debate,* edited by David Held and Anthony McGrew, 99–104. Cambridge: Polity, 2000.

Beck, Ulrich, and Natan Sznaider. "Unpacking Cosmopolitanism for the Social Sciences: A Research Agenda." *The British Journal of Sociology* 61, no. s1 (2010): 381–403.

Briggs, Laura. "Mother, Child, Race, Nation: The Visual Iconography of Rescue and the Politics of Transnational and Transracial Adoption." *Gender & History* 15, no. 2 (2003): 179–200.

Calhoun, Craig. "The Class Consciousness of Frequent Travelers: Towards a Critique of Actually Existing Cosmopolitanism." In *Conceiving Cosmopolitanism: Theory, Context, and Practice,* edited by Steven Vertovec and Robin Cohen, 86–109. Oxford: Oxford University Press, 2002.

Cartwright, Lisa. "Images of 'Waiting Children': Spectatorship and Pity in the Representation of the Global Social Orphan in the 1990s." In *Cultures of Transnational Adoption,* edited by Toby Alice Volkman, 185–212. Durham, NC: Duke University Press, 2005.

Cohen, Mitchell. "Rooted Cosmopolitanism: Thoughts on the Left, Nationalism and Multiculturalism." *Dissent* 39, no. 4 (Fall 1992): 478–83.

---

67. Yngvesson, "'Un Niña de Cualquier Color,'" 199.

Delanty, Gerard. "The Cosmopolitan Imagination: Critical Cosmopolitanism and Social Theory." *The British Journal of Sociology* 57, no. 1 (2006): 25–47.

Dorow, Sara. "Racialized Choices: Chinese Adoption and the 'White Noise' of Blackness." *Critical Sociology* 32, nos. 2–3 (2006): 357–79.

———. *Transnational Adoption: A Cultural Economy of Race, Gender, and Kinship.* New York: New York University Press, 2006.

Dorow, Sara, and Amy Swiffen. "Blood and Desire: The Secret of Heteronormativity in Adoption Narratives of Culture." *American Ethnologist* 36, no. 3 (2009): 563–73.

Emerson, Robert M., Rachel I. Fretz, and Linda L. Shaw. *Writing Ethnographic Fieldnotes.* Chicago: University of Chicago Press, 1995.

Eng, David L. "Transnational Adoption and Queer Diasporas." *Social Text* 21, no. 3 (2003): 1–37.

Grotevant, Harold D. "Toward a Process Model of Identity Formation." *Journal of Adolescent Research* 2, no. 3 (1987): 203–22.

Hollinger, David A. *Postethnic America: Beyond Multiculturalism.* New York: Basic Books, 1995.

Howard, Judith A. "Social Psychology of Identities." *Annual Review of Sociology,* no. 26 (2000): 367–93.

Hübinette, Tobias. "Adopted Koreans and the Development of Identity in the 'Third Space.'" *Adoption & Fostering* 28, no. 1 (2004): 16–24.

Hübinette, Tobias, and James Arvanitakis. "Transracial Adoption, White Cosmopolitanism and the Fantasy of the Global Family." *Third Text* 26, no. 6 (2012): 691–703.

Huh, Nam Soon, and William J. Reid. "Intercountry, Transracial Adoption and Ethnic Identity." *International Social Work* 43, no. 1 (2000): 75–87.

Kaldor, Mary. "Cosmopolitanism and Organized Violence." In *Conceiving Cosmopolitanism: Theory, Context, and Practice,* edited by Steven Vertovec and Robin Cohen, 268–78. Oxford: Oxford University Press, 2002.

Kim, Eleana. "Wedding Citizenship and Culture: Korean Adoptees and the Global Family of Korea." In *Cultures of Transnational Adoption,* edited by Toby Alice Volkman, 49–80. Durham, NC: Duke University Press, 2005.

Lamont, Michèle, and Sada Aksartova. "Ordinary Cosmopolitanisms: Strategies for Bridging Racial Boundaries among Working-Class Men." *Theory, Culture, and Society* 19, no. 4 (2002): 1–25.

Levy, Daniel, and Natan Sznaider. *Human Rights and Memory.* University Park: Pennsylvania State University Press, 2010.

———. "The Institutionalization of Cosmopolitan Morality: The Holocaust and Human Rights." *Journal of Human Rights* 3, no. 2 (2004): 143–57.

———. "Memory Unbound: The Holocaust and the Formation of Cosmopolitan Memory." *European Journal of Social Theory* 5, no. 1 (2002): 87–106.

Malcomson, Scott. "The Varieties of Cosmopolitan Experience." In *Cosmopolitics: Thinking and Feeling Beyond the Nation,* edited by Pheng Cheah and Bruce Robbins, 233–45. Minneapolis: University of Minnesota Press, 1998.

Melosh, Barbara. *Strangers and Kin: The American Way of Adoption.* Cambridge, MA: Harvard University Press, 2002.

Mohanty, Jayashree, Gary Keokse, and Esther Sales. "Family Cultural Socialization, Ethnic Identity, and Self-Esteem: Web-Based Survey of International Adult Adoptees." *Journal of Ethnic and Cultural Diversity in Social Work* 15, no. 3/4 (2006): 153–72.

Morse, Alan. "Returning to China." *Adoptive Families.* Accessed August 2, 2005. https://web. archive.org/web/20041223233645/http://www.adoptivefamilies.com/articles.php?aid=1000.

Nussbaum, Martha C. "Patriotism and Cosmopolitanism." In *For Love of Country: Debating the Limits of Patriotism,* edited by Martha C. Nussbaum, 3–20. Boston: Beacon, 1996.

Rée, Jonathan. "Cosmopolitanism and the Experience of Nationality." In *Cosmopolitics: Thinking and Feeling Beyond the Nation,* edited by Pheng Cheah and Bruce Robbins, 77–90. Minneapolis: University of Minnesota Press, 1998.

Rios-Kohn, Rebecca. "Intercountry Adoption: An International Perspective on the Practice and Standards." *Adoption Quarterly* 1, no. 14 (1998): 3–32.

Robbins, Bruce. "Introduction Part I: Actually Existing Cosmopolitanism." In *Cosmopolitics: Thinking and Feeling Beyond the Nation,* edited by Pheng Cheah and Bruce Robbins, 1–19. Minneapolis: University of Minnesota Press, 1998.

Shiao, Jiannbin Lee, Mia Tuan, and Elizabeth Rienzi. "Shifting the Spotlight: Exploring Race and Culture in Korean-White Adoptive Families." *Race and Society* 7, no. 1 (2004): 1–16.

Shome, Raka. *Diana and Beyond: White Femininity, National Identity, and Contemporary Media Culture.* Chicago: University of Illinois Press, 2014.

Soysal, Yasemin Nuhoglu. *The Limits of Citizenship: Migrants and Postnational Membership in Europe.* Chicago: University of Chicago Press, 1994.

Traver, Amy E. "Becoming a 'Chinese American' Parent: Whiteness, Chinese Cultural Practice, and American Parents of Children Adopted from China." In *Race in Transnational and Transracial Adoption,* edited by Vilna Bashi Treitler, 226–41. London: Palgrave Macmillan, 2014.

———. "Home(land) Décor: China Adoptive Parents' Consumption of Chinese Cultural Objects for Display in Their Homes." *Qualitative Sociology* 30, no. 3 (2007): 201–20.

———. "Mothering Chineseness: The Gendered Nature of American China Adoptive Parents' Ethnic Efforts." In *Adoption and Mothering,* edited by Frances Latchford, 103–18. Toronto: Demeter, 2012.

———. "Towards a Theory of *Fictive Kin Work*: China Adoptive Parents' Efforts to Connect Their Children to Americans of Chinese Heritage." *International Journal of Sociology of the Family* 35, no. 1 (2009): 45–67.

Vertovec, Steven, and Robin Cohen. "Introduction: Conceiving Cosmopolitanism." In *Conceiving Cosmopolitanism: Theory, Context, and Practice,* edited by Steven Vertovec and Robin Cohen, 1–22. Oxford: Oxford University Press, 2002.

Volkman, Toby Alice. "Embodying Chinese Culture: Transnational Adoption in America." *Social Text* 21, no. 1 (2003): 29–55.

Yoon, Dong Pil. "Intercountry Adoption: The Importance of Ethnic Socialization and Subjective Well-Being for Korean-Born Adopted Children." *Journal of Ethnic & Cultural Diversity in Social Work* 13, no. 2 (2004): 71–89.

Yngvesson, Barbara. "Going 'Home': Adoption, Loss of Bearings, and the Mythology of Roots." *Social Text* 21, no. 1 (2003): 7–27.

———. "'Un Niña de Cualquier Color': Race and Nation in Inter-Country Adoption." In *Globalizing Institutions: Case Studies in Regulation and Innovation,* edited by Jane Jenson and Boaventura de Sousa Santos, 169–204. Burlington, VT: Ashgate, 2000.

CHAPTER 5

Black American Adoption Advocates and the Origins of Intercountry Adoption

KORI A. GRAVES

On February 14, 1953, the front page of the Black newspaper the *Afro-American* featured two stories about intercountry adoption that celebrated Black American families' efforts to rescue vulnerable foreign-born children. The first described the arrival of two German "brown babies" whose adoptions had been arranged by a member of the newspaper's staff, Mabel Alston Grammer. The second announced the first adoption of a Korean child by a Black American family, and it mentioned the Private Act of Congress that Dr. Sylvester Booker had obtained to bring Rhee Song Wu to the US. While the placement of these articles on the first page was unusual, the paper's coverage of adoption was not. Since the end of World War II, the Black press had encouraged Black Americans to adopt the children of Black soldiers born in countries including England, Germany, and Japan. After the Korean War, Black newspapers and popular magazines continued to promote the personal, humanitarian, and political merits of intercountry adoption. Like the people featured in the *Afro-American*'s Valentine's Day issue, many families relied on the ingenuity and skills of social workers and adoption advocates to adopt thousands of the so-called brown babies of World War II and hundreds of Korean GI babies.[1]

---

1. For more on Black Americans' intercountry adoptions after WWII and the Korean War, see Fehrenbach, *Race after Hitler*; Green, *Black Yanks in the Pacific*; Kim, *Adopted Territory*; Lemke Muniz de Faria, "'Germany's "Brown Babies" Must Be Helped!'"; Oh, *To Save the Children*; Peña, "From Both Sides of the Atlantic"; and Plummer, "Brown Babies." See also the contributions of Hackenesch, Patton, and Peña in this volume.

Throughout the 1950s and 1960s, articles about intercountry adoption frequently directed Black Americans to contact local social welfare agencies or some official agency to begin the adoption process. Many also endorsed the methods of nonprofessional adoption advocates like Harry Holt and Pearl S. Buck. Child welfare officials employed the term *non-professionals* when referring to adoption advocates who lacked professional child welfare credentials. They were particularly wary of Holt and Buck. Holt was an Oregon farmer whose religious convictions had led him first to adopt eight Korean children and then to carry out some of the first baby lifts that brought hundreds of Korean children to the US. Buck was a Pulitzer and Nobel Prize–winning author and social activist who opened an adoption agency to place US and foreign-born "mixed race" children of Asian descent even though she had no formal social work training. Adoption scholars have chronicled many of the ways such nonprofessionals influenced the development of intercountry adoption at a time when child welfare officials attempted to exert greater control over transnational child placements. Less studied are the ways that child welfare officials' efforts to limit nonprofessionals affected Black American adoption advocates. This piece adds to the growing body of intercountry adoption scholarship through an evaluation of two Black American adoption advocates who endeavored to increase adoptions of foreign-born, "mixed race" children fathered by Black American soldiers.[2]

Many child welfare officials insisted that trained professionals were best equipped to coordinate intercountry placements because they followed policies designed to protect the best interests of all parties involved. Mabel Alston Grammer and an adoption advocate I call Alice Warren did not agree. These women questioned whether conventional adoption methods could work for the "mixed race" children of Black American soldiers born in Germany and South Korea. Their skepticism was understandable given how inadequately child welfare systems served Black American and "mixed race" children in the US. Throughout the twentieth century, child welfare professionals developed standards for legal adoptions that evolved, in large part, to assist white clients. By midcentury, most agencies that coordinated adoptions did not work with Black American women seeking to relinquish a child or Black Americans interested in adopting a child. Black Americans who did attempt to legally adopt faced obstacles that revealed the ways some child welfare officials hoped

---

2. For more on Holt and his role in the development of Korean international adoption, see Choy, *Global Families*, 81–95; Kim, *Adopted Territory*, 43–82; Oh, *To Save the Children*, 89–111; Pate, *From Orphan to Adoptee*, 101–25; and Winslow, *Best Possible Immigrants*, 70–141. For more on Buck's adoption reform work in the US and South Korea, see Briggs, *Somebody's Children*, 151–52; Herman, *Kinship by Design*, 204 and 209–16; Klein, *Cold War Orientalism*, 123, 135, 143–44, and 178; and Oh, *To Save the Children*, 88 and 96–97.

to engineer ideal adoptive families. In general, social workers wanted an adoptive couple to include a breadwinning father and stay-at-home mother who were younger than forty, financially stable, and living in a residence that included a separate bedroom for an adopted child. De jure and de facto segregation made it difficult for many Black Americans to meet these requirements because they could not access the employment, education, or housing options that were available to the white families that agencies preferred to approve for adoption.[3]

Grammer and Warren believed that adoption standards like those mentioned above and the persistence of segregation in child welfare institutions caused social workers to unnecessarily impede adoptions involving Black Americans. So they established independent programs to address what they saw as lacking in adoption strategies devised by child welfare officials. To accomplish this goal, they adapted the child welfare strategies Black communities had developed in the States to care for the Black and "mixed race" children that many agencies did not accommodate. The procedures involved in completing intercountry adoptions meant that Black American adoption advocates also needed some assistance from professionals to navigate adoption and immigration regulations. Consequently, Grammer and Warren worked to connect parallel adoption systems—one formal and one informal—that co-existed and clashed in the years before intercountry adoption became highly regulated.

In November 1952 Mabel Alston Grammer gave readers of the *Afro-American* magazine section step-by-step instructions on how they could adopt a German "brown baby." This article was a follow-up to two pieces she had written in September and October of the same year that described the requests of German mothers who wanted Black American families to adopt their "mixed race" children. Grammer explained that the mothers loved their children but turned to intercountry adoption because they could no longer care for them. Black Americans had been reading about the struggles of such women since the Allied occupation of Germany began in the summer of 1945. Some Black Americans stationed in Germany or living with family members there endeavored to help these families with donations of food and clothing. The wives of Black American officers stationed in Mannheim had been assisting

---

3. For more on the obstacles Black Americans faced when they pursued formal adoptions in the twentieth century, see Billingsley and Giovannoni, *Children of the Storm*; Briggs, *Somebody's Children*; Herman, *Kinship by Design*; Melosh, *Strangers and Kin*; Potter, *Everybody Else*; and Solinger, *Wake Up Little Susie*.

"brown babies" since 1948 through their Kinder Welfare Club, also known as the Brown Baby Club.[4]

When Grammer reported on the Kinder Welfare Club's fundraising activities and charity ventures in September 1952, she likely knew that Black American clubwomen had been engaging in this type of social uplift work since the women's club movement began in the late nineteenth century. It is also possible that she saw her adoption work as an extension of the club's mission to "promote cultural and welfare activities."[5] It is certain that Grammer's encounters with the mothers and "mixed race" children, as well as mothers' and grandmothers' tearful requests for help, inspired Grammer to begin the Brown Baby Plan to arrange adoptions with the help of the *Afro-American*.[6] The activities of Grammer and the Kinder Welfare Club were reminiscent of the strategies Black American reformers developed to address community problems in the decades before the founding of the nation's first Black American schools of social work. The following description of these reformers' strategies and the early years of Black Americans' involvement in social work shows how Grammer and Warren fit the mold of respected nonprofessionals who had assisted Black American children in need for decades.

Black Americans and the Community Approach to US Child Welfare

In the early twentieth century, several educated Black American reformers embraced the idea that volunteers and trained professionals had important roles to play in the struggle to uplift the race. Black American women's roles in uplift gained recognition especially when their activism conformed to middle-class conceptions of domesticity, and their reforms promised to strengthen Black families and communities.[7] This generation of reformers was born

---

4. Yara-Colette Lemke Muniz de Faria notes that the Black American wives of officers stationed in Mannheim founded the Culture and Welfare Group of Mannheim in 1948. This group coordinated donations of food and clothing for "one hundred fifty Afro-German children and their mothers" in 1950 as one strategy to assist this population. Lemke Muniz de Faria, "'Germany's "Brown Babies" Must Be Helped!,'" 347.

5. "Army Wives in Germany Turn Their Hours to Working for Tan Babies," *Afro-American*, September 13, 1952, 10.

6. Mabel Alston, "Daddy Will Send For Me," *Afro-American* Magazine Section, July 26, 1952, 3; "What Happens to Brown Babies?," *Afro-American* Magazine Section, October 18, 1952, 4; and Mabel Alston, "How to Adopt a German Brown Baby," *Afro-American* Magazine Section, November 8, 1952, 9.

7. Gaines, *Uplifting the Race*, 129–40.

during or soon after the Civil War and came of age as Jim Crow laws in the South and discrimination in the North institutionalized Black Americans' inequality. In response, they resisted exclusion and oppression by working with existing organizations or creating their own. Some became involved in settlement-house work or joined organizations like the Young Women's Christian Association (1855), the National Association of Colored Women's Clubs (1896), and the National Urban League (1910). Others found ways to pool community resources and coordinate with professionals to deliver services to Black Americans. In cities throughout the North and South, this approach also characterized efforts to resolve child welfare issues.[8]

The founding of the Gate City Free Kindergarten Association (GCFKA) in Atlanta, Georgia, is one of the best documented examples of early twentieth-century reform work that involved Black American trained professionals and volunteers in the care of vulnerable children. Many of the strategies GCFKA leaders implemented remained integral to the success of other programs created to meet the needs of Black American children well into the mid-twentieth century. Therefore, a description of these strategies and the circumstances that led to the creation of GCFKA helps explain why women like Grammer believed they could and should establish independent adoption programs for vulnerable "mixed race" children. GCFKA began in 1905 because educators like W. E. B. Du Bois at Atlanta University reached out to influential community members, including the wives of several educators, to get volunteers involved in programs to assist working mothers.[9] In Atlanta, middle-class volunteers had worked to establish and maintain that city's Black American neighborhood day nurseries and kindergartens, and they influenced the organization of the nation's first Black American school of social work. Some of the women that served on committees and raised funds to support such initiatives had backgrounds in organized reform work, but, as historian Stephanie J. Shaw explains, they "were moved more by social conscience than by social science."[10] These women were pragmatic, and they attempted to devise practical solutions to the problems that were right around them.

Lugenia Burns Hope was one of the women who organized volunteers and trained professionals to address the needs of the poor and working-class

---

8. Shaw, *What a Woman Ought to Be*, 166–74; and White, *Too Heavy a Load*, 29. For more on Black American women's club work and involvement in the YWCA, see Cash, *African American Women and Social Action*; and Weisenfeld, *African American Women and Christian Activism*.

9. Cash, *African American Women and Social Action*, 75; and Shaw, *What a Woman Ought to Be*, 139–40.

10. Shaw, *What a Woman Ought to Be*, 140.

families in her Atlanta neighborhood. Burns Hope was the wife of educator and then president of Atlanta Baptist College John Hope, who would go on to become the first Black American president of Morehouse College. While John Hope was making a name for himself among Atlanta's Black American educators, Burns Hope was establishing herself in reform circles. Though not professionally trained in social work, she had done settlement work in Chicago, Illinois, before marrying John Hope in 1897. She used this training in Atlanta when she joined the GCFKA and then helped establish the Neighborhood Union in 1908. Through this organization, Black American female reformers advanced a model of comprehensive community service that would influence trained professionals' and volunteers' ideas about child welfare.[11]

Founders of the Neighborhood Union based their interventions on the settlement-house model. Their efforts also incorporated elements of community development that went well beyond the objectives and organizational structure associated with the settlement-house movement. According to Shaw, the Union drew on the skills of poor, working-class, and middle-class members. This characteristic distinguished the Union's activities from other forms of settlement work because the middle-class reformers "anticipated, encouraged, and received the help of people who were often less able but equally interested."[12] These reformers believed that the widespread involvement of diverse families would allow the organization to thrive.[13] The Union did thrive. By the 1920s it had branches throughout the city that offered an array of services, programs, and clubs. Its success attracted the attention of local and national leaders in social work. When participants at the 1920 National Conference of Social Workers became interested in establishing a school of social work for Black Americans, leaders in Atlanta's white and Black American social welfare organizations and universities took up the challenge, in part because of the strong base for study and implementation that the Neighborhood Union provided. These leaders established a program called the Atlanta School of Social Service, and some who had been involved with the Neighborhood Union became instructors at the school. First affiliated with Morehouse College, the school became independent in 1925 before it became the Atlanta University School of Social Work in 1938.[14]

---

11. Cash, *African American Women and Social Action*, 74–75; and Rouse, *Lugenia Burns Hope*, 26–31 and 65–90.

12. Shaw, *What a Woman Ought to Be*, 170.

13. Cash, *African American Women and Social Action*, 74–77; Rouse, *Lugenia Burns Hope*, 66–73; and Shaw, *What a Woman Ought to Be*, 168–71.

14. Rouse, *Lugenia Burns Hope*, 83–85; Gary and Gary, "History of Social Work Education," 74–75.

The school's bulletins from the 1920s show that the curriculum emphasized case work, investigation, and survey methods. The courses offered in the program's first decade also addressed specific community issues like health, hygiene, housing, recreation, crime, and education. By 1931 the bulletins included classes with a specific focus on issues of child welfare. These courses provided academic and fieldwork training to students interested in the care of children in their homes and in foster care or institutional settings. In 1936 the school dropped the class "Foster Care of Children" and replaced it with the more comprehensive course "Children under Substitute Parental Care." The school would add more courses to prepare students for the challenges associated with childhood mental health and behavioral issues in the 1940s, but there were no specific courses on adoption listed in the bulletins during the school's first thirty years.[15]

One reason the school of social work did not emphasize training in adoption service delivery was that legal adoptions were uncommon in the first half of the twentieth century. Instead, volunteers associated with sectarian and nonsectarian benevolent organizations relied on foundling homes for babies and orphanages for children. They also placed children with families using formal and informal arrangements that resembled indentures or foster care. These organizations often used race and religion to determine which children received services. Because of segregation in the South, Black Americans had to create options for Black children needing short-term or long-term care.[16] Indeed, Atlanta was home to the Carrie Steele Orphans' Home, one of the oldest homes for Black American orphans run by Black Americans in the US. Founded in 1888 by Carrie Steele, the home grew out of her efforts to help children abandoned at Union Station in Atlanta, where she worked as a maid. Originally Steele arranged to keep the children in a boxcar while she worked. Then she took them to her home at night. When this plan became unsustainable, Steele raised money to purchase a home to begin her orphanage, which she ran until her death, in 1900.[17] As social work became an established pro-

15. Atlanta University School of Social Work Bulletins, Box Atlanta University School of Social Work Bulletin, 1927–1949, folders: 1925–1926, 1927–1928, 1929–1930, 1931–1932, 1933–1934, 1934–1935, 1936–1937, 1940–1941, 1943–1944, 1945–1946, 1948–1949, and 1949–1950, Atlanta University School of Social Work Records.

16. Balcom, *Traffic in Babies*; Herman, *Kinship by Design*; and Rymph, *Raising Government Children*.

17. Sloan, "Carrie Steele-Pitts Home," 2–4. The orphanage became the Carrie Steele-Pitts Home in the 1950s to honor the organization's founder and third director, Clara Maxwell Pitts. Other cities also opened orphanages for Black American children, but white reformers often established and ran these institutions. For more on nineteenth- and early twentieth-century orphanages for Black American children, see Ramey, *Child Care in Black and White*; and Seraile, *Angels of Mercy*.

fession in the 1920s and 1930s, the Black Americans who ran kindergartens, day nurseries, and orphanages like the Steele Orphans' Home represented a mix of professional, often highly educated reformers, and volunteers who were committed to community service. These professional and volunteer partnerships made possible a community approach to the care of abandoned children in the decades before adoption became more widely practiced.

It is also likely that schools for Black American social workers did not prioritize adoption because many Black Americans made informal arrangements to care for vulnerable children. Historian Ellen Herman has described that "formal and informal, commercial and sentimental, deliberate and impulsive" methods characterized adoption for many people in the first half of the twentieth century.[18] While it is impossible to know how many Black Americans adopted informally, reports of organizations including the Child Welfare League of America and the National Urban League indicate that these practices were common.[19] In fact, several Black American female professional reformers informally adopted children.[20] The prevalence of informal, black-, and gray-market arrangements led a number of child welfare professionals to implement adoption standards throughout the 1930s, 1940s, and 1950s. These professionals were particularly concerned about black- and gray-market adoptions because they could involve baby-selling or baby-stealing, and because private citizens, doctors, lawyers, and others who lacked any social work training often brokered these arrangements.[21] Although the laws governing adoption varied from state to state, efforts to standardize adoption policies allowed professionals to exert more control over the assessment of families and the placement of children. In the wake of these changes, formal adoptions increased, especially among white adoption seekers. But Black American adoption seekers and child welfare professionals continued to face obstacles when they attempted to work with many of the agencies that arranged formal placements.[22]

---

18. Herman, *Kinship by Design*, 22.

19. Fanshel, *Study in Negro Adoption*; and Hill, *Informal Adoption among Black Families*.

20. Shaw, *What a Woman Ought to Be*, 221–37.

21. For more on professionals' efforts to regulate black- and gray-market adoptions, see Balcom, *Traffic in Babies*, 166–94; and Herman, *Kinship by Design*, 31–41.

22. For more on the professionalization of social work and adoption in the first half of the twentieth century, see Berebitsky, *Like Our Very Own*; and Kunzel, *Fallen Women, Problem Girls*.

Black American Advocates and Intercountry Adoption Programs

The preceding examples describe just a few of the ways Black Americans worked to care for vulnerable children and resist the multiple forms of discrimination at work in US child welfare institutions. Given the obstacles Black American social workers encountered, it is not surprising that volunteers were vital to the successes of all these efforts.[23] It is also possible to imagine that Black American volunteers' responses to the needs of children in their communities influenced the ways women like Grammer and Warren reacted to the circumstances of children fathered by Black American soldiers in Germany and South Korea. Both women reasoned that since the children faced racism and discrimination because of their Black American ancestry, Black Americans were uniquely suited to design programs to provide for their care. This belief suggests ways that ideas about self-help and racial solidarity, which were aspects of the racial uplift ideology described by historian Kevin Gaines, evolved to address challenges faced by Black Americans and their children in and outside the US.[24] Their confidence in these traditions would bring Grammer and Warren into conflict with white child welfare professionals that considered untrained adoption advocates' methods to be illegal in some cases, questionable in most cases, and always potentially dangerous.

Mabel Grammer's disputes with child welfare professionals began in 1953 because of her very public adoption efforts. By August of that year, Grammer had written numerous articles telling couples how to adopt a German child. While she directed her appeal to families in the US and Germany, she frequently described the many happy families that resulted when soldiers' families stationed in Germany adopted. In one article, she recounted the stories of several Black American adoptive mothers who were thrilled with their children but insisted that their identities remain anonymous. These women had no intention of telling people in the States that they had adopted a child,

---

23. Throughout the first half of the twentieth century, Black American social workers completed graduate work at prominent schools like the University of Chicago and New York University and undergraduate training at the growing number of Black American schools with social work programs. By the 1930s Black Americans could complete a social work program at Atlanta University; Howard University in Washington, DC; Fisk University, in Nashville, TN; and the Bishop Tuttle School, in Raleigh, NC, which only admitted female students. According to social work scholars Robenia Baker Gary and Lawrence E. Gary, students with training from these programs found jobs in a number of Black American organizations prior to the 1930s. During the Great Depression, these opportunities diminished. Gary and Gary, "History of Social Work Education," 70.

24. Gaines, *Uplifting the Race*, 1–12.

because they wanted their families to appear to be biologically related. Such secrecy was common among adoptive parents in the States and possible for families stationed in Germany.[25]

Families in the US who received help from Grammer had no such anonymity, because they had to agree to allow the *Afro-American* to publicize their names. The paper printed lengthy lists of the couples from all regions of the nation who adopted a child from Germany. Grammer claimed that she personally replied to the hundreds of letters she received requesting help to adopt a German child with the kind of information she included in an August 15, 1953, article, "How You Can Adopt a Baby." In that article, Grammer explained the requirements of US-German adoption. She made it clear that readers should only attempt the process if they owned or planned to own a home, had savings, and could get personal and professional references attesting to their character and employment history. Grammer also instructed couples to get a recommendation from a board of social welfare in the US. Yet she indicated that adoptive couples should be more concerned about getting the approval of child welfare officials in Germany.[26]

Couples that followed the steps in Grammer's articles received considerable assistance from her and the staff at the *Afro-American*. Grammer made phone calls and submitted the necessary paperwork to the appropriate officials. She estimated that each adoption would cost three hundred fifty dollars. This fee paid for a child's visa, nursery care in Germany, payments to the *Afro-American* for administrative services, and airfare on Scandinavian Airlines. Adopting couples also received a discount on their child's airfare and a free plane ticket for the adult accompanying the child to the US. This was possible because Grammer and the *Afro-American* had negotiated a deal with officials of Scandinavian Airlines.[27]

---

25. Mabel Alston, "U.S. G.I.s Adopt German Kids," *Afro* Magazine Section, August 30, 1952, 10; Mabel Alston, "Army Wives in Germany Turn Their Hours to Working for Tan Babies," *Afro-American*, September 13, 1952, 10; Mabel Alston, "What Happens to Brown Babies?" *Afro-American*, October 18, 1952, 4; and Mabel Grammer, "Ex-GIs May Find Their Children Thru the AFRO," *Afro* Magazine Section, May 16, 1953, 9.

26. Mabel Grammer, "How You Can Adopt a Baby," *Afro* Magazine Section, August 15, 1953, 3; James L. Hicks, "AFRO Arranges Adoption of First Brown Babies," *Afro-American*, January 24, 1953, 1; James L. Hicks, "Two More War Babies Arrive for Adoption," *Afro-American*, February 28, 1953, 1 and 9; James L. Hicks, "500 Greet 11th War Baby," *Afro-American*, June 6, 1953, 1–2; James L. Hicks, "DC Couple Adopts Third Brown Baby," *Afro-American*, July 11, 1953, 14; and James L. Hicks, "No Interpreters Needed When Germany Met Brooklyn," *Afro* Magazine Section, August 1, 1953, 1. In 1953 the *Afro-American* changed the title of its letters-to-the-editor page from "What Our Readers Say" to "What AFRO Readers Say."

27. Mabel Grammer, "How You Can Adopt a Baby," *Afro* Magazine Section, August 15, 1953, 3; and R.C.M., "Against German Brown Babies," *Afro-American*, June 20, 1953, 4.

Grammer had no social work training, but she felt qualified to assess adoptive couples and help them navigate immigration restrictions. As Yara-Colette Lemke Muniz de Faria has explained, until June 1952 the few families that completed an adoption of a "mixed race" German child used the orphan provision of the 1948 Displaced Persons Act (DPA). When this law expired in June 1952, families had to request a Private Act of Congress that would allow the child to enter the country as the "natural born alien child" of a US citizen.[28] Throughout the fall of 1952, Grammer included a description of this process in her instructions for adoptive families. After the passage of the 1953 Refugee Relief Act (RRA), she directed families to apply to get a visa through that law's orphan provision that set aside four thousand nonquota visas for children under ten years of age. The RRA also allowed couples to choose a proxy—a person to represent them legally in a foreign court—to complete the requirements of the child's birth country. Although it is not clear how many of Grammer's families used the proxy method, enough did to attract the attention of officials with agencies like International Social Service (ISS) who were concerned that independent adoption plans like Grammer's were dangerous.[29]

The success of her efforts caused ISS officials in the US and Germany to investigate Grammer and some of the families she recruited. ISS was a social work organization established in 1924 to help individuals and agencies resolve social welfare challenges across national borders. The questions ISS officials posed to Grammer in March 1954 caused her to write a letter of complaint about the treatment she received. Grammer relayed that in October 1953, Ann Marie Korner of ISS-German Branch stopped by her home to report that ISS-American Branch considered some of Grammer's families unfit to adopt. Korner also wanted to know how Grammer had "obtained 700 children to send to the United States" and why she was sending them to a nation where racial discrimination was pervasive. Korner had heard that there were already enough "colored" people in the US and that Black Americans would discriminate against "mixed race" German children because they had white mothers. Korner's comments stunned and angered Grammer.[30]

---

28. For a discussion of the gaps and interconnections between adoption and immigration legislation, see the piece by Eleana J. Kim and Kim Park Nelson in this volume.

29. "How to Adopt a German Brown Baby," 9; and Muniz de Faria, "'Germany's "Brown Babies" Must Be Helped!,'" 356. Muniz de Faria notes that at least thirty of Grammer's families used the proxy method. For more on Grammer's adoption program, see Fehrenbach, *Race after Hitler*, 147–56; and Lemke Muniz de Faria, "'Germany's "Brown Babies" Must Be Helped!,'" 354–58.

30. Mabel Grammer to ISS–America Branch, 18 March 1954, Box 10 Folder: Children-Independent Adoption Schemes-Grammer, Mabel, 1953, ISS records.

Grammer clarified how and why she got involved in US-German adoptions by explaining that the children's German national identity was secondary and mutable while their racial identity was primary, fixed, and tied them to Black American communities. Much like "mixed race" children in the US, "mixed race" German children did not fit neatly into one racial category. However, many people considered them to be Black based on the legacy of the one-drop rule. This principle evolved as a legal and social category that defined any person with a Black American ancestor as Black, whether or not they appeared phenotypically Black. Because many of the "mixed race" German children had brown complexions and coarse hair textures like their Black American fathers, they experienced ostracism. Grammer described her shock at seeing the children "with their hair standing straight on top of their heads [. . .] because of head-lice and the lack of care: and asking, 'where is my N***r papa?'" These scenes convinced her that the children needed to be with Black American families.[31]

Grammer countered ISS officials' disapproval of some of the families she recruited by arguing that she had found good homes. These families included "qualified teachers [and] physicians." She defended two mothers ISS criticized by explaining that one worked in child care and the other was a schoolteacher. Grammer declared that she would testify in any court that these women were respectable. She assumed that one of the prospective mothers had "objected to some high-handed methods from a Social Worker," which led the social worker to label that woman unfit. Grammer sympathized with the families whom child welfare officials seemed to patronize, and she rejected the premise that Black Americans were in any way inferior to other adoptive families. Instead, she insisted that Black American adoptive parents were "coloured Americans and no savages who must permanently be guarded, only because they try to serve a good purpose."[32]

Grammer also addressed the rumors that people were sending the children to the States to be slaves of white southerners. She called these ideas "COMMUNIST PROPAGANDA" [emphasis in original text], and she turned the red-baiting tactics that opponents of civil rights activists and organizations used into an element of her defense. Grammer asserted that the families who adopted "mixed race" German children were "outstanding citizens who could pass any test, loyalty, physical and fitness." She acknowledged that racism was a problem in the US but claimed that race relations were improving.

---

31. Mabel Grammer to ISS–America Branch, 18 March 1954. For more on the history of race matching and constructions of race based on the one-drop rule, see Herman, *Kinship by Design*; Kennedy, *Interracial Intimacies*; and Pascoe, *What Comes Naturally.*

32. Mabel Grammer to ISS-America Branch, 18 March 1954.

In her estimation, "mixed race" children were better off with Black families because of Germany's history of violent and oppressive treatment of minorities. Further, Grammer objected to Germans' use of vicious racist epithets when referring to the children. She ended her letter with a promise to try to resolve these issues when she returned to the States. Her assurances were not persuasive. ISS officials continued to suspect that Grammer's methods were putting "mixed race" German children in jeopardy.[33]

Grammer and the families she assisted likely considered her methods to be in line with the child welfare strategies described above that Black Americans had practiced for much of the twentieth century. Some of the formal and informal adoptions that involved grandparents, aunts, uncles, and unrelated people grew out of Black Americans' understandings of extended kinship networks and obligations. People like Grammer imagined that the foreign-born children of Black GIs were a part of these networks.[34] Several officials with the West German government agreed. They believed that Black American women were better suited to raise "mixed race" children than their white German mothers. They also supported Grammer's work because intercountry adoptions made Americans responsible for children fathered by Black soldiers. According to Heide Fehrenbach, this support allowed Grammer to place as many as one thousand children between 1952 and the early 1960s.[35]

The legal and social circumstances that informed adoption strategies for children fathered by Black soldiers in Germany and Korea were different. One key difference was that West Germany recognized the citizenship of German-born "mixed race" children whereas South Korea did not extend citizenship to Korean-born "mixed race" children.[36] But similar attitudes about race shaped Black Americans' responses to Afro-German children and Afro-Korean children. Black American advocates of intercountry adoption emphasized the children's vulnerability because many Germans and Koreans considered them to be racially Black, which indicated that the children would be outsiders in the countries of their births. They also insisted that Black Americans could provide the children stable homes and give them a sense of racial pride. These ideas said more about how Black Americans understood their status in the US and the effectiveness of their struggles to obtain racial equality than about

33. Mabel Grammer to ISS-America Branch, 18 March 1954.

34. Fanshel, *Study in Negro Adoption*; and Hill, *Informal Adoption among Black Families*.

35. Fehrenbach, *Race after Hitler*, 133 and 163. Fehrenbach estimates that Black Americans adopted around seven thousand Afro-German children between 1945 and 1968.

36. For more on the legal status of "mixed race" children in Germany after WWII, see Fehrenbach, *Race after Hitler*; and Plummer, "Brown Babies." For more on the legal status of "mixed race" children in South Korea, see Oh, *To Save the Children*; Pate, *From Orphan to Adoptee*; and Winslow, *Best Possible Immigrants*.

the challenges of adopting children from nations recovering from devastating wars. But they are instructive because they reveal that Black Americans understood the challenges associated with German and Korean intercountry adoption as fundamentally rooted in inequalities they were familiar with and had worked to destabilize for decades. Therefore, Black Americans' responses to the Korean crisis incorporated many of the strategies they had already developed to address the needs of abandoned, displaced, and orphaned children in the US and Germany.

When the Korean War ended, several Black American publications, including *Ebony, Jet,* and *Sepia,* popularized stories about the desperate circumstances of Afro-Korean children using many of the same tactics that newspapers and magazines were using to increase adoptions of World War II "brown babies." Articles often described the requirements for intercountry adoption and outlined the steps families needed to take to conform to US and Korean regulations. Some articles directed prospective adoptive parents to work with adoption advocates who lacked social work training and ran private agencies. Many described the economic and bureaucratic reasons that Black Americans were willing to work with adoption advocates. The story of Alice Warren's adoption program shows how race motivated Black Americans' choices, too. Warren's case also highlights the reasons child welfare professionals believed such programs put adoptees and adoptive families at risk.[37]

Warren's efforts to bring Afro-Korean children to the US drew the attention of officials with the US Children's Bureau and ISS in 1957. Officials with the State Department of Social Welfare of Kansas began investigating Mrs. Warren in January of that year when they learned that she was attempting to place Afro-Korean children with families in her community. These officials suspected that Warren's methods were unsafe because they had worked with Warren in the past when licensing her to provide transitional care for children in Kansas City. At the time of the investigation, Warren was not boarding any children, because of an incident involving a child she had tried to keep after the Division of Child Welfare attempted to retrieve the child.[38]

The first time that public health nurse Mrs. Brady tried to investigate Warren to determine the status of her Korean children, Warren would not

---

37. J. Morgan, "Adoption by Proxy: Red Tape Abolished in Case of Koreas," *Sepia,* July 1959; Pearl S. Buck, "Should White Parents Adopt Brown Babies?" *Ebony,* June 1958, 26–28, and 31; and Welcome House Ledgers, Inquiries, August 1950–1962, Archives of Pearl S. Buck International, Perkasie, PA.

38. Ruth Graves to State Department of Social Welfare, Kansas City, 22 January 1957, Box 675, Folder 7-3-1-3 September 1957 1953–1957 Interstate Placement, Non-Resident Problems, Juvenile Immigration Transient Boys, Records of the Children's Bureau.

allow Brady to enter her home. When Brady and the nurse for the Division of Maternal and Child Health, Ruth Graves, finally gained access to the home, they learned that Warren first became involved with US-Korean adoption when responding to an appeal in a magazine. She then contacted the US State Department and, according to Warren, representatives at the State Department referred her to Harry Holt's Holt Adoption Program (HAP). HAP was popular among Black Americans because the agency charged low fees, conducted minimal investigations, and sponsored proxy adoptions.[39] Warren adopted two children through HAP. When Brady and Graves asked about her adoption work, Warren claimed that after her first inquiry, Holt asked her to help him place children in Kansas City. Warren explained that Holt paid for her to travel to South Korea, where she collected eight Afro-Korean children, whom she placed with families in and around Kansas City. She brought five more children back with her after a second trip, and she placed some in Kansas City and others across state lines in Missouri. Warren also used the clothes, food, and money that families gave her to support the children they wanted to adopt.[40]

During their visit, Brady and Graves saw two of the children Warren brought back to the States whom she identified as her adopted children. Both nurses agreed that they appeared to be in good health. They also noted that Warren was making an effort to help them adapt to their new surroundings, even trying to communicate with them using the Korean word list the US State Department provided adoptive families. Based on a picture she showed the nurses, it was clear that one of her children had gained weight since arriving in the States. Warren told the nurses that she was introducing new foods into the children's diets that included dairy and vegetables. She was also addressing the children's medical needs and working with her physician to rid her adopted son of worms in his digestive tract. She even retrieved one of the worms to give to the doctor, which she showed the nurses. Warren was proud of the care she gave the children, and she showed Brady and Graves pictures of the children's first Christmas in her home.[41]

The nurses' report of their visit did not include any overtly negative comments about Warren's care of the children, but they did not like her living arrangements. There were several unrelated people living in the home, including a person Warren had raised and a child she called her grandson. There were also two elderly men living on the third floor of her house that, according to Warren, officials with the County Welfare Department had placed in her

39. Oh, *To Save the Children*, 104–11.

40. Ruth Graves to State Department of Social Welfare, Kansas City, 22 January 1957.

41. Ruth Graves to State Department of Social Welfare, Kansas City, 22 January 1957.

care. These circumstances confirmed the nurses' decision to discourage the Division of Child Welfare from working with Warren. Instead, they planned to pretend that they were simply nurses interested in the health of Warren's adopted Korean children so that they could keep track of her activities.[42]

At one point, Warren contacted officials with the Kansas State Department of Social Welfare to get their help with the intercountry adoption program she wanted to establish. After making her initial request, Warren met with several staff members of the Division of Child Welfare who were willing to conduct home studies of the families she recommended. These officials made it clear that they could only help if ISS approved Warren's adoption plan. This stipulation meant that they would not allow her to place a child adopted by proxy. It seems that the Department of Social Welfare's stance against proxy adoptions led Warren to continue arranging her own placements. When asked, Warren confirmed that she conducted the investigations of the families who received a child from her. She explained that she tried to ensure that each couple had savings, owned a home, had a steady job, were no older than forty years of age, and had medical proof of infertility.[43] The requirements on Warren's checklist were similar to the basic standards professionals used to screen prospective families, which indicates her superficial familiarity with adoption policies. Warren's knowledge of some adoption standards was not reassuring to officials with the Kansas Department of Social Welfare. They became even more alarmed when Warren disclosed that social workers had already rejected several of the families she approved (and planned to approve) when these families had applied to complete a domestic adoption. Some families sought Warren's help to adopt a Korean child after they had grown tired of waiting to hear whether they could adopt a child in the States. Neither of these circumstances was unusual for families attempting to adopt a child from Europe or Asia, but they raised child welfare officials' level of concern regarding Warren's activities.[44]

Child welfare officials in Kansas became even more concerned about Warren's adoption work when they learned that she was planning to get more children from Child Placement Services (CPS) in South Korea. Oak Soon Hong, the director of CPS, was optimistic about Warren's work, and in March 1957, she contacted officials with the Kansas State Board of Health regard-

---

42. Ruth Graves to State Department of Social Welfare, Kansas City, 22 January 1957.

43. Dorothy W. Bradley to Anna E. Sundwall, 27 June 1957, Box 675, Folder 7-3-1-3 September 1957 1953–1957 Interstate Placement, Non-Resident Problems, Juvenile Immigration Transient Boys, Records of the Children's Bureau; and Ruth Graves to State Department of Social Welfare, Kansas City, 22 January 1957.

44. Ruth Graves to State Department of Social Welfare, Kansas City, 22 January 1957.

ing Warren's plan. Hong had met Warren during her visit to Korea and had agreed that Afro-Korean children had better prospects in the States. She had been the director of CPS since the South Korean government established the agency in 1954. Officials with ISS were complimentary of her devotion to the children and her commitment to getting them placed. However, they worried that Hong was not qualified to run an adoption program because she was a nurse, not a social worker. Given her lack of social work experience, and her intimate awareness of the poor treatment Afro-Korean children experienced, her desire to work with Warren makes sense.[45] But child welfare officials in Kansas remained convinced that Warren's methods were definitely unsound, if not altogether illegal.

In April 1957 Dr. G. Martin, director of the Division of Maternal and Child Health for the State Department of Social Welfare in Kansas, discouraged Hong from placing any confidence in Warren or assuming that the children were better off in the US. In his short reply to her letter that mentioned Warren, Dr. Martin explained that Warren was not qualified to investigate families or to place children. He warned Hong that Warren's approach would create problems of adjustment for the children and their adoptive families that would require social welfare agency intervention in the future. His predictions were grim. Dr. Martin believed that the adoptive parents Warren selected would either abandon or neglect the children, predisposing some to "severe mental illness and others [to] great difficulties with schools and police courts." He closed his letter by informing Hong that, regarding Afro-Korean children, he and his staff believed she "should feel more responsible for their welfare in this country."[46] This reprimand must have struck Hong as unnecessarily patronizing. After all, her concern for the children's welfare in the States was what caused her to reach out to the Department of Social Welfare in the first place.

Hong was caught between two competing philosophies concerning the intercountry adoption of Korea's "mixed race" children. She was under pressure from officials in South Korea who encouraged her not to rely on "one particular agency" to place "mixed race" Korean orphans. Hyo Sun Shin, vice minister of the Ministry of Health and Social Welfare, further advised Hong to continue to use the proxy adoption method that was "preferably recommended by this Ministry." It was the vice minister's understanding that there were more families applying to adopt than there were "mixed race" children

45. Kim, *Adopted Territory*, 60–69; and Oh, *To Save the Children*, 56.

46. G. Martin to Oak Soon Hong, 1 April 1957, Box 675, Folder 7-3-1-3 September 1957 1953–1957 Interstate Placement, Non-Resident Problems, Juvenile Immigration Transient Boys, Records of the Children's Bureau.

to place, and he wondered why there was a delay in getting adoptions finalized "in the earliest as possible date."[47] Yet ISS officials shared Dr. Martin's
misgivings. They believed Warren was a fraud and an unstable religious kook
who had lied about her activities and credentials. A memo from ISS-Korean
Branch to ISS Assistant Director Susan T. Pettiss claimed that Warren, not
Harry Holt, had paid for her first trip to Korea. Pettiss was certain that Warren was not working with Holt. She also claimed that after Warren's first trip
to South Korea, the bank had returned all her checks because of insufficient
funds. According to the same memo, Warren had misled people by saying she
had a letter from President Eisenhower supporting her plan to get all Afro-
Korean children to families in the US.[48]

Warren put her plan into action in the summer of 1958, when she established the International Love of Humanity Aid Society, Inc. She did not
explain how her plan would work, but she did inform ISS officials that she
was "divinely guided into this work and that this was why she would succeed
in her project." The charter for the society stipulated that the agency would
have legal guardianship over the "destitute, friendless, foreign-born children
of African descent," which would allow Warren to make all decisions about
their care, education, and eventual placement with an adoptive family in the
US. Warren planned to open more branches of the society in other states and
countries to make it easier to arrange adoptions across state and national borders. She rented a house in Kansas City, Missouri, to begin placing children
in that state. But she did not receive a license to operate an adoption agency
in Missouri or in her home state of Kansas.[49]

As president of the society, Warren received money from families who
applied to adopt an Afro-Korean child, and it seems that she used some of
those funds to pay for a house in South Korea to care for the children she
planned to bring to the States. It is possible that Warren used some of the
money to pay for a trip to promote her plan in Oakland, California, and to
cover the costs of another trip to South Korea in January 1959.[50] As a result of
inquiries into Warren's activities from adoption advocates, complaints from

---

47. Hyo Sun Shin to Oak Soon Hong, 14 January 1958, Box 885, Folder 7-3-1-3 1958–1962
Non-Resident Problems, Records of the Children's Bureau.

48. ISS-Korea Branch to ISS-American Branch, 17 September 1957, Box 10, Folder: Children, Independent Adoption Schemes, Clemmons, Mrs. Leroy 1957, ISS records.

49. ISS-Korea Branch to ISS-American Branch, 17 September 1957.

50. Anna E. Sundwall to Proctor Carter, 10 November 1958, Box 884, Folder: 7-3-1-3 September 1959 Non-Resident Problems (Include Juvenile Immigrant, Transient Boys), Records of
the Children's Bureau; and Anna E. Sundwall to Chief, Program Development Branch, 5 February 1959, Box 884, Folder: 7-3-1-3 September 1959 Non-Resident Problems (Include Juvenile
Immigrant, Transient Boys), Records of the Children's Bureau.

prospective adoptive families, and Warren's sketchy history with child welfare agencies in Kansas and Missouri, representatives of the Kansas Division of Child Welfare stopped her from bringing more Korean children to the States.[51] Investigations into Warren's activities in South Korea also jeopardized adoptions she had already arranged and her own adoptions. While she was in Korea, the court ordered child welfare officials to remove her two Korean children from her home. Warren was able to get the children back, but she had to appear in court to answer questions about legal custody. These measures effectively ended her Korean adoption plan.[52]

Warren's response to the needs of Afro-Korean children highlights a few issues that drew Black Americans into US-Korean adoptions, why many chose to work with adoption advocates, and why their adoption numbers remained low. Warren's vision of an agency that could rescue all Afro-Korean children suggests how unsettling the circumstances in Korea were that shaped her conviction that Black American families had to intervene. Even though racial inequality structured Black Americans' lives in the US, she thought Afro-Korean children would thrive in the States, and in some ways her efforts replicated the informal strategies Black Americans had used to help displaced children in the US and World War II "brown babies." Some Black Americans agreed with Warren's (and Mabel Grammer's) assessment of the children's prospects. Many perceived or experienced discrimination when they interacted with professional adoption and child welfare agencies, which constrained their abilities to adopt. These circumstances exaggerated a fundamental distrust of child welfare officials among Black Americans who considered social workers to be biased gatekeepers that hindered adoptions involving Black American families in the US and abroad.

Given the negative experiences of many Black Americans with child welfare agencies, it is understandable that some chose to work with people like Grammer and Warren to complete an intercountry adoption. But the adoption programs established by Black Americans did not have the longevity or achieve the results of agencies like those run by Harry Holt and Pearl S. Buck. Instead, Black American adoption advocates struggled to secure resources, institutional support, and alliances with trained professionals that had been

---

51. N. G. Walker to Patricia T. Schloesser, 30 June 1959, Box 884, Folder: 7-3-1-3 September 1959 Non-Resident Problems (Include Juvenile Immigrant, Transient Boys), Records of the Children's Bureau; and Erwin W. Raetz to Kansas State Department of Welfare, 17 January 1959, Box 884, Folder: 7-3-1-3 September 1959 Non-Resident Problems (Include Juvenile Immigrant, Transient Boys), Records of the Children's Bureau.

52. Josephine Thomas to Paul R. Shanahan, September 1959, Box 884, Folder: 7-3-1-3 September 1959 Non-Resident Problems (Include Juvenile Immigrant, Transient Boys), Records of the Children's Bureau.

a hallmark of Black Americans' child welfare strategies for the first half of the twentieth century. Throughout the 1950s and 1960s, Black Americans would continue to pursue assistance to complete intercountry adoptions, and the Black press would chronicle both the successes and the failures of these endeavors. But Black American adoption advocates would become increasingly marginalized as child welfare officials with agencies, including the US Children's Bureau and ISS, worked to standardize the policies they believed would create more safeguards for intercountry adoptees and adoptive parents.

Bibliography

Balcom, Karen. *The Traffic in Babies: Cross-Border Adoption and Baby-Selling between the United States and Canada, 1930-1972.* Toronto: University of Toronto Press, 2011.

Berebitsky, Julie. *Like Our Very Own: Adoption and the Changing Culture of Motherhood, 1851–1950.* Lawrence: University of Kansas Press, 2001.

Billingsley, Andrew, and Jeanne M. Giovannoni. *Children of the Storm: Black Children and American Child Welfare.* New York: Harcourt, Brace, Jovanovich, 1972.

Briggs, Laura. *Somebody's Children: The Politics of Transracial and Transnational Adoption* Durham, NC: Duke University Press, 2012.

Cash, Floris Loretta Barnett. *African American Women and Social Action: The Clubwomen and Volunteerism from Jim Crow to the New Deal, 1896-1936.* Westport, CT: Greenwood, 2001.

Choy, Catherine Ceniza. *Global Families: A History of Asian International Adoption in America.* New York: New York University Press, 2013.

Fanshel, David. *A Study in Negro Adoption.* New York: Child Welfare League of America, 1957.

Fehrenbach, Heide. *Race after Hitler: Black Occupation Children in Postwar Germany and America.* Princeton, NJ: Princeton University Press, 2005.

Gaines, Kevin K. *Uplifting the Race: Black Leadership, Politics, and Culture in the Twentieth Century.* Chapel Hill: University of North Carolina Press, 1996.

Gary, Robenia Baker, and Lawrence E. Gary. "The History of Social Work Education for Black People 1900-1930." *The Journal of Sociology & Social Welfare* 21, no. 1 (March 1994): 67–81.

Green, Michael Cullen. *Black Yanks in the Pacific: Race in the Making of American Military Empire after World War II.* Ithaca, NY: Cornell University Press, 2010.

Herman, Ellen. *Kinship by Design: A History of Adoption in the Modern United States.* Chicago: University of Chicago Press, 2008.

Hill, Robert. *Informal Adoption among Black Families.* Washington, DC: National Urban League, 1977.

Kennedy, Randall. *Interracial Intimacies: Sex, Marriage, Identity, and Adoption.* New York: Vintage, 2003.

Kim, Eleana J. *Adopted Territory: Transnational Korean Adoptees and the Politics of Belonging.* Durham, NC: Duke University Press, 2010.

Klein, Christina. *Cold War Orientalism: Asia in the Middlebrow Imagination, 1945-1961.* Berkeley: University of California Press, 2003.

Kunzel, Regina G. *Fallen Women, Problem Girls: Unmarried Mothers and the Professionalization of Social Work, 1890–1945*. New Haven, CT: Yale University Press, 1995.

Lemke Muniz de Faria, Yara-Colette. "'Germany's "Brown Babies" Must Be Helped! Will You?': US Adoption Plans for Afro-German Children, 1950–1955." *Callaloo* 26, no. 2 (Spring 2003): 342–62.

Melosh, Barbara. *Strangers and Kin: The American Way of Adoption*. Cambridge, MA: Harvard University Press, 2002.

Oh, Arissa. *To Save the Children of Korea: The Cold War Origins of International Adoption*. Stanford, CA: Stanford University Press, 2015.

Pascoe, Peggy. *What Comes Naturally: Miscegenation Law and the Making of Race in America*. New York: Oxford University Press, 2009.

Pate, SooJin. *From Orphan to Adoptee: U.S. Empire and Genealogies of Korean Adoption*. Minneapolis: University of Minnesota Press, 2014.

Peña, Rosemarie. "From Both Sides of the Atlantic: Black German Adoptee Searches in William Gage's Geborener Deutscher (Born German)." *Genealogy* 2, no. 4 (2018): 40.

Plummer, Brenda Gayle. "Brown Babies: Race, Gender, and Policy after World War II." In *Window on Freedom: Race, Civil Rights, and Foreign Affairs, 1945–1988*, edited by Brenda Gayle Plummer, 67–91. Chapel Hill: University of North Carolina Press, 2003.

Potter, Sarah. *Everybody Else: Adoption and the Politics of Domestic Diversity in Postwar America*. Athens: University of Georgia Press, 2014.

Ramey, Jessie B. *Child Care in Black and White: Working Parents and the History of Orphanages*. Champaign: University of Illinois Press, 2012.

Rouse, Jacqueline Anne. *Lugenia Burns Hope: Black Southern Reformer*. Athens: University of Georgia Press, 1989.

Seraile, William. *Angels of Mercy: White Women and the History of New York's Colored Orphan Asylum*. New York: Fordham University Press, 2013.

Shaw, Stephanie J. *What a Woman Ought to Be and to Do: Black Professional Women Workers During the Jim Crow Era*. Chicago: University of Chicago Press, 1996.

Sloan, Albert J. H., II. "The Carrie Steele-Pitts Home and the Church Partners in Mission." Master's thesis, the Interdenominational Theological Center, 1969.

Solinger, Rickie. *Wake Up Little Susie: Single Pregnancy and Race before Roe v. Wade*. New York: Routledge, 1992.

Weisenfeld, Judith. *African American Women and Christian Activism: New York's Black YWCA, 1905–1945*. Cambridge, MA: Harvard University Press, 1997.

White, Deborah Gray. *Too Heavy a Load: Black Women in Defense of Themselves*. New York: Norton, 1999.

Winslow, Rachel Rains. *The Best Possible Immigrants: International Adoption and the American Family*. Philadelphia: University of Pennsylvania Press, 2017.

CHAPTER 6

Love across the Color Line?

Pearl S. Buck and the Adoption of Afro-German Children after World War II

SILKE HACKENESCH

In June 1958 the acclaimed American writer Pearl S. Buck published an article in *Ebony* magazine entitled "Should White Parents Adopt Brown Babies?"[1] The question Buck posed to the Black American readership was rhetorical, for she had already adopted several children of color, including a Black girl from Germany. She had also facilitated the adoption of children who were considered "hard to place" with white families through her own agency, Welcome House.

Analyzing the *Ebony* article along with other pieces by Buck on "the children of war" as well as her correspondence with civil rights leaders sheds light on the dynamics of race in early international adoption discourses and on Buck's own shifting position on race and transracial adoption. Scholars have insightfully explored Buck's activism on behalf of "Amerasian" children and her own adoption service.[2] Less attention has been paid to her relationship to the Black American community, the Black press, and civil rights activists such as Walter White. This chapter offers an analysis of selected articles by Buck that address issues of matching and transracial adoption as well as her writing on the so-called war babies. These publications explain and justify her own adoptions across the most impervious color line and were intended to encour-

---

1. Buck, "Should White Parents Adopt Brown Babies?"
2. Klein, *Cold War Orientalism*; Herman, *Kinship by Design*; Oh, *To Save the Children*; Choy, *Global Families*; Conn, *Pearl S. Buck*; Shaffer, *Pearl S. Buck and the American Internationalist Tradition*.

age Black Americans to likewise consider the adoption of "racially mixed" children. They illustrate how Buck's own perspective on race evolved from a belief in matching to an embracing of colorblind adoption principles over the course of the 1940s and 1950s. It also shows that Buck's close connection to civil rights activists influenced her adoption of the Afro-German girl Henriette and her work as an advocate for transracial and transnational adoption.

The internationalism of the postwar period as well as the galvanizing civil rights movement and a belief in colorblind social policies challenged previous processes of standardization and rationalization in adoption practices. These processes included matching children with adoptive parents in terms of race and religion: in short, in ways that should mimic "natural" families as much as possible. Failure to do so would entail great risks for the families, social workers believed.[3] The public discussions and controversies that transnational and transracial adoptions elicited because they violated the matching paradigm reflect the paradoxes inherent in American family formation and the formation of the American nation: on the one hand, a liberal pluralist understanding—families can be made through voluntary association, a nation can be made through immigration and naturalization—and, on the other hand, the belief that blood ties determine belonging to the family as well as to the nation. Beginning in the late 1940s, transracial adoptions especially touched on these notions in new and challenging ways.

Because of a prevalence of media reports on "war orphans" that began during World War II and continued well through the Korean and Vietnam wars, American affective responses ranged from pity to responsibility, and—in tune with Cold War ideology—many embraced the idea of welcoming such children into their homes.[4] Most were not orphans in the literal sense, and the definition of *orphan* widened considerably in those years. In close connection, the term *GI baby* emerged as a new identity category, one that also seems to suggest who was to be responsible for the children: if not the fathers themselves, then at least their home country.[5] "Rescuing" an orphan from a fascist or communist country was a means of performing American democratic citizenship, and the narrative of rescue proved central to the discourse on intercountry adoption throughout the 1950s.[6] Historian Donna Alvah has perhaps optimistically noted: "Thanks to [Pearl S.] Buck and other American leaders, Americans came to see the adoption of children from Germany, Japan, China, Korea, and other key sites of the Cold War, as a way to demon-

---

3. Herman, *Kinship by Design*.
4. Oh, *To Save the Children*.
5. Winslow, *Best Possible Immigrants*, 76.
6. On the "rescue narrative," see also Choy, "Race at the Center," 164.

strate support for U.S. Cold War goals of opposing the spread of communism and winning allies."[7]

Children born to white German women and Black American soldiers during the Allied occupation represent the first organized transnational adoptions to the US primarily on the basis of race yet have received comparatively little scholarly attention so far.[8] While most of these children remained in Germany and grew up with their mothers or extended family or in orphanages, some were adopted by (mostly Black) American families between the mid-1940s and the end of the 1950s. These transracial intercountry adoptions provoked contentious debates among social welfare workers, nonprofessional adoption advocates, and civil rights activists.[9] What these debates reveal is that the civil rights movement, discourses on the hegemonic notions of the American family and on American citizenship, and a Cold War rhetoric all intersected in the social practice that became international adoption. Lobbying for the adoption of Black German children must also be analyzed with regard to the integrationist discourse of a colorblind society and the domestic adoption landscape in the US. For the purpose of this chapter, I zoom in on Pearl S. Buck as one nonprofessional adoption advocate in particular and examine her understanding of transracial and transnational family-making, seen as progressive by some and as misguided and dangerous by others.

Pearl S. Buck's Politics of Matching and Race

In 1892 Pearl S. Buck was born in Hillsboro, West Virginia, to a Presbyterian missionary couple on home leave from China. When Buck was three months old, her family took her back to China, where she would spend most of the next forty-plus years of her life before eventually returning to the US.[10] As an adult, and after getting divorced from her first husband, Buck came to reject

---

7. Alvah, "'I Am Too Young to Die,'" 26.

8. Works that address the history of Black German "occupation children": Lemke Muniz de Faria, *Zwischen Fürsorge und Ausgrenzung*; Lemke Muniz de Faria, "'Germany's "Brown Babies" Must Be Helped!'"; Fehrenbach, *Race after Hitler*; Plummer, "Brown Babies"; Kraft, *Kinder der Befreiung*.

9. I use the term *nonprofessional* to distinguish between professional social workers like those at the International Social Service and the Child Welfare League, and laypeople or adoption activists like Pearl S. Buck and Mabel A. Grammer. Such a distinction is warranted not least because it was important to both sides: to the social workers in their ongoing critique of laypeople who seemingly did not understand the "science of adoption and family making," and for adoption advocates who used terms like *professionals* almost derogatorily as a reference to red tape and unnecessary paperwork.

10. Conn, *Pearl S. Buck,* 22–24.

the religious fundamentalism that had shaped her and risen to prominence in the US. Now largely relegated to oblivion and excluded from most canons of American literary studies, Pearl Buck had become a hugely popular and successful writer. In 1932 she had won a Pulitzer for her novel *The Good Earth* (1931), and in 1938 she was the first American woman to win the Nobel Prize for Literature (joined by Toni Morrison in 1993).[11] She also gained prominence and notoriety for her political activism. Buck was involved in numerous human rights struggles at once, among them the Indian independence movement, women's rights, China relief, an end to Chinese exclusion and racial inequality in the US, and the liberation of Korea.[12] Growing up in China as a minority, she claimed, deeply affected her perspective on race relations and the practice of segregation in Jim Crow America.

In 1949 she had founded Welcome House and was an early advocate for adoptions of "Amerasian" children.[13] Buck frequently explained that an adoption agency had turned to her for help when they were unable to find a family for a child of "mixed parentage." Without Buck's assistance, the agency would have to transfer this child of Asian and American descent to an orphanage for Black American children. At that time, most orphanages did not house white children and children of color together. The agencies' officials also sought Buck's guidance because by then she had already adopted a "mixed race" daughter. "And so Welcome House was established." According to a Welcome House information brochure that narrates the history of what turned from a foster home into an internationally operating adoption agency, it was "a family-size home with permanent foster parents, where a group of Asian-American children could grow up naturally in a normal family and community environment."[14] In its first two years, Welcome House facilitated more than forty adoptions.[15]

From its start, Buck framed Welcome House as a response to what was, in her mind, the inadequate work of social workers in the US.[16] In her 1955 article "The Children Waiting: The Shocking Scandal of Adoption" for *Woman's Home Companion,* she addressed the contested practice of transracial adoption:

---

11. Conn, *Pearl S. Buck,* 143, 207.

12. Conn, *Pearl S. Buck,* 262–64.

13. On American Asian adoptions in general, and adoptions from Korea in particular, as an anticommunist goodwill project, see Holt, *Cold War Kids,* 110.

14. Buck, "Story of Welcome House" see also Graves, *War Born Family,* 192–93.

15. "Welcome House Statistics on Number of Children, March 1956–February 1957."

16. A major source of contestation between Buck and social workers was her reliance on proxy adoption, which the CWLA and ISS were highly critical of. On Buck and the issue of proxy adoption, see most notably Choy, *Global Families.*

All things being equal, it is undoubtedly best for him [the child] to be adopted by people who are like him racially. But if parents cannot be found of such similarity, he should not be kept an orphan because of his race. The family who wants him and who is best able to make him happy should be his family. There are American couples of loving hearts who do not care what a child's race is.[17]

To Buck, matching was still the preferred social welfare paradigm, yet she insisted that transracial adoption should be preferred to the child having to live in an orphanage. In the text, Buck also challenges the alleged superiority of "blood relationships" and the widespread notion that biological kinship was superior: "There is no magic in blood relationship when parents alienate their children by neglect or desertion. Yet under our laws and our customs blood still takes precedence, blood instead of the reality of love." In statements like these, she voiced a progressive view of parenthood and family-making in tune with her critique of matching. She further seems to suggest that that first/birth parents, who were (temporarily) unable to care for their children and thus placed them in orphanages, were unfit for parenting and should have no legal claims to their child. According to Buck, a variety of factors led to children "languishing" in orphanages while "loving American couples" were trying to "rescue" them. The most obvious was the practice of matching based on religion, race, and socioeconomic background between adoptee and prospective adoptive parents. Apart from that was the adherence to "misguided adoption standards," which Buck often disparagingly referred to as "red tape," as well as the alleged lack of experience of the social workers involved. Further, she accused social workers of having unrealistic expectations:

And how [. . .] could we ever get so many children adopted when our social agencies cannot cope with what we have? I submit a controversial answer. It could be done if the red tape of adoption procedures were eliminated and only essentials kept. There are, I am sure, sincere and unselfish social workers and religious persons in the field of child welfare and adoption who honestly believe that they are doing the best that can be done, unaware that they themselves are the hindrances because they are faithful to red tape and encrusted in tradition.[18]

---

17. Buck, "Children Waiting"; see also Graves, "Amerasian Children, Hybrid Superiority."
18. Buck, "Children Waiting."

Buck speculated that young, inexperienced social workers were part of the problem, not the solution, by implementing standards that they failed to see as inappropriate and retrogressive ("encrusted in tradition"). Such statements elicited critical responses from the social work establishment. Agencies including the Child Welfare League of America (CWLA) pursued critical interventions to correct the image Buck created for the profession.[19] As a response to the article in the *Woman's Home Companion*, Joseph Reid of the CWLA wrote an indignant reply to the journal and asked for a correction in their next issue:

> Miss Buck's article contains many statements which are inaccurate and grossly misleading. [. . .] The article is at best not factual and at worst verges on the slanderous. The general impression is that child welfare agencies for a variety of unsupported reasons are refusing to make available children who are clamoring for adoption. This is not true. [. . .] The average age of children in institutions today is approximately 10.7 years. There are very few adoption agencies in the United States which possess the financial resources necessary to cover the greater costs involved in finding adoptive homes for children this age. The nation's childcare programs reflect what the public is willing to pay for. It is misleading to talk about this problem without discussing costs.[20]

Reid stressed that not all children who were temporarily taken care of in foster homes or orphanages were up for adoption, and that orphanages were by no means a job creation scheme for social workers. On the contrary, he argued, such institutions were chronically underfinanced and could barely keep up with the work they faced. He thus responded to Buck by highlighting institutional challenges and a lack of willingness to allocate more funds to child welfare in general. Yet Buck's prominence and popular activism made it difficult for social workers to draw attention to the more structural problems they were facing.

The social workers from the CWLA and the International Social Service (ISS), a nongovernmental organization founded in 1924 to assist refugees and unaccompanied minors after World War I, helped coordinate intercountry adoptions. They frequently accused Buck of a "naïve humanitarianism" and scolded her for propagating easy solutions to more complex problems.[21] Yet upon a closer look at Buck's perspective, it becomes obvious that her attitude

---

19. On the CWLA, see Lindenmeyer, *"A Right to Childhood"*; on foster care, see also Rymph, *Raising Government Children*.

20. Letter by Joseph Reid / CWLA to Paul Smith, Editor-in-Chief, *Woman's Home Companion*, September 15, 1955.

21. Conn, *Pearl S. Buck*, 270.

as articulated in the *Woman's Home Companion* piece was close to the one on race by the Child Welfare League of America, even though she was an outspoken critic of social welfare agencies. These parallels are evident in the CWLA's 1958 publication *Standards for Adoption Service,* the product of the CWLA's 1955 conference on adoption. This was the first conference exclusively devoted to the issue of adoption, and *Standards* continued to emphasize the importance of matching in the making of families. What is interesting, however, is its position on race:

> Racial background in itself should not determine the selection of the home for a child. It should not be assumed that difficulties will necessarily arise if adoptive parents and children are of different racial origin. At the present time, however, children placed in adoptive families with similar racial characteristics, such as color, can become more easily integrated into the average family group and community.[22]

Against the backdrop of the civil rights movement, especially the 1954 *Brown v. Board of Education* Supreme Court decision and the fight to end segregation, race relations were prominently and contentiously debated. The CWLA felt compelled to reconsider its own standards and to draft a modestly progressive stance. The statement implies that race is a social construct, not a biological reality, and should not determine the placement of children in adoptive homes. However, it goes on to state that the resistance to adoption across the color line was so profound and so widespread that such adoption might harm a child's development and should thus not be pursued—articulating a position later voiced with more vehemence by the National Association of Black Social Workers (NABSW).[23]

Looking at Buck's writings suggests that her position on matching evolved over time. In the 1948 article "An Interview with My Adopted Daughter," published in *Cosmopolitan,* Buck described a conversation with her first adopted daughter, Janice, a white American girl who had come to live with her in 1924.[24] Buck emphasized the importance of matching physical and character traits when she wrote, "The child's racial backgrounds should be as near as possible to those of the adoptive parents. Even the basic national strains should be as near as possible. If you come of warm Italian blood, do not adopt a child of cool Scandinavian ancestry—unless you happened to have married

---

22. Child Welfare League of America, *Standards for Adoption Service,* 24.

23. See the position statement on "Trans-Racial Adoption" from September 1972.

24. Graves, *War Born Family,* 191.

someone like that—for love."[25] Her stance recalls earlier discourses on eugenics and conflates race and nation as well as cultural and biological assumptions about race and identity, skin color, and intellectual capacities. When asked what she considered important in adoption, Janice replied that finance, age, and love were crucial: "Only people who love children ought to be allowed to adopt them."[26] The emphasis on love is a recurrent theme in Buck's writing and seems to work as an alternative vision to standards and regulation in Buck's view. Appealing to one's love for children thus serves as the only prerequisite for a successful adoption procedure, something to be addressed again in my discussion of Buck's article in *Ebony*.

Buck on Transnational and Transracial Adoption

Pearl Buck was not only concerned with children in the domestic foster system and the handling of domestic adoptions. She also closely followed the news on so-called war babies and addressed the intercountry adoption of these "occupation children" in her book *Children for Adoption*, published in 1964. The situation of children fathered by (Black) American GIs in various theaters of war across Europe and Asia might have pushed Buck to reconsider her own outlook on race. In her book, she described the conditions into which many of these children were born once the immediate military conflict was over:

> There was both horror and excitement among the populace when an army
> approached, and when the battle was over, the ensuing rape of women was
> the grand finale, after which the curtain went down. [. . .] The same situation
> prevailed in Germany after the war ended, and if the crop of babies was not
> so obvious as it was in Asian countries it was only because both parents were
> white. When the American father was Negro, exactly the same displacement
> occurred and the half-Negro child found neither welcome nor status in the
> land of his birth. The Germans were not accustomed to dark Germans, and
> the half-Negro children suffered much until some provision could be made
> for them, mainly orphanages. It remains to be seen what will happen to
> them as they grow into adulthood. Germany does not have a good record of
> absorbing special peoples.[27]

---

25. Buck, "Interview with My Adopted Daughter," 97.
26. Buck, "Interview with My Adopted Daughter," 97.
27. Buck, *Children for Adoption*, 37–38.

That white Germans were unaccustomed to Black people is incorrect: after World War I, the Allied forces had occupied the Rhineland and France had deployed African colonial troops. The presence of these Black soldiers was regarded as especially humiliating in the German public and highly controversial. Their presence, however, also resulted in the birth of Black German children who grew up in Germany.[28] But Buck is certainly right in voicing some profound skepticism toward the integration of Black German children into German society, and in contrast to many civil rights leaders, this prompted her to advocate for their adoption. Interestingly, Walter White, executive secretary of the National Association for the Advancement of Colored People (NAACP) from 1931 to 1955, felt more optimistic about the integration of Black German children into the predominantly white German society and watched news about them closely from afar. Moreover, White as well as Lester Granger, of the National Urban League (NUL), expressed the opinion that their own funds and efforts should not go to adoption services or to the support of Black German children. Instead, they should be directed to Black American children in the US, primarily in the South, who were possibly worse off. Granger also articulated some skepticism about the acceptance of these Black *German* children into the Black American community.[29] To him, the fact that these children were "racially mixed" and of white German heritage posed a possible hindrance to their acceptance. Pearl Buck and Walter White exchanged several letters on the so-called brown babies in Germany in 1952 and 1953. Buck had reached out to White because of information on the situation in Germany that White had received from Oscar Lee, of the National Council of the Churches of Christ. Based on Lee's reporting, White evaluated the situation of Afro-German children as much less desperate or bleak than Buck did. His optimism was partly based on the fact that the first cohort of Black German children had started with elementary school and were schooled along with their white German classmates. In the wake of the fight against school segregation at home, a desegregated educational system in Germany and publications for teachers about how to best "integrate" these children made him

---

28. On the history of these Black Germans, see Campt, *Other Germans*; Koller, "*Von Wilden aller Rassen niedergemetzelt*"; Roos, "Racist Hysteria to Pragmatic Rapprochement?"; Wigger, *Die "Schwarze Schmach am Rhein."*

29. Protocol of the *Committee to Consider Possibilities and Resources for Immigration and Resettlement of Colored Children from Germany,* January 29, 1951; see also Hackenesch, "'I Identify Primarily as a Black German in America.'" Brenda Gayle Plummer suggests that Black Americans were reluctant to adopt Black German children because of their white ancestry. While Granger and other members of the committee did voice some skepticism, the Black press and large parts of its readership seem to have endorsed their adoption.

hopeful.[30] Accordingly, the NAACP never participated in adoption programs and never officially endorsed the adoption of "brown babies" from Europe or Asia, instead referring to its own community programs that should benefit underserved children in the US. Yet the question of who was supposed to be responsible for these children and where they would fare best had been put before the NAACP. In the summer of 1949, for example, a letter from the NAACP branch in Ithaca, New York, to Roy Wilkins, then assistant secretary and the editor of its magazine *The Crisis,* described how the chapter had followed the news coverage on the Afro-German babies and now wanted to organize aid. The letter asked the NAACP to officially endorse such efforts and to pressure President Harry Truman to support these children financially.[31] In his reply to the Ithaca branch, Wilkins wrote:

> The matter of the so-called brown babies in Europe has been before us on numerous occasions. The Association has taken no position with regard to this question and as far as I know the government has not set up any program either. While the problem is a worthy and deserving one, it would be our feeling that our branches would have just as much as they can do in working on actual NAACP program and work. [. . .] While it is very gratifying to see such a fine evidence of desire on the part of the Ithaca branch to work on the matter in question, we do not feel that such a matter is within the scope and purview of NAACP program.[32]

According to Wilkins as well as Walter White, the organization officially viewed these children primarily as German; thus, German postwar society needed to accommodate them.

Buck, too, had received letters from Germany asking for her help in finding homes for Black German children, a fact she recounted in a Welcome House publication in 1951:

> I have even had letters from Germany asking to know how Welcome House is run, for there the problem is with the little German-American babies of color, the fathers having been American Negro soldiers. Good Germans

---

30. Simon, *Maxi;* Eyferth et al., *Farbige Kinder in Deutschland;* Frankenstein, *Soldatenkinder.*

31. William Heidt Jr., Letter to Roy Wilkins, June 17, 1949.

32. Jones, Madison S., Reply to William Heidt Jr., June 21, 1949; for letters sent to the NAACP on behalf of or by German birth mothers looking for Black families to adopt their children, see *The NAACP Records, Part II: General Office File, 1940–1956,* Box II: A642 United States Army Forces; Folder 7: "Brown Babies in Europe," 1945–49; and Folder 8: "Brown Babies in Europe," 1950–55.

are fearful that unless they can establish now a proper attitude in Germany toward these little brown babies, there is real danger that they will not be allowed to live after the occupation is over.[33]

In 1951, at the age of 59, Pearl Buck herself adopted an Afro-German girl, Henriette, and raised her in her home in Pennsylvania.[34] Buck's adopting of Henriette is unusual insofar as the great majority of Black German children brought to the US were adopted by Black American families. Estimates suggest that in the 1940s and 1950s, about 7,000 "racially mixed" children from Germany were adopted by (Black) American families. The adoption of these children, despite their dual heritage, was often considered not to be transracial but transnational. Buck, however, used her personal experience of having adopted Henriette (along with a Black Japanese girl) to publicly comment on transracial adoptions and advocate her colorblind politics.[35]

In June 1958 Buck published the article "Should White Parents Adopt Brown Babies?" in *Ebony* magazine. That question triggered less of a controversy than one might assume, and it certainly did not foreshadow the critique on transracial adoption that the NABSW would issue fourteen years later.[36] The article spans several pages and is accompanied by photographs depicting Buck and her adopted children, other children relinquished for adoption, and families who had already adopted children from abroad. In that piece, Buck concerned herself with the situation of American-fathered so-called war babies in Korea and Japan, whom she feared were unwanted and "doomed" because of the ways they were ostracized in their countries of birth and also because of the immigration laws that Buck critiqued as too narrow.[37] She believed there were enough white American families to adopt "the strong and intelligent" of these "war children" but worried that not enough Black families could be found for "the half-Negro children." She explicitly addressed a Black American readership in the *Ebony* article and encouraged them to adopt "racially mixed" children fathered by Black American servicemen stationed abroad. Ignoring the discrimination that Black families were historically con-

---

33. Buck, "Welcome House Letter."

34. Sherk, *Pearl S. Buck*, 151.

35. See also Fehrenbach, *Race after Hitler*, 133.

36. For a discussion of the NABSW statement, see the contribution by Laura Briggs in this volume.

37. See a letter from ISS to *Ebony* in response to Buck's article. The letter reveals that the ISS was familiar with the article prior to its publication but refused to endorse it: "We sincerely regret that we were unable to assist you [. . .] in the promotion of Pearl Buck's article on intercountry adoption." A major criticism was the use of photographs that violated the children's right to privacy, according to the ISS.

fronted with by mainly white social welfare agencies, the writer speculated that Black Americans were not considering adopting these children because of colorism: "Even the Negro, it seems, prefers to be light colored, or to adopt a light colored child, rather than dark. I do not know why this is. To me a brown skin, or a pure ebony, is as handsome as white [. . .] I do not understand prejudice." Buck's statement reveals a lack of understanding of the complex ways of race and ideology in American history.[38] She evades a discussion of slavery, of the sexual violence that Black women were historically exposed to, and white supremacy—in short, the forces that were the foundation for a social phenomenon like colorism to evolve. With transracial adoptions, the color line was often negotiated in the smallest social unit, the family; hence, Buck was pushed to navigate complex terrain. On the one hand, she had adopted across the color line multiple times herself; on the other hand, she specifically reached out to Black Americans to adopt children fathered by Black military service members.

Moreover, she does not mention that Black Americans were, indeed, adopting dual-heritage children for a decade at the time she published her article. Mabel A. Grammer, for instance, a journalist for the Baltimore *Afro-American,* and the wife of an army officer stationed in Germany, had initiated the so-called Brown Baby Plan, which had facilitated the adoption of Black German children by Black American families.[39] After coming to Germany in 1951, Grammer had visited an orphanage and found herself surrounded by Black German children pleading for a "mummy." Grammer recounted: "It nearly broke my heart and of course we decided to adopt a child ourselves. And we just kept on."[40] The Grammers adopted several children and helped thousands of Black Americans adopt an Afro-German child by proxy—a contested practice that elicited criticism of the ISS but was widely covered and favorably commented on in the Black press. Adults who were interested in adopting a child through the Brown Baby Plan were asked to contact the *Afro-American,* submit papers to them similar to those required by an agency (proof of income, letter of recommendation, proof of adequate housing, etc.), and agree that their story be covered in the paper.[41] Given how closely Buck followed the news on children affected by war in Europe and Asia, and given that she had adopted a Black German girl herself, any reference to Grammer

---

38. Fields, "Slavery, Race, and Ideology."

39. See also the chapter by Kori Graves in this volume.

40. Stoneman, "German Waifs Find a Friend."

41. Grammer, "How You Can Adopt a Baby," *Afro* Magazine Section, August 15, 1953; Lemke Muniz de Faria, *Zwischen Fürsorge und Ausgrenzung,* 108–10; see also Clark, "Overlooked No More."

and other Black adoption advocates, or to the news coverage in other outlets such as the *Pittsburgh Courier* or the Baltimore *Afro-American*, is curiously absent from her piece. Instead, she encouraged readers of *Ebony* to reach out to her and her own agency, Welcome House, and again referred to the "biracial" heritage of these children and her own colorblindness: "I know from practical human experience that skin color is irrelevant. I know from my own experience in adoptive work that children are welcome in loving families, whatever their color." She continued:

> Above all, I know from my own personal experience that color of skin does not mean anything at all. One of my own adopted children happens, quite by chance, to be the child of an American Negro soldier and a German mother. She came to us as a little refugee child from Germany, and she has stayed because we love her too well to let her go. She is our living answer to prejudice. [. . .] To all criticism I have but one reply. She is happy with us and we are happy with her.[42]

The quotation is interesting for several reasons. Skin color did carry a lot of meaning in the fifties, and multiracial families were far from a common occurrence, despite all the colorblind rhetoric. And Pearl Buck knew this; otherwise, she would not have used her adopted daughter to deliver a message to the readers of *Ebony* magazine. The point Buck was trying to make here, I contend, and which obviously appealed to the readership of *Ebony*, is that she was seemingly able to see beyond skin to value people's character ("My brown child has qualities which are congenial to me").[43] The text thus illustrates how appealing and prevalent colorblind discourses were in the mid-1950s, especially against the backdrop of the civil rights movement and the fight against racial segregation. Such colorblindness appealed to both liberal Black and white Americans, who seemed to believe that such a stance could be a social force against racism and racial discrimination. Buck continued, stating that "many families can accept and love children of other races and colors— *if they love children*" (her emphasis). Again, an intriguing quote given that there was enough "practical human experience" to suggest that skin color did indeed matter and was far from irrelevant, especially as these children grew into adulthood. The quote also reveals an essentialized notion of love. Yet love

---

42. Buck, "Should White Parents Adopt Brown Babies?"; as a response to Buck's piece, letters to the editor were published two issues later, in August 1958 and September 1958.

43. Buck also referred to the alleged "hybrid superiority" of "racially mixed" children, possibly in an attempt to counter negative stereotypes about them; see Graves, "Amerasian Children, Hybrid Superiority."

is not universal or without presuppositions. Who is capable of giving love, of extending it across the color line? Whose love matters here? The photographs accompanying Buck's piece give us some hints. Two feature Buck with her daughter Henriette, playing chess and playing the piano together; others show Buck reading to her adopted children, and other adoptive families, Black and white, welcoming their children at the airport, reading to them, watching their children as they joyfully unwrap presents. In short, the visuals accompanying the text feature heteronormative middle-class nuclear families, seemingly capable of offering safe homes, economic safety, *and* love. Obviously, love also included a relative economic independence and certain ways of raising a child, and only parents who met these criteria were considered capable of opening their "hearts and homes." As Kori Graves has argued about normative families in general, and about Buck's transracial family in particular, "While dominant popular cultural representations defined the ideal family as white, nuclear, and middle-class, Buck believed people would accept her family because it conformed to postwar family ideals in all ways except for race."[44]

Buck's adopting across racial lines was not only a reaching out to the Black American community, and a powerful message to segregationists and racists in the US, but also a way to counter the negative images of US race relations during the Cold War. Moreover, she suggests intercountry and transracial adoptions as a means to overcome institutional racism.[45] For Buck, transracial adoptions were the most powerful and visible answer to race prejudice. She had repeatedly highlighted the contradiction between the democratic ideal and the reality of racial inequality as a central vulnerability of the US during the Cold War.[46] While such statements labeled her a communist by critics, she argued that it was exactly her patriotism that made her hold the US to its foundational principles.[47] According to Robert Shaffer, Buck was left-wing but not a communist.[48] Indeed, in her own writings, she employed a common strategy of stating that she did not criticize the US because she was unpatriotic and that it was exactly her patriotism and her love for the country and its proclaimed ideals that made racism unbearable to her: "I love my country with a fierce and jealous love. Nothing that is American is a matter of course to me. I put the Constitution and the Bill of Rights into my spiritual life. The inscription on the Statue of Liberty is sacred to me. I suffer when Americans

44. Graves, *War Born Family,* 196.
45. Graves, *War Born Family,* 189; and Dudziak, *Cold War Civil Rights.*
46. Conn, *Pearl S. Buck,* 249.
47. Conn, *Pearl S. Buck,* 249, 260; "Story of Welcome House."
48. Shaffer, "Women and International Relations," 152.

are mean-spirited and prejudiced and deny their country by un-American traits."[49]

In tune with what Ruth Feldstein has called *racial liberalism*, Buck believed that racism was inherently un-American and undemocratic, and she thereby seemingly failed to grasp that racism was indeed an inherent and institutional part of US history.[50] And she herself had exposed such beliefs in her attack on social workers who adhered to the matching paradigm and were slow to consider Black Americans as potential adoptive parents. In 1937 leaders of the National Urban League's New York chapter invited Buck to speak to its members. She used this opportunity to explain that her sense of racial equality was in large part due to her upbringing in China. Since she had not grown up in the US or been socialized to understand the nation's gender and race hierarchy, her idealized notions of the US had been little tested.[51] In her address, Buck compared China with the US and concluded that racial harmony had been achieved in China but not in the US, where racial animus was pervasive. Buck made it clear that this situation was unacceptable to her. Besides her own thoughts on race and racism, her speech also illustrates the origins of her long-standing close connections to various civil rights organizations, civil rights activists, and Black American intellectuals. She wrote a book with Eslanda Goode Robeson, the wife of singer and activist Paul Robeson, on being an American woman, on living abroad, and on marriage, Russia, and world politics, and she frequently contributed to the NUL's *Opportunity* and the NAACP's *Crisis*. Buck received an honorary degree from Howard University in 1942 and was a lifelong member of the NAACP and a board member of NUL.[52] Walter White considered her a friend and famously declared that there were only two white Americans he trusted: Eleonore Roosevelt and Pearl S. Buck. And according to her Afro-German adopted daughter Henriette Walsh, Buck "was very active in civil rights long before it was fashionable to be."[53]

It is evident that her involvement in civil rights activism informed her involvement in and ideas about transracial adoption, too. In her piece "I Am the Better Woman for Having My Two Black Children," published in 1972, Buck reflects on the circumstances that led her to adopt Henriette. Henriette's American father had been killed, and her German mother felt unable to provide for her in their small German town. Her mother had thus reached out

---

49. Buck, "Story of Welcome House"; see also Graves, *War Born Family*, 205.

50. Feldstein, *Motherhood in Black and White*.

51. Conn, *Pearl S. Buck*, 250; see also Buck's essay "Letter to Colored Americans."

52. Buck, *American Argument*; see also Umoren, *Race Women Internationalists*, 98–100; and Ransby, *Eslanda*.

53. Davidson and Rogosin, *East Wind—West Wind*, 00:45 min.

to Howard University, where the birth father had been a student. Buck was a trustee of Howard, and the president turned to her for help. What is revealing is how candidly Buck describes her first encounter with Henriette:

> She arrived at our house on Thanksgiving Day—five years old, bone-thin, weighing only 35 pounds, speaking only German. She had been airsick, she was unwashed, she was terrified, but she did not cry. Later, years later, she told me her German mother had simply put her on the plane without telling her where she was going. She had promised to return in a moment but had never come back. [. . .] She did not cry. She was too frightened.[54]

The description complicates the popular rescue narrative of the time by giving what is probably a more realistic description of the girl's traumatic experience and her fears. In this regard, it differs from the popular adoption reports in, for example, the *Baltimore Afro-American*.[55] Although Buck probably knew that most Black German children were adopted by Black Americans, she nonetheless contended that "from experience we knew that the little black children from Germany had difficulty adjusting to black mothers."[56] Here, Buck acknowledged that many of these children had been raised and socialized in a predominantly white environment before their adoption and that they did not necessarily (depending on their age) identify as Black. Yet, again emphasizing "love" in this piece, she argued that if these children were brought up with "basic love," their parents' racial identity was not relevant. She continued to encourage white couples to adopt Black children if they could love them and deal with their own prejudices. The article emphasized the political dimension of this kinship formation across the color line. Buck repeatedly stated how all individuals involved, Black and white, benefited from these transracial adoptions. Given that this piece was published in 1972, this conclusion is revealing. Amid the Black Power movement and the growing tensions surrounding transracial adoption that would culminate later that year in the National Association of Black Social Workers' statement condemning transracial adoption, Buck's writing can very well be interpreted as a defense not only of her personal choices but of transracial adoptions as such. Her daughter Henriette thus grew up to become "in the deepest, truest sense a bridge between two peoples, to both of whom she belongs by birth." Indeed, as such a "bridge," she taught Buck "much I could not otherwise have known." Buck concluded

---

54. Davidson and Rogosin, *East Wind—West Wind*, 00:45 min.

55. See "War Babies Romp in New U.S. Home," *Baltimore Afro-American*, March 10, 1953, 5; "Eight New Americans," *Baltimore Afro-American*, October 6, 1953, 1.

56. Buck, "I Am the Better Woman," 21.

her piece thus: "I am the better woman, the wiser human being, for having my two black children. And I hope and believe they are the better, too, and more understanding of me and my people because of their white adoptive parents."[57] While birth mothers relinquished their children because of their racial identities and the intensity of discrimination that their sex across the color line generated, it was now also the adoptees' racial identities that affected their adoptive mothers, yet in very different ways. Buck believed that for adoptive mothers like herself, adoption across the color line might overcome racial prejudice and discrimination. In her view, only mutual understanding could be gained from transracial adoption. Practiced to a larger extent, it could even be a force for a fully integrated society. This colorblind stance, however, which may very well sound misguided and naïve from the perspective of our contemporary discussions about race, also erased the racialized origins of such adoptions and put the experiences of birth mothers and the adoptive mothers in an uneasy relation.

To some social workers, Buck's statements were troubling; they preferred white adoptive parents who saw their children as "kin and not as projects in racial reconciliation."[58] Moreover, Black social workers argued that "love" for the Black child was not sufficient or constructive for developing a racial identity or for developing tools to survive in a white supremacist society. In the words of Ellen Herman: "Individualistic conceptions of how children grew up were luxuries associated with majority group membership, not accurate descriptions of the hurdles that black children faced in a racist society. [. . .] Instead of promoting their interests, transracial adoption made children even more vulnerable victims of racism."[59] Yet it was especially white middle-class families who were encouraged to adopt a child out of desolate postwar societies. Black families were not less interested in adopting a child from another country, yet they were often discriminated against by adoption agencies. Many agencies privileged white families by, for instance, spreading much less information about their work in Black neighborhoods and by implementing requirements that were difficult for Black American couples to meet since they usually presupposed middle-class status, residence in a certain neighborhood, a stay-at-home wife and working husband, and proof of infertility.[60] As Simon and Altstein explain: "The difficulty lay in the ability of white-administered adoption agencies to attract enough black adopters into 'the system' in order

57. Buck, "I Am the Better Woman," 64. Her use of the bridge as metaphor reminds me of the feminist publication by Moraga and Anzaldua, *This Bridge Called My Back*.

58. Herman, *Kinship by Design*, 244.

59. Herman, *Kinship by Design*, 249.

60. McRoy and Zurcher, *Transracial and Inracial Adoptees*, 9.

to establish credibility."[61] This speaks to the fact that most social workers in the US were white and that social work services were historically racially segregated. The lack of a diverse staff in most adoption agencies resulted in inadequate outreach to nonwhite families. Consequently, most agencies and social workers were inexperienced in recruiting Black families. It is certain that this lack of familiarity with Black Americans led most white social workers inaccurately to believe that they were unwilling to adopt. Yet Black Americans who could legally adopt a child did. In lieu of formal adoptions, many traditionally adopted informally, by taking in children from relatives or neighbors who were unable or unwilling to care for a child.[62] But since many of these adoptions were not finalized in courts or documented in statistics, the distorted perception that Black Americans were unwilling to adopt persisted.[63]

Historically, Blacks have long taken care of nonbiological kin. During slavery, the family unit was not protected, since mothers, fathers, and siblings could be sold away at any time. In this case, other members of the slave community stepped in and took care of abandoned children and children whose parents had to leave them behind. In his study *Efforts for Social Betterment among Negro Americans,* published in 1909, W. E. B. DuBois wrote that "among the slaves the charitable work was chiefly in the line of adopting children and caring for the sick. The habit of adoption is still wide-spread and beneficent."[64] The misconception that Black Americans were unwilling to adopt thus applied largely to the urban North, where agencies failed miserably in recruiting Black families. In the South, most Black children continued to be adopted informally, independent of an agency.[65] That the families were not considered by adoption agencies reflects their biased standards with regard to religion, class, and race. In tune with that, Black children were also often regarded as outside the scope of most adoption agencies and excluded from foster care, a discrimination that only slowly began to wane in the 1950s.[66] At the same time, overtly strict standards were applied to Black families that represented white middle-class values and made it hard for them to be considered as possible adopters.[67]

---

61. Simon and Altstein, *Adoption, Race, and Identity,* 10.
62. Ladner, *Mixed Families,* 56.
63. Ladner, *Mixed Families,* 64.
64. Du Bois, *Efforts for Social Betterment,* 11.
65. Ladner, *Mixed Families,* 66–68.
66. Ladner, *Mixed Families,* 57–60; see also Rymph, "Looking for Fathers," 179; and Rymph, *Raising Government Children.*
67. Rymph, *Raising Government Children,* 143.

Contrary to dominant adoption historiography, the NUL, for example, did lead widespread efforts to recruit Black prospective adoptive families to find homes for dependent Black children. Their Adopt-A-Child program was based on less strict regulations insofar as it did not require birth certificates, took no issue with working mothers, and accepted homes in Black neighborhoods that were not too congested for children.[68] These efforts, however, were short-lived. In tune with Buck, the NUL believed in a fully integrated society and shifted its emphasis on interracial adoption during the mid- and late 1960s. The unintended consequences of the new paradigms of integration and colorblindness were the negligence of special efforts to recruit Black families.[69] It is telling that as transracial placements increased in the US, the NABSW insisted that if adoption agencies and the social workers on their staffs did a better job recruiting Black families and strengthening Black communities, there would be no need for such adoptions.[70]

Conclusion

To some, Buck's advocacy of colorblind adoption seems misguided from today's perspective. It can also be read as an expression of white privilege and as a denial of racism. Yet, against the backdrop of the Double Victory campaign launched by the *Pittsburgh Courier* (which repeatedly reported on children fathered by Black American military service members abroad since the mid-1940s) and the civil rights movement, integration and colorblindness were powerful paradigms. Pittsburgh Urban League Executive Director Alexander Allen insightfully commented on transnational and transracial adoption as promoted by Buck when he stated: "It is an interesting commentary on prevailing American attitudes on race that white families are able to adopt across international racial lines, for example the fairly widespread adoption of Korean war orphans, but it is not yet possible to give serious or widespread consideration to domestic interracial adoption."[71]

In a December 1959 article, *Ebony* announced "The Problem of America's Brown Babies." Commenting on the wide news coverage on "war orphans" and "brown babies" after the Second World War and because of the Korean

---

68. Spence, "Whose Stereotypes and Racial Myths?," 152.

69. Spence, "Whose Stereotypes and Racial Myths?," 145–46.

70. Simon and Altstein, *Transracial Adoptees and Their Families*, 9; see also Simon and Altstein, *Adoption, Race, Identity*, 17–18.

71. Alexander Allen, "Study in Negro Adoption," 1957, 89; cited in Spence, "Whose Stereotypes and Racial Myths?"

War, the text stated: "But long overlooked is a booming homegrown market of such children. [. . .] They are what we call unusual babies, children of mixed parentage who are harder to place because of their unusual looks. They are too fair for many Negroes and too Negroid for most whites."[72] The slow acceptance of transnational adoptions that happened to be transracial as well did not result in more progressive domestic adoption practices. While race attitudes progressed considerably in one area—the incorporation of "racially mixed" Asian children into white families—most of these families would not have considered adopting a Black child domestically. Put another way, the adoption of children fathered by American GIs was a way to demonstrate and perform responsible citizenship. Adoption across the color line domestically, however, was regarded as dangerous "miscegenation" until the mid-1960s. These children were not only "mixed race" at a time when adoptions still heavily relied on matching; they were also the offspring of relationships deemed illegitimate and even unlawful in most US states until the US Supreme Court ruled anti-miscegenation laws unconstitutional in *Loving vs. Virginia* in 1967.

Moreover, international and transracial adoption has often been framed in narratives of need and rescue. Yet this framing did not extend to the domestic adoption of Black American children, where the parents' "failure" loomed in the back, echoing Buck's statement on "unfit" parents who should lose their claim on their child. In this regard, international adoption seemed easier for adopters because they were less concerned about possible disruptions or custody claims once the adopted children were out of their birth countries.[73] In her 1958 *Ebony* piece, Buck stressed the love she feels for her daughter Henriette. With statements like this, Buck demonstrated that the offspring of relationships deemed illegitimate and derogatorily labeled miscegenation could be seen as a potential force in the fight against racism and segregation. Given the normative power of matching and social engineering criteria in the making of modern families, transnational and transracial adoption was indeed progressive, maybe even revolutionary—if problematic—yet it did not result in the multiracial, colorblind society Pearl Buck envisioned. Buck did not develop an adoption plan for Black German children like Mabel Grammer did, or like she herself developed one for the "Amerasian" children with her agency Welcome House. But through her writings and her popularity with Black and white Americans, she shaped the discourse on transnational and transracial adoption in significant ways. Her adoption activism represents Cold War politics put into practice, and she clearly rejected contemporary gendered and racial norms to suit her interests.

72. "The Problem of America's Brown Babies."
73. Callahan, *Kin of Another Kind*, 36–37.

Bibliography

Alvah, Donna. "'I Am Too Young to Die': Children and the Cold War." *OAH Magazine of History* 24, no. 4 (2010): 25–28.

Buck, Pearl. S. With Eslanda Goode Robeson. *American Argument*. New York: John Day, 1949.

———. *Children for Adoption*. New York: Random House, 1964.

———. "The Children Waiting: The Shocking Scandal of Adoption." *Woman's Home Companion* 33 (September 1955): 129–32.

———. "I Am the Better Woman for Having My Two Black Children." *Today's Health*, January 1972, 21–22, 64.

———. "An Interview with My Adopted Daughter." *Cosmopolitan* 120 (April 1946): 38–39, 97–99.

———. "A Letter to Colored Americans." In *American Unity and Asia*, by Pearl S. Buck, 34–42. 1942. Reprint, Freeport, NY: Books for Libraries Press, 1970.

———. "Should White Parents Adopt Brown Babies?" *Ebony*, June 1, 1958, 26–31.

———. "The Story of Welcome House" (1955). Welcome House History Collection, Pearl S. Buck Archives, Perkasie, PA.

———. "Welcome House Letter" (1952). Welcome House History Collection, Pearl S. Buck Archives, Perkasie, PA.

———. "Welcome House Statistics on Number of Children, March 1956–February 1957." Folder 5: Adoption Statistics and Finances 1958–1984, Pearl S. Buck Archives, Perkasie, PA.

Callahan, Cynthia. *Kin of Another Kind: Transracial Adoption in American Literature*. Ann Arbor: University of Michigan Press, 2011.

Campt, Tina. *Other Germans: Black Germans and the Politics of Race, Gender, and Memory in the Third Reich*. Ann Arbor: University of Michigan Press, 2005.

Child Welfare League of America. *Standards for Adoption Service*. New York: Child Welfare League of America, 1958.

Choy, Catherine Ceniza. *Global Families: A History of Asian International Adoption in America*. New York: New York University Press, 2013.

———. "Race at the Center: The History of American Cold War Asian Adoption." *Journal of American-East Relations* 16, no. 3 (2009): 163–82.

Clark, Alexis. "Overlooked No More: Mabel Grammer, Whose Brown Baby Plan Found Homes for Hundreds." *New York Times*, February 2, 2019. Accessed April 28, 2022. https://www. nytimes.com/2019/02/06/obituaries/mabel-grammer-overlooked.html.

Conn, Peter. *Pearl S. Buck: A Cultural Biography*. Cambridge: Cambridge University Press, 1998.

Davidson, Craig, and Donn Rogosin, dirs. *East Wind—West Wind: Pearl Buck, The Woman Who Embraced the World*. Refocus Films. 1993. VHS.

Du Bois, W. E. B. *Efforts for Social Betterment among Negro Americans*. Atlanta, GA: Atlanta University Press, 1909.

Dudziak, Mary. *Cold War Civil Rights: Race and the Image of American Democracy*. Princeton, NJ: Princeton University Press, 2002.

Eyferth, Klaus, Ursula Brandt, and Wolfgang Hawel, eds. *Farbige Kinder in Deutschland: Die Situation der Mischlingskinder und die Aufgaben ihrer Eingliederung*. Munich: Juventa Verlag, 1960.

Fehrenbach, Heide. *Race after Hitler: Black Occupation Children in Postwar Germany and America*. Princeton, NJ: Princeton University Press, 2005.

Feldstein, Ruth. *Motherhood in Black and White: Race and Sex in American Liberalism, 1930–1965.* Ithaca, NY: Cornell University Press, 2000.

Fields, Barbara Jeanne. "Slavery, Race and Ideology in the United States of America." *New Left Review* 1, no. 181 (May/June 1990): 95–118.

Frankenstein, Luise. "Soldatenkinder: Die unehelichen Kinder ausländischer Soldaten mit besonderer Berücksichtigung der Mischlinge." In *Unsere Jugend* 10, by Internationale Vereinigung für Jugendhilfe (Genf), München, 1954.

Graves, Kori A. "Amerasian Children, Hybrid Superiority, and Pearl S. Buck's Transracial and Transnational Adoption Activism." *Pennsylvania Magazine of History and Biography* 143, no. 2 (April 2019): 177–209.

———. *A War Born Family: African American Adoption in the Wake of the Korean War.* New York: New York University Press, 2020.

Hackenesch, Silke, "'I Identify Primarily as a Black German in America': Race, Bürgerrechte und Adoptionen in den USA der 1950er Jahre." In *Kinder des Zweiten Weltkrieges: Stigmatisierung, Ausgrenzung, Bewältigungsstrategien,* edited by Elke Kleinau and Ingvill C. Mochmann, 115–35. Frankfurt; New York: Campus Verlag, 2016.

Herman, Ellen. *Kinship by Design: A History of Adoption in the Modern United States.* Chicago: University of Chicago Press, 2008.

Holt, Marilyn Irvin. *Cold War Kids: Politics and Childhood in Postwar America, 1945–1960.* Lawrence: University Press of Kansas, 2014.

Kirk, William. Letter to Erabelle Thompson, June 11, 1958. International Social Service United States of America Branch records, Box 23, Folder 34. International Social Service USA Branch Papers. Social Welfare History Archives, Minneapolis, MN.

Klein, Christina. *Cold War Orientalism: Asia in the Middlebrow Imagination, 1945–1961.* Berkeley: University of California Press, 2003.

Koller, Christian. *"Von Wilden aller Rassen niedergemetzelt": Die Diskussion um die Verwendung von Kolonialtruppen in Europa zwischen Rassismus, Kolonial- und Militärpolitik (1914–1930).* Stuttgart: Franz Steiner Verlag, 2001.

Kraft, Marion, ed. *Kinder der Befreiung. Transatlantische Erfahrungen und Perspektiven Schwarzer Deutscher der Nachkriegsgeneration.* Münster: Unrast, 2015.

Ladner, Joyce A. *Mixed Families: Adopting across Racial Boundaries.* Garden City, NY: Anchor/Doubleday, 1977.

Lemke Muniz de Faria, Yara-Colette. "'Germany's "Brown Babies" Must Be Helped! Will You?': US Adoption Plans for Afro-German Children, 1950–1955." *Callaloo* 26, no. 3 (2002): 342–62.

———. *Zwischen Fürsorge und Ausgrenzung: Afrodeutsche "Besatzungskinder" im Nachkriegsdeutschland.* Berlin: Metropol, 2002.

Lindenmeyer, Kriste. *"A Right to Childhood": The U.S. Children's Bureau and Child Welfare, 1912–46.* Urbana: University of Illinois Press, 1997.

McRoy, Ruth G., and Louis A. Zurcher. *Transracial and Inracial Adoptees: The Adolescent Years.* Springfield, IL: Thomas, 1983.

Moraga, Cherrie, and Gloria Anzaldua. *This Bridge Called My Back: Writings by Radical Women of Color.* New York: Kitchen Table, 1984.

National Association of Black Social Workers. "Position Statement on Trans-Racial Adoptions." September 1972. https://cdn.ymaws.com/www.nabsw.org/resource/collection/E1582D77-E4CD-4104-996A-D42D08F9CA7D/NABSW_Trans-Racial_Adoption_1972_Position_(b).pdf.

Oh, Arissa H. *To Save the Children of Korea: The Cold War Origins of International Adoption.* Stanford, CA: Stanford University Press, 2015.

Plummer, Brenda Gayle. "Brown Babies: Race, Gender, and Policy after World War II." In *Window on Freedom: Race, Civil Rights, and Foreign Affairs, 1945–1988,* edited by Brenda Gayle Plummer, 67–91. Chapel Hill: University of North Carolina Press, 2003.

Protocol of the *Committee to Consider Possibilities and Resources for Immigration and Resettlement of Colored Children from Germany,* January 29, 1951. The NAACP Records, Part II: General Office File, 1940–1956, Box II: A642 United States Armed Forces, Folder 8: "Brown Babies in Europe, 1950–55." National Association for the Advancement of Colored People Papers, Library of Congress, Washington, DC.

Ransby, Barbara. *Eslanda: The Large and Unconventional Life of Mrs. Paul Robeson.* New Haven, CT: Yale University Press, 2014.

Roos, Julia. "Racist Hysteria to Pragmatic Rapprochement? The German Debate about Rhenish 'Occupation Children,' 1920–30." *Contemporary European History* 22, no. 2 (2013): 155–80.

Rymph, Catherine E. "Looking for Fathers in the Postwar U.S. Foster Care System." In *Inventing the Modern American Family: Family Values and Social Change in 20th Century United States,* edited by Isabel Heinemann, 177–95. Frankfurt: Campus Verlag, 2012.

———. *Raising Government Children: A History of Foster Care and the American Welfare State.* Chapel Hill: University of North Carolina Press, 2018.

Shaffer, Robert. *Pearl S. Buck and the American Internationalist Tradition.* Rutgers, NJ: Rutgers University Press, 2003.

———. "Women and International Relations: Pearl S. Buck's Critique of the Cold War." *Journal of Women's History* 11, no. 3 (Autumn 1999): 151–75.

Sherk, Warren. *Pearl S. Buck: Good Earth Mother.* Philomath, OR: Drift Creek, 1992.

Simon, Rita J., and Howard Altstein. *Adoption, Race, and Identity: From Infancy through Adolescence.* New York: Praeger, 1992.

———. *Transracial Adoptees and their Families: A Study of Identity and Commitment.* New York: Praeger, 1987.

Simon, Alfons. *Maxi, unser Negerbub.* Bremen, 1952.

Spence, Matine T. "Whose Stereotypes and Racial Myths? The National Urban League and the 1950s Roots of Colorblind Adoption Policy." *Women, Gender, and Families of Color* 1, no. 2 (2013): 143–79.

Stoneman, William. "German Waifs Find a Friend!" *Chicago Daily News,* May 15, 1953.

Umoren, Imaobong D. *Race Women Internationalists.* Oakland: University of California Press, 2018.

Wigger, Iris. *Die "Schwarze Schmach am Rhein": Rassistische Diskriminierung zwischen Geschlecht, Klasse, Nation und Rasse.* Münster: Westfälisches Dampfboot, 2007.

Winslow, Rachel Rains. *The Best Possible Immigrants: International Adoption and the American Family.* Philadelphia: University of Pennsylvania Press, 2017.

CHAPTER 7

I Want to Show You My New Family

Race, Rejection, and Reunion in Postwar Germany

TRACEY OWENS PATTON

Helga and her twin, Heidi (my mother), are *afrodeutsche Nachkriegskinder* ("mixed raced" Black German postwar children), the so-called colored occupation children.[1] Helga and Heidi (aliases for the twins), whose visible phenotype is white, were wrapped up in the diasporic exodus that purged *afrodeutsche Nachkriegskinder* from Germany and into seemingly more diverse locales. There were "approximately 95,000 children born in Germany shortly after WWII," and of that, Helga and her twin represent "an estimated three to four thousand Black German children born between 1946 and 1953" who were either raised in Germany, adopted by German families, or adopted outside of Germany (for example, Denmark and the US).[2] "Mixed race" Black Germans, in reclaiming an identity for themselves, call themselves Afro-German, or Black German. However, as Rosemarie Peña has noted, "No ethnographic study exists that examines the diverse childhood experiences by the thousands of Black German children comprising the finite cohort of adoptees that Yara-Colette Lemke Muniz de Faria identifies in her seminal texts about Afro-

This chapter is part of a larger monograph, *A Nation's Undesirables: Mixed Race Children and Whiteness in the Post-Nazi Era*, currently under review with publishers. The author thanks the editor, Dr. Silke Hackenesch, Dr. Nancy Small, and Heidi for their suggestions for change.

1. Not all children born of Black US GIs and white German women during and after WWII were "occupation children."

2. "German Brown Babies"; Sollors, *Temptation of Despair,* 222.

German 'occupation children.'"[3] To answer this call, I use my family as an example, particularly since Helga and Heidi, and likely other adoptees during this period, felt the effects of and lived the close connection between race and nation in Germany, as well as the connection between nationalism, nation-building, and whiteness.

Helga's and Heidi's personal narratives are important additions to the scholarship on *afrodeutsche Nachkriegskinder* and the overall understanding of identity and identity formation during the postwar era. Many Black German children, if they were adopted, tended to be adopted as infants-to-toddlers. This was not the case for Helga and Heidi. With long-standing German familial connections and detailed memories, Helga and Heidi's personal narratives share the experience of being born into liminality and ultimately erased from their German biological family. The lived rejection and racism these preteens experienced was transnational, involved two continents, and ultimately affected the next generation. This research explores memory and postmemory through an autoethnographic centering as it relates to race, citizenship, family, and memoried erasure.

Memory and Postmemory

The nefarious effect of memory is that it is treated as fact. Events on a global scale are often reduced to the "winner" and the "losers," and those who do not fit neatly into the binary divides are easily erased from the official memoried recounting. Memories are larger than what is recounted in history books and recited in classrooms, and this includes places and spaces that, too, hold memories. Visual artifacts can include, exclude, and shape what we know or do not know, since it is people who craft the narratives that surround what happened in place, space, and territory, and it is people who can control absences and erasures. As Frances Yates noted, "The artificial memory is established from places and images [. . .] the stock definition to be forever repeated down the ages."[4] And these official memories become collective cultural frameworks, as Maurice Halbwachs has noted: "Collective frameworks are, to the contrary, precisely the instruments used by the collective memory to reconstruct an image of the past, which is in accord in each epoch, with the predominant thoughts of the society."[5]

---

3. Peña, "Stories Matter," 244.
4. Yates, *Art of Memory*, 6.
5. Halbwachs, *On Collective Memory*, 40.

If Halbwachs is correct, memory can be regarded as an artifact, remembered, reproduced, and reinterpreted to function as an aspect of one's lived experiences, both collectively and individually. Thus, the root and the routes these narratives take become part of our collective memories. The question then becomes, What kind of present do we hope to make out of strategically remembering the past? How does one tell a story of race, racism, adoption, and rejection in ways that make visible liminal and erased experiences? Postmemory may be one way.

Marianne Hirsch created the concept of postmemory and argued that it can be applied to traumatic events but also affects the lives of those who did not directly experience the trauma itself, for example, descendants of Holocaust survivors.[6] "The postwar world would accept only certain kinds of stories, making it doubly hard to render a truly authentic account."[7] Therefore, the use and recovery of postmemory experiences are action-oriented in design because their articulation of the memories allows for an alternative way of knowing which allows space for disenfranchised narratives to take root. Postmemory is the process of meaning-making that can be used as cognitive tools to challenge the hegemonic hierarchies often supported by language, thought, and interaction.

The narrative I share here is a collection of stories and experiences that are subjective. There is no "official history" recounted here, and, as such, my narrative experiences fit with postmemory. Through an examination of our lived and communicative processes, it is important to understand the meaning-making in identity formation that occurs as we situate ourselves in our lived experiences. This resituating allows for reimagining the narratives we tell ourselves and the narratives we tell others about ourselves.

A memory and postmemory accounting of my own story is important in critical adoption studies where the voices of the orphaned and adopted, particularly during iconic events like world wars, are often excluded from discourse because of their age and racial identity, which leads them to be erased. Therefore, I weave in my own family's experience to ask what happens when we view these "mixed race" German children of the postwar generation not only through the actions of the biological mother but also through the experiences of the children affected. It was memory, postmemory, and curiosity that led Anna (alias for my grandmother) to respond to a letter from us after fifty-two years.

---

6. See Hirsch, *Generation of Postmemory.*

7. Roseman, *Lives Reclaimed,* 8–9.

Constructions of Race and Nation: Anti-Blackness in Colonial Germany, 1884–1918

Fatima El-Tayeb and other scholars such as Adam Blackler, Michelle Moyd, Britta Schilling, Helmuth Stoecker, and Susanne Zantop have shown how race and national belonging are inextricably linked in German history, having their roots in Germany's colonialist politics and practice (1884–1918). German citizenship laws were designed to maintain whiteness as the default Germanness, and the idea that to be German meant to be white deeply impacted the twins.[8] The legalization for connecting Germanness and whiteness was seen as early as July 22, 1913, when the Imperial and State Citizenship law in Germany was passed, which excluded Black colonial subjects, and this continued under the Weimar Republic and the Nazi regime. Visually persuasive images, like postcards, were one way for colonialists to ensure a connection to Germany and whiteness, as well to provide a visual representation of the law. There were "a billion picture postcards [. . .] sent from the German Empire in 1900."[9] As part of the post-WWI agreement with the signing of the Treaty of Versailles on June 28, 1919, Germany lost its colonies, but debates continued about Black Germans and any "mixed raced" children created during this time. Nearly thirty years later, "mixed race" children embodied a liminal German/non-German existence. The twins Helga and Heidi embodied the fear of *Verkafferung* ("going native") because even decades later they are the visual embodiment of and "symbol for everything foreign."[10]

The Weimar Republic (1919–33) was the form of government put into place after Germany's WWI defeat, and it solidified anti-Black sentiment in Germany. The Weimar Constitution highlighted that "all Germans are equal and have the same civil rights and responsibilities," but this right reinforced

---

8. See Axster, "'Will Try to Send You'"; Blackler, "After the Herero 'Uprising'"; El-Tayeb, *Schwarze Deutsche*; Moyd, *Violent Intermediaries*; Schilling, *Postcolonial Germany*; Stoecker, *German Imperialism in Africa*; Zantop, *Colonial Fantasies*; Steinmetz, *Devil's Handwriting*.

9. Axster, "'Will Try to Send You,'" 55–56.

10. Axster, "'Will Try to Send You,'" 55–56. Axster detailed the fear of going *Verkafferung* in his research as related to the persuasive messaging and propaganda of postcards. *Verkafferung* was a term from the colonial era used as a way to discourage interracial coupling and the potential for "mixed race" children. "Postcards played a major role in communicating the mental cohesion between people and army. [. . .] The fear of an impending *Verkafferung*, a 'going native' of the settlers far away from home and without sufficient contacts, was a prominent topic in the colonial discourse in the German Empire" (60). The fear of *Verkafferung* was the nation-state fear of losing the privilege of being a so-called white nation by "racially mixing" with the so-called Black Other. To be marked as *Verkafferung* placed someone outside the compact of Germanness and whiteness, much like many *afrodeutsche Nachkriegskinder* children were put out, including Helga and Heidi.

Black people as outside the compact of white Germany.[11] In distinction to colonial Germany, where the threat of "Black pollution" of the white German race was placed *outside* the German national body, the Rhineland occupation by approximately 30,000 to 40,000 primarily African French colonial soldiers resulted in a threat from *within* the national body.[12] The presence of these Black troops, as authority figures within Germany, upset the boundary between whiteness (cultural supremacy) and Blackness (cultural inferiority). The "Black Shame Campaign" produced stereotypical images of hypersexualized Black colonial soldiers as polluted genetic stock and threats to the white women of Germany, and "the children were depicted as the carriers of the infectious diseases of their fathers, in particular sexually transmitted diseases."[13]

Black German children became the bodies on which anti-Black discourses played out throughout Germany. Subjected to forced sterilization as early as 1919, "biracial" German children of African French colonial soldiers and white German women were constructed as victims of their own circumstances and simultaneously unacceptable threats to the homogenous white German citizenry.[14] For Anna, as a youth, the presence of post-WWI African occupying soldiers was frightening: "You know, after the war [World War I] during the Occupation, we had a Negro down the street from us. I was afraid. Then my mother said, 'A person is a person. Don't be frightened by his skin color. He is probably just as afraid of you as you are of him'" (Anna, personal interview).[15] This early construction of Black as "other" affected how Anna would understand race and white privilege in later life.

Hitler and the Third Reich (1933–45) stripped citizenship and civil rights from Jewish Germans: "A citizen of the Reich is that subject only who is of German or kindred blood and who, through his conduct, shows that he is

---

11. Constitution of the German Reich.

12. Knowing the anti-Black racism that ran through German society, the French government intentionally placed their African colonial soldiers there to police Germany and its government as well as to antagonize Germany and its racist citizenry. See Oguntoye, Opitz, and Schultz, *Showing Our Colors*; see also Koller, "Recruitment of Colonial Troops in Africa"; Wigger, *Black Horror on the Rhine*.

13. Wigger, "'Black Shame'"; see also Florvil, *Mobilizing Black Germany*; Campt, "Converging Specters of an Other Within," 336–37.

14. Oguntoye, Opitz, and Schultz, *Showing Our Colors*; see also Campt, "Converging Specters of an Other Within."

15. The term *Negro* is a highly stigmatized word that is no longer used to refer to Black people in the US. *Black*, which is used more as a diasporic term to refer to Black peoples worldwide, replaced *Negro* in the 1970s, and *African American* became popular beginning in the 1990s.

both desirous and fit to serve the German people and Reich faithfully."[16] By the wording of this anti-Semitic law, Black Germans, too, were excluded from citizenship by default because of the "white blood boundary" of citizenship that defined Germany's colonial era. These anti-Semitic and racist provisions led the way to the 1935 establishment of the Nuremberg Laws, which were repealed in 1945 under Allied occupation. In 2000 Germany's citizenship law was amended, making it easier for long-term migrants and their children to obtain German citizenship. Then, in 2016, and again in 2021, Article 116 made it easier for Jewish Germans and their descendants who had fled Nazi Germany to regain their citizenship rights.[17] None of these citizenship amendments applies to *afrodeutsche Nachkriegskinder* adopted out of Germany who lost their German citizenship.

Hitler developed a robust sterilization program that targeted Black Germans and resulted in hundreds of these children being sterilized and hundreds of other youths moved to concentration camps.[18] Black female Holocaust survivors described the scientific experimentation on their bodies and the racist epithets they survived as part of the larger racist ideology that shaped Black German experiences.[19] The scientific justification for sterilization and extermination of Black people, and other people who did not meet the standard of a so-called superior being, took off with the eugenics movement that was embraced throughout the Western world, including the US and Germany. "Soon after Hitler was appointed chancellor on 30 January 1933, he made it clear that he would not retreat from the nationalist and racist elements of his vision of this 'community.'"[20] The use of eugenics justified Nazi violence against Black bodies, which paved the way for the passage of the "Law for the Prevention of Genetically Diseased Offspring" to be passed in Germany in 1933. Eugenics intricately linked "scientific and colonial discourses of racial purity" and "gendered and sexualized discourses" of the German body politic, wherein the "German national body is a raced body made vulnerable through the female body as the conduit of racial pollution."[21]

The research of Eugen Fischer (German professor of anthropology and father of the eugenics movement) informed the 1935 Nuremberg Laws, which

---

16. See Article 2 of the Nuremberg Laws. See also "German Imperial and State Citizenship Law."

17. "Germany Passes New Citizenship Law."

18. Okuefuna, *Hitler's Forgotten Victims.*

19. Lusane, *Hitler's Black Victims.*

20. Gellately and Stolzfus, "Social Outsiders," 3.

21. Campt, "Converging Specters of an Other Within," 327; see also Gellately and Stolzfus, "Social Outsiders," 4.

included so-called antimiscegenation laws and also targeted Jewish people, people with disabilities, those having mental health conditions, "and anyone else who did not resemble the blond and blue-eyed Nordic ideal the eugenics movement glorified."[22] "Most of their targets were individuals and groups long regarded as outsiders, nuisances, or 'problem cases,'" and this included Black Germans, who were seen as outside the compact of whiteness and, therefore, outside of Germany and not German.[23]

The Nazi regime established a coercive pronatalist policy that called for a significant increase in births from white German ("Aryan") women. In 1935 young white German women were encouraged to have as many children as possible and formed the group the Hitler Maidens (a female division of the male group, the Hitler Youth), in which all German women over the age of ten were mandated to participate. Anna was an active member of the Hitler Maidens. The group's primary focus was to teach girls how to be good German citizens and the importance of motherhood. After the 1936 Nuremberg rally, 900 young German women left pregnant.[24] As Oguntoye et al. have noted, "Aryan women who brought Aryan offspring into the world were glorified. Those who bore Afro-Germans, Sinti-Germans, or half-Jewish children were excluded from the cult of motherhood and were denounced as 'whores' in public and often by their closest relatives."[25] Men, on the other hand, were not sanctioned for having sexual relationships with nonwhite women if it was for nonreproductive purposes.[26]

Postwar Germany, 1945–1955: Democratizing Anti-Blackness in Germany

Previous research on *Heimat* (home) from Germany's colonial period forward highlighted that Germany had both anti-Semitic and anti-Black racist foundations for belonging and for who and who is not considered German. By 1949 the Republic of West Germany was constitutionally established and expressly prohibited racial discrimination, and "by 1950 West German federal and state Interior Ministry officials explicitly constructed the postwar prob-

---

22. Black, *War against the Weak*, xvi.
23. Gellately and Stolzfus, "Social Outsider," 4.
24. Rittenmeyer and Skundrick, *Third Reich*.
25. Oguntoye, Opitz, and Schultz, *Showing Our Colors*, 50; see also Campt, "Converging Specters of an Other Within."
26. Fehrenbach, "Black Occupation Children," 34.

lem of race around skin color and, even more narrowly, blackness."[27] Newly established West Germany conducted its first census of the population and used skin color as a central characteristic (similar to the US), establishing a postwar preoccupation with color/Blackness in German bureaucracy and the larger public discourse "regarding the reproductive consequences of defeat and occupation."[28] Again, "mixed race" children were a reminder of how far Germany had fallen from their military might to yet another military defeat.

Helga and Heidi became haunted by racist definitions of Blackness. They were never physically sterilized like some of the Rhineland-born "biracial" children. They were allowed to exist, but only through their absence in a dormitory, out of the family home. Put in one of several Catholic housing facilities for white and *afrodeutsche Nachkriegskinder*, the twins had a right to life, but between the ages of one and three, they were placed in a Catholic institution. The dormitory/orphanage they lived in operated much like a boarding school, where parents visited their children during the week and some of the children stayed in the family home on the weekends. Some children were adopted, and others not—it depended on the desires of the mother. Helga and Heidi were integrated into their white German family, knew their biological family, and often on the weekends stayed with family in the apartment. "I picked [the twins] up in the morning [Friday or Saturday] and returned [them back to the dormitory] on Sunday night" (Anna, personal interview) (see figure 7.1). Picked up and returned: what an interesting concept and liminal space to live in. Loved by family but put out of one's home. Visited by family who could leave and go on with life. Their liminal identity exposed during weekend home visits.[29]

The 1952 movie *Toxi* brought issues of Black American GIs, "biracial" German children after World War II, and orphanages to the big screen.[30] While Toxi (the young Black German main character) stays with a white German family for most of the film, it is the conclusion that drives home the ultimate message about "biracial" postwar children: despite being born to German mothers, children whose fathers were Black American GIs were seen as American, not German, as Black, not "biracial," and a parental identification the children seemingly longed for due to phenotype was the Black American father.

---

27. Fehrenbach, "Black Occupation Children," 38.

28. Fehrenbach, "Black Occupation Children," 38.

29. It was not uncommon for German children of young unmarried mothers to be placed in dormitories whether or not they were put up for adoption. Many German children, after WWII, regardless of ethnicity or racial identity, were placed in these Catholic facilities because of housing shortages or for economic reasons.

30. For more on *Toxi*, see Fenner, *Race under Reconstruction*; Stemmle, *Toxi*.

FIGURE 7.1. Helga (*left*) and Heidi (*right*) with Anna in Germany. They were coming from their kindergarten graduation holding balloons and had gingerbread hearts hanging from ribbons around their neck. Author's private collection.

Anti-Black racism in Germany was intricately linked to the processes of democratization in postwar West Germany, and much of it was learned and incorporated from the relationships developed between German citizens and segregated American forces.[31] A point of cooperation between Germany and the US, German women and Black GIs who dated and desired to marry met stiff opposition in both Germany and the US. The US military was entrenched in its anti-Black and antimiscegenation position and most often denied Black GIs' marriage applications, leaving hundreds of German women and children without their partners and fathers.[32] In some cases not only was the application for marriage licenses denied, the soldiers were immediately transferred to other military bases and barred from contact with their partners.[33] US military officials justified this behavior by stating that Black servicemen's relationships with white women in Germany would be unacceptable in the US and thus undermine domestic social cohesion when the troops were to return.[34]

31. See Fehrenbach, "Black Occupation Children"; Goedde, *GIs and Germans*.
32. See Fehrenbach, "Black Occupation Children"; Goedde, *GIs and Germans*.
33. Oguntoye, Opitz, and Schultz, *Showing Our Colors*, 89–90.
34. Oguntoye, Opitz, and Schultz, *Showing Our Colors*, 89–90.

The US War Brides Act (1945) did not offer German mothers and their "bira-cial" children an opportunity to immigrate to the US because American visas for Germans from 1945 to 1951 were capped and often quickly filled by many of the acknowledged victims of the Shoah.[35]

Point of Origin: An Illicit Inception

A Person Is a Person

Anna was twenty-three years old by the time WWII ended, and her notions of race and Blackness would have been shaped by another round of foreign occu-pation and another shift in the discourse of race, gender, and citizenship. As Black American soldiers developed relationships with white German women, West Germany was pushed to deny its Nazi past and move toward American-ized Jim Crow democracy. Anna met one "mixed race" American GI (Peter, an alias), who produced a cognitively dissonant shift in Anna's understanding of race when she said "a person is a person." This WWII American soldier gave her things like "chocolate and stockings" and was "nicer than the German soldiers" (Anna, personal communication). As historian Maria Höhn stated in *GIs and Fräuleins*: "Many Germans preferred the black GIs to the white sol-diers, because black GIs were more generous with their food rations."[36] Peter also provided an apartment for the two of them to live in, which was cru-cial because Anna had previously lived in a two-bedroom apartment that was crowded because of the postwar housing shortage.

For Anna to be with Peter is quite a departure for a woman who was once an active member of the Hitler Maidens. When I asked her about how she fell in love with him, she smiled and said, "Peter swept me off my feet, literally. He danced like an angel. He twirled me around. I never knew I could dance like that. He was very nice, we were friends. He was very light skinned with slightly curly hair and very proud of his Native American heritage. Race never mattered to me. It was always the person, never the color" (personal inter-view). When I pushed Anna on Peter's ethnic origin, she continuously stressed that he was Native American and resisted any Black label.[37] It was safer, more acceptable, for Peter to be anything but Black.

---

35. Fehrenbach, "Black Occupation Children."

36. Höhn, *GIs and Fräuleins*, 91.

37. Based on results of a DNA test Heidi took, she has no Native American ancestry but is one-third African.

I'm Pregnant

"I'm pregnant." Anna expected a marriage proposal from her American GI; instead, he said: "'I have a wife back in the US' and he broke up with me, choosing the other woman. I never heard from him again" (personal interview). He left. Anna never forgave him for his silence or his disappearance. Unbeknownst to Anna, he died.[38] Because of her pregnancy and Peter's leaving, Anna could not afford the rent for their apartment. She was forced to move back to the overcrowded apartment where her mother and her sisters lived. Attempting to hide the pregnancy from her family, Anna sought advice from the local Catholic priest in their city, who condemned her for premarital sex, and for sex with an American GI. "The priest told me he could not and would not help me and then kicked me out of the church. He told me I was no longer part of the Catholic Church and to leave. [. . .] After that, I was in denial about the whole pregnancy" (Anna, personal interview). Similar to the German colonial era, these racist terms reinforced a white supremacist hierarchy. Therefore, having sexual relations with a Black man meant that Anna was no longer seen as equal to other white people and had violated white racial norms. Anna chose silence to deal with her unplanned pregnancy and continued with the pregnancy.

> When I went to the hospital I asked, "What did I have, a boy or a girl?" I was absolutely shocked when the nurse told me, "Twins! Twin girls!" [see figure 7.2]. When I tried to give the girls up for adoption immediately after they were born, [my mother] said no. "They're family. Family stays with family." (Anna, personal interview)

Anna had several white German families interested in the twins but was forced to decline their offers of adoption. When I asked her about this experience, she said of birthing the twins and becoming a mother, "Having children was awful, the worst day of my life" (personal interview).

Helga and Heidi's skin color was light enough for Anna to likely pass them off as white children when they were in the US, since they were marked as white German children.[39] Only when Anna chose to place Helga and Heidi in

---

38. Peter died in 1953 and had no biological children apart from the twins. Apparently not as a love match, Peter married an older friend of the family, a widow with one child from her first marriage. Because they were married before Peter headed off to fight in WWII, she received Peter's pension when he died.

39. Cameras from the late 1940s and '50s are vastly different from the advanced cameras made today, and in the images of the twins in this chapter, it may appear to some that Helga and Heidi look like children with a darker phenotype. However, the photographic difference in

FIGURE 7.2. Heidi (*left*) and Helga (*right*) as infants in matching knit cardigans and bonnets, 1948. Author's private collection.

the California foster care system were they assigned a social worker who suddenly declared they were Black.

Anna had motherhood thrust upon her and was forced to parent two children she wanted to adopt out immediately. So one day, in an act of reclaiming her agency and power, Anna left. She had prearranged international sponsorship and passage to the US in 1955, becoming one of many immigrants to go through Ellis Island on her way to California. Anna left her seven-year-old twin daughters behind in Germany to be raised by their grandmother, her sisters, and the orphanage and told no one she was leaving. Later, she contacted her youngest sister, telling her that she was safely ensconced in the US, embracing the freedom she had lost as a young mother.

When I asked Anna about how her ideas around race had changed over time, even in 2012 she used antiquated and racist terminology: "I am surprised that racism happens in this day and age. I am sheltered from all that as you know. To me, a Negro is no different than anyone else" (personal interview). The sentiment she expressed is hard to believe, since Peter's "secret" ethnicity and evidence of her past sexual activity proved too much for her

phenotype is more likely due to shadows and lighting (overexposed or underexposed), shading and white balancing the camera, and the optical illusions a camera creates depending upon the wavelengths available from various light sources (e.g., indoor versus outdoor lighting) rather than a change in phenotype or skin color.

to bear, and I was her ghost and evidence of her secret "shame" knocking on her door. Her literal "guess who's coming to dinner" moment and her "mixed race" granddaughter.

New Life, New Family

The grandmother who said "family stays with family" was undermined when she discovered that Anna, unbeknownst to her, had worked with the nuns at the German orphanage to have the twins put on a plane to the US, permanently severing their relationship with her. It is difficult to comprehend why Anna would arrange for her children to eventually be with her, when she did not want to be a mother. Why would she want to bring her haunted memoried past forward, into the postmemory identity she was trying to create?

Anna, like many immigrants who established a foothold in the US, was sponsored by a wealthy Bostonian family who moved out west, the Duvenecks, who Anna said were German-speaking. Anna eventually told Frank and Josephine Duveneck that she had twin daughters. Once Helga and Heidi arrived in California, they lived together with Anna at the Duvenecks' ranch, Hidden Villa Ranch. Helga and Heidi loved the Duvenecks, whom they called *Opa* and *Oma* (grandpa and grandma), and the Duvenecks longed to adopt the twins, "but I said no" (Anna, personal interview). Eventually Anna met a white American man, who became her boyfriend and was involved in the twins' lives, but in 1958 her world changed: Anna's mother unexpectedly died. Her death allowed Anna a choice she had never had before: keep Helga and Heidi or have them adopted out. Her choice was made when Anna's boyfriend proposed and said "I'll marry you, but I don't want another man's children" (Anna, personal interview). Anna conceded.

Learning about the engagement, the Duvenecks once again offered to adopt the twins, and inexplicably Anna turned them down. Instead, she announced to them that she and her fiancé had begun parental rights termination paperwork, which they had already filed with the court; the twins would be entering the California foster care system. Furious, the "Duveneck family never spoke to me again. They never forgave me" (Anna, personal interview). Anna experienced a level of freedom in the US that she could only dream about in Germany. She was immune to the racial terrorism of Jim Crow, and she was free from being labeled a "w*****" or "n***** lover" in the US.[40] Even

---

40. "Wigger" is "a white person who befriends black people or adopts aspects of their culture or both[; . . .] its derivation from white n***** leaves little doubt of its pejorative origins." See Herbst, *Color of Words*, 233.

her twin daughters were immune, as they were seen as and labeled white. I could not understand why Anna kept turning down a family who loved and eagerly wanted to adopt the twins. Perhaps having a German family adopt the children, a German family knowing Anna's shame, would have kept her secret alive. To begin again with new memories, Anna had to sever the old ones.

The papers terminating parental rights were finalized in July 1958, and Anna was a married woman in October 1958. The push-pull of the liminal space of Helga and Heidi's existence had been decided. "We wanted to begin anew like any newly married couple" (Anna, personal interview). In Anna's new postmemory creation, ten-year-old Helga and Heidi were not invited to the wedding, and Anna began to make new memories of her new life as a married woman with no children in her new home with her new husband. This new life included the ability to live a wealthy lifestyle where she did not have to work, frequent travel, and a weekly housecleaner and gardener. Helga and Heidi in foster care became an afterthought whom Anna would "visit monthly" until their adoption (Heidi, personal interview). In honor of the twins, Anna planted a tree in her new yard and around the base of the tree placed two abalone shells containing artificial flowers, almost like a memorial to the dead. At ten years old, Helga and Heidi were stripped of another stable environment, became wards of the state in July 1958, and eventually were citizens of no country.[41] The Children's Home Society placed the twins in the Ming Quong orphanage in Los Gatos, California.[42] The twins were in a precarious situation because their only documents, which they had no control over, were their German passports. Since Helga and Heidi were not placed for adoption in Germany, the US viewed them as German citizens with German passports. The twins were brought to a new country beyond their control; today, they would be labeled Dreamers. As was demonstrated with the other postwar children who were adopted out of Germany and into international

41. "Biracial" German children, after the founding of the West German Federal Republic in 1949, were afforded German citizenship as part of the democratization effort. It was argued that the children should not have to pay for the sins of their mothers, but those children in orphanages were stripped of their citizenship. See Fehrenbach, "Black Occupation Children."

42. "The Ming Quong Home, translated as 'Radiant Light,' opened in 1915 in Oakland and in 1936 in Los Gatos, serving Chinese American girls of all ages. The home was the first institution of its kind in the United States to admit Chinese children. Ming Quong was part of a network of Presbyterian Mission Homes created in San Francisco in 1874 whose initial purpose was to intervene on behalf of young, Asian, immigrant females who had become vulnerable upon arrival into the United States. Although Ming Quong was referred to as an orphanage, it functioned more as a custodial home for girls with families that could not care for them financially or emotionally" ("Radiant Light"). Initially a home for children of Chinese descent in 1953, Ming Quong actively operated as an orphanage for all children. Helga and Heidi were placed in Ming Quong from 1958 to 1960. See also Peterson, "Ming Quong."

locales, the termination of their German citizenship was automatic, and the application for citizenship in their new country began. However, this was not the case for Helga and Heidi, who were never available for adoption in Germany. No one ever attempted to make Helga and Heidi naturalized citizens of the US. In the simplest terms, Helga and Heidi were undocumented.[43]

Undocumented immigrants are "foreign-born people who do not possess a valid visa or other immigration documentation, because they entered the US without inspection, stayed longer than their temporary visa permitted, or otherwise violated the terms under which they were admitted."[44] Being undocumented and a Black German adopted child was not unusual. "All the children were eligible for United States citizenship upon their arrival into the US, but individual testimonies reveal that not all families were properly informed of the naturalization procedure, or perhaps some just neglected to follow up. Thus, some children did not receive their US citizenship until much later, if at all."[45] Under Section 27 of the German Nationality Act, a minor who is a German citizen, when adopted by a foreign parent, will automatically lose their German citizenship, but *only* if they automatically acquire the citizenship of the adoptive parent because of the adoption. As Rosemarie Peña shared about her own situation, her parents wanted to conceal her adoption and did not initiate naturalization until she "was twelve years old, only after they received an official notification from the federal government threatening my deportation. Prior to that time, as I discovered much later, I had been legally *staatenlos* [stateless]."[46] Once Helga and Heidi were adopted, responsibility for the twins' naturalization as US citizens fell to the adoptive family and was not completed until 1967, when they were nineteen, long after their German passports expired, and only because they and the people who adopted them were deployed back to Mainz, Germany. *Staatenlos*, Helga and Heidi had no official paperwork at a state or national level (for example, a general ID, driver's license, or valid passport) noting who they were; and at least on paper, they did not exist.

---

43. As shown in Eleana Kim and Kim Park Nelson's chapter in this volume, the example of Germany is similar to the situation of Korean and other adoptees in the US in that their citizenship status is particularly precarious as a result of the complicated and exclusionary logics of racial identity and national belonging.

44. Washington State Department of Social and Health Services, "What's the Difference?," para. 1.

45. Peña, "Stories Matter," 247. See also Rosemarie Peña's contribution in this volume.

46. Peña, "Stories Matter," 247.

Justification and Adoption

Anna relinquished her parental rights, reinvented herself as a thirty-six-year-old newlywed, and now suddenly revealed to the California social worker assigned to her case that the father may have been a Black American, which allowed for sympathy and understanding from social and government agencies that otherwise would have judged her harshly for having had premarital sex. The social worker paperwork showed that Anna vacillated on the race of the father, from "White to Native American to Negro." The social worker seized on "Negro," thus thrusting US race binaries and white supremacist division onto the twins.[47] In the US, the so-called one-drop rule reigned: one drop of Black blood makes one Black.[48]

In assessing Anna, the social worker was impressed by her success in life: "She had the equivalent of two years of college, was a manager in [Germany] and earned a very good salary." She was impressed with her "above-average intelligence" and her "definite accent and good command of the English language." She was impressed with her beauty: "[Anna] had a very fair complexion [. . .] and is attractive and capable." But most of all, the social worker was impressed that Anna took care of her twin ten-year-old daughters despite their "biracial" status and the accompanying challenges and was "working through her feelings of past experiences."[49] The social worker's representation of Anna is inconsistent with how Anna characterized her memoried class positionality in Germany as someone struggling to make ends meet with two jobs.

The different postmemory narratives told illuminate how Anna crafted her now-immigrant story of survival. Because of this story of survival, Anna was afforded all the benefits of whiteness, including beauty and intelligence, apparently attributes that are synonymous with whiteness. In Germany, Anna's white privilege would have been secure had she not bore "biracial" children, and her cultural value, worth, and status would have been confirmed. The children, on the other hand, were the anchors weighing her down, preventing her from accessing white privilege.

---

47. Social worker, Children's Home Society of California, once-sealed adoption records, accessed 2012. Heidi and I petitioned the court in the state of California, through Homeland Security, to have these records opened.

48. To be classified as Black under the one-drop rule, a person had to have 1/32 or more Black ancestry, or as recently as five generations ago, and that person would not benefit from whiteness and all the privileged notions that come with being white. The one-drop rule is a unique racial qualifier in the US: it applies to no racial or ethnic group in the US other than those classified as Black / African American and is not found elsewhere. See Davis, *Who Is Black?*

49. Social worker, Children's Home Society of California, accessed 2012.

The twins, thrust into the California foster care system, were reeling from loss of culture, country, home, language, and now family. In referencing Heidi, the social worker noted: "[Heidi] often mentioned [her] birth mother. [Heidi] drew pictures of [her] birth mother," longing for her return.[50] But Anna never reclaimed the twins. The twins were deemed "Negro" and as having all the racist, negative phenotypical associations the social worker highlighted—slow wit and intelligence, thick lips, dark skin, and kinky hair—and Anna worked hard in her postmemory creation of self to distance herself from that.

With the twins, the social worker noted that "there are language barriers for both," but in commenting on their features and phenotype, she used language and visual observation that echoed back to the eugenics movement. In noting their skin color, she said, "Helga had a light complexion [with a] brighter rosy cast, and a round fat appearing face," whereas Heidi had "a medium to dark complexion, thick lips, and a long narrow face." In commenting on their hair texture, the social worker said, Helga had "kinky textured light brown and blond hair," whereas Heidi had "dark brown hair and less kinky textured hair." In referencing their intelligence, she said that Helga "related easily, was outgoing and succeeded in being the leader," whereas Heidi was "seriously thoughtful [. . .] (but) a slow learner. [. . .] [She] seemed to be well liked and accepted [. . .] but slow to be a leader." In remarking on their nationality, the social worker said that Helga "described herself as an American and a German but prefers to call herself an American," whereas Heidi "was stubborn," indicating that she refused the American label. In referencing "racial" categorization in the US, the social worker said that Helga "cop[ed] with the recent information that her birth father was of Negro descent," whereas when Heidi was "told of [her] part Negro heritage [she] reported [she was] German, thus embracing her liminal German identity."[51]

In speaking with Helga and Heidi about their next steps in the California foster care system, the social worker said that their "biracial heritage" was a problem for their mother's new marriage and that Anna found it emotionally difficult to cope with. And when Anna relinquished the twins, she "met with [them] sensitively and sweetly and said her final goodbyes. She was emotional and this seemed to have meaning for [them]."[52] This goodbye is the opposite of what Anna said at the orphanage, when she said that she and her fiancé relinquished the twins, severed Anna's parental rights, and informed the Duvenecks of their decision. This was also the complete antithesis of the goodbye that Heidi remembered too:

50. Social worker, Children's Home Society of California, accessed 2012.

51. Social worker, Children's Home Society of California, accessed 2012.

52. Social worker, Children's Home Society of California, accessed 2012.

I thought it was a visiting day. We were sitting outside on a bench at Ming Quong. My mother was very stoic. There was no handholding and no conversation. No motherly loving exchange. It was just "let me get this off my chest and let me go." [Anna] said, "You know I am not coming back. This is the last time we are going to see each other." I stared at her, trying to read her. My reaction was "she doesn't mean that. It couldn't be that." She always visited us in Germany and in Ming Quong. Then she left. Unbeknownst to us, she had already married and begun a new life. (Heidi, personal interview)

In these varied memory events of the final goodbye, the memories function to allow each person to go on with life. Helga and Heidi were relinquished to the state of California because their "biracial" background was too much for Anna to cope with. How can being who you are be too much? Helga and Heidi had seen their mother for most of their lives, yet Anna's nonvirginity and sex with a Black man was what had to be erased. Helga and Heidi's memory of Anna's departure is a goodbye told through a child's eyes. The twins express a level of betrayal in which they do not understand why they are being left. They only understand that they are being abandoned. They do not understand why Anna is leaving forever; in the past she always came back. Drawing pictures of her mother is the only way Heidi can keep her alive in her memory.

Anna had several offers of adoption from white families in the US who wanted Helga and Heidi, but she consistently declined these. Only when the social workers brought a sole offer from a Black American military family did Anna approve of placement. Why would Anna say "yes" to this adoption by a Black American couple who were strangers, as opposed to the Duvenecks, who loved the twins? Perhaps Anna made the choice based on the one-drop rule; or she perhaps followed adoption protocol, according to which race matching was common and transracial adoptions rare for most of the twentieth century.[53]

Anna also likely saw the media campaigns from *Jet* and *Ebony* magazines and/or heard about Mabel Grammer's efforts, which could have meant holding out for a Black American family. Grammer facilitated the adoption of at least 500 "biracial" German children because "she personally witnessed [racist] discrimination against Afro-German children and their mothers on the streets of Mannheim. Many of them found themselves in altered circumstances: Their husbands had returned from POW camps, or they were in new marriages in which the Afro-German child was no longer wanted."[54] After

53. Herman, *Kinship by Design.*
54. Lemke Muniz de Faria, "'Germany's "Brown Babies" Must Be Helped!,'" 355.

the war, the German government relaxed adoption laws for German children, not to help Black German children as much as to help other displaced ethnic Germans.[55] The German government pushed for the adoption of children of Black American GIs by Black American families where the children could find that they "fit" into the community, thus formalizing denial or refusal of their German belonging and citizenship.[56]

Regardless of Anna's reason, in 1960, at nearly twelve years old, Helga and Heidi were adopted by a Black American family whom both twins described as "emotionally, physically, and sexually abusive." Anna, who never had more children, was thirty-eight, married, and in a well-off, stable home environment by the time the twins were adopted by abusers. Anna was able to make new memories and was no longer haunted by her past in Germany. There were no more echoes and hauntings of a life that once removed her white privilege, her access to white privilege, and her white womanhood. The adoption of the twins served Anna well as she constructed her new identity and embraced her postmemory future with "prescriptive forgetting" whereby forgetting or erasing a past is a gain: "Not to forget might provoke too much cognitive dissonance: Better to consign some things to a shadow world."[57] The adoption of the twins embodied generational trauma, and they were haunted by the past and placed in a liminal and erased existence by Anna, Germany, and the US through stereotypes of Blackness. As Gordon aptly noted, "To be haunted is to be tied to historical and social effects."[58] The twins were haunted by the racist stereotypes about Black people that cloaked them in Germany and the racist stereotypes about Black people that enveloped them in the Jim Crow US.

Reunion

On July 13, 2012, Anna's first words on the telephone after fifty-two years were "I always hoped you'd forgive me." During our reunion, which Helga chose not to attend but Heidi and I did, Anna sat us down and before any questions were asked said, "I thought if you were unhappy in your new home, you would be returned to me. That's what the adoption agency said. They refused to give you back to me. I was threatened with arrest if I took [you girls] back. I did it so you could be in a home that was financially stable, but I hung around the area just in case you decided to come back." And then, "The day that I found

55. Fehrenbach, "Black Occupation Children," 46.
56. Fehrenbach, "Black Occupation Children," 45–48.
57. Connerton, "Seven Types of Forgetting," 63.
58. Gordon, Ghostly Matters, 190.

out I was pregnant was the worst day of my life" (personal interview). Silence. Heidi and I had no words. The pregnancy, the twins—all of it unwanted. The twins were born into liminality. They were only seen in juxtaposition to the pain they caused her physically and the pain they caused her life.

During our visit we learned that we were unwanted and learned about a life that had not included us for fifty-two years. Over the next couple of years, we had weekly phone calls, video calls, and in-person visits, yet the twins and I were forced into a space of liminal existence and never publicly acknowledged to other German family members (sans one aunt) or strangers. Shame and racism haunted any kind of long-term relationship after the initial reunion. Tired of being the secret "kept in the closet," I asked for a full family reunion, and Anna emphatically said "no" and exclaimed, "Because we're embarrassed! I'm sorry I have such a crummy family. To me people are people." If Anna was no longer ashamed and race/racism was no longer a concern, she did not stand up to the rest of the family. Since 2012 there have been family reunions, family cruises, and vacations to exotic locales, but not one that included the twins or me. Rather, Anna and the family excluded the twins and then sent happy pictures of who they consider to be their only family—aunts, uncles, and in-laws.

Conclusion

Once the twins were adopted, Anna told people that she was "unable to have children" (Anna, personal interview). Moving from a public narrative that included the inability to have children to one where the daughter and granddaughter show up on one's doorstep creates quite a cognitive dissonance. How does one navigate that public narrative? How does one circumnavigate a memoried event that, when one digs a little deeper, falls apart? How does Anna navigate her decision to drop off her children on the orphanage doorstep because of some invisible drop of Black blood? What about the twins and their claim to culture, language, and homeland?

Unlike South Korea, where the Global Overseas Adoptees' Link successfully lobbied the government in 2011 to "offer adoptees F-4 visas, which allow them to live and work in the country indefinitely [and] now adoptees can also apply to become dual citizens," Germany never made such an offer to its *afrodeutsche Nachkriegskinder* who were adopted out of Germany.[59] There has never been a German government apology or recognition for those chil-

---

59. Jones, "Why a Generation of Adoptees," para. 33.

dren who were adopted out of Germany; stripped of country, citizenship, and language; and brought to a foreign country. Article 116 of the German Constitution is supposed to correct for and "restore the citizenship of thousands of people descended from [Jewish] victims of Nazis."[60] However, in 2021, the German government amended the April 1, 1953, law which stated that "German citizenship could be derived from the father only. If only the mother was a German citizen, citizenship was not passed on to the children."[61] As of August 20, 2021, there appears to be a route to declaration for children like Helga, Heidi, and I to attempt to regain German citizenship: "Anyone who was excluded from birth due to earlier gender-discriminatory parentage regulations can acquire German citizenship by declaration (declaration of acquisition according to § 5 StAG)."[62]

This new law addresses, in part, Black German marginalization and *afrodeutsche Nachkriegskinder* claims of belonging. Through this law, *afrodeutsche Nachkriegskinder* and the second generation of Black Germans who are their children should finally be able to access their German citizenship and call Germany home. This is my hope, as Heidi and I pursue this avenue for ourselves.

The sin of interracial sex, embarrassment, adoption, and erasure continued at Anna's funeral in 2015. The twins and I were not allowed to attend the memorial and initially were told that there would not even be a memorial. There was a memorial. The fear of what others would say coupled with the vast wealth the other family members inherited were the driving factors. Issues of race, racism, and societal shame superseded family and the continued legacy of embarrassment, shame, and whiteness that keeps us in the closet.

Bibliography

Axster, Felix. "'Will Try to Send You the Best Views from Here': Postcards from the Colonial War in Namibia (1904–1908)." In *German Colonialism, Visual Culture, and Modern Memory*, edited by Volker M. Langbehn, 55–70. New York: Routledge, 2010.

Black, Edwin. *War against the Weak: Eugenics and America's Campaign to Create a Master Race*. Washington, DC: Dialog, 2012.

Blackler, Adam. "After the Herero 'Uprising': Child Separation and Racial Apartheid in German Southwest Africa." *Age of Revolutions*, March 30, 2020. https://ageofrevolutions.com/2020/03/30/after-the-herero-uprising-child-separation-and-racial-apartheid-in-german-southwest-africa/#_ftnref4.

---

60. Whitehouse, "Fight to Get Citizenship," para. 1.
61. "Restoration of German Citizenship."
62. See Bundesverwaltungsamt, "Nationality Law Changed."

Bundesverwaltungsamt. "Nationality Law Changed." August 20, 2021. https://www.bva.bund.de/DE/Services/Buerger/Ausweis-Dokumente-Recht/Staatsangehoerigkeit/_documents/Meldung/Meldung_Gesetzesaenderung.html.

Campt, Tina. "Converging Specters of an Other Within: Race and Gender in Prewar Afro-German History." *Callaloo* 26, no. 2 (2003): 322–41.

Connerton, Paul. "Seven Types of Forgetting." *Memory Studies* 1, no. 1 (2008): 59–71.

Constitution of the German Reich. http://reader.library.cornell.edu/docviewer/digital?id=nur01840#mode/1up.

Davis, James F. *Who Is Black? One Nation's Definition.* University Park: Pennsylvania State University Press, 2001.

El-Tayeb, Fatima. *Schwarze Deutsche: Der Diskurs um Rasse und Nationale Identität 1890–1933.* Frankfurt: Campus, 2001.

Fehrenbach, Heide. "Black Occupation Children and the Devolution of the Nazi Racial State." In *After the Nazi Racial State: Difference and Democracy in Germany and Europe,* edited by Rita Chin, Heide Fehrenbach, Geoff Eley, and Atina Grossman, 30–54. Ann Arbor: University of Michigan Press, 2009.

Fenner, Angelica. *Race under Reconstruction in German Cinema: Robert Stemmle's Toxi.* Toronto: University of Toronto Press, 2011.

Florvil, Tiffany N. *Mobilizing Black Germany: Afro-German Women and the Making of a Transnational Movement.* Champaign: University of Illinois Press, 2020.

Gellately, Robert, and Nathan Stolzfus. "Social Outsiders and the Construction of the Community of the People." In *Social Outsiders in Nazi Germany,* edited by Robert Gellately and Nathan Stolzfus, 3–19. Princeton, NJ: Princeton University Press, 2001.

"German Brown Babies." Black German Cultural Society. http://afrogermans.us/german-brown-babies-2/.

"German Imperial and State Citizenship Law. July 22, 1913." *The American Journal of International Law* 8, no. 3 (1914): 217–27.

"Germany Passes New Citizenship Law for Descendants of Nazi Victims." *BBC News,* June 25, 2021. https://www.bbc.com/news/world-europe-57618755.

Goedde, Petra. *GIs and Germans: Culture, Gender, and Foreign Relations, 1945–1949.* New Haven, CT: Yale University Press, 2003.

Gordon, Avery F. *Ghostly Matters: Haunting and the Sociological Imagination.* Minneapolis: University of Minnesota Press, 2008.

Halbwachs, Maurice. *On Collective Memory.* Translated, edited, and with an introduction by Lewis A. Coser. Chicago: University of Chicago Press, 1992.

Herbst, Philip H. *The Color of Words: An Encyclopedic Dictionary of Ethnic Bias in the United States.* Yarmouth, ME: Intercultural Press, 1999.

Herman, Ellen. *Kinship by Design: A History of Adoption in the Modern United States.* Chicago: University of Chicago Press, 2008.

Hirsch, Marianne. *The Generation of Postmemory: Writing and Visual Culture after the Holocaust.* New York: Columbia University Press, 2012.

Höhn, Maria. *GIs and Fräuleins: The German-American Encounter in 1950s West Germany.* Chapel Hill: University of North Carolina Press, 2002.

Jones, Maggie. "Why a Generation of Adoptees Is Returning to South Korea." *New York Times Magazine,* January 14, 2015. https://www.nytimes.com/2015/01/18/magazine/why-a-generation-of-adoptees-is-returning-to-south-korea.html.

Koller, Christian. "The Recruitment of Colonial Troops in Africa and Asia and Their Deployment in Europe during the First World War." *Immigrants & Minorities: Historical Studies in Ethnicity, Migration, and Diaspora* 26, no. 1–2 (2008): 111–33.

Lemke Muniz de Faria, Yara-Colette. "'Germany's "Brown Babies" Must Be Helped! Will You?': U.S. Adoption Plans for Afro-German Children, 1950–1955." *Callaloo* 26, no. 2 (2003): 342–62.

Lusane, Clarence. *Hitler's Black Victims: The Historical Experience of European Blacks, Africans and African Americans during the Nazi Era.* New York: Routledge, 2003.

Moyd, Michelle R. *Violent Intermediaries: African Soldiers, Conquest, and Everyday Colonialism in German East Africa.* Athens: Ohio University Press, 2014.

Okuefuna, David, dir. *Hitler's Forgotten Victims.* UK: SpiritWorld Entertainment, 1997.

Oguntoye, Katharina, May Opitz, and Dagmar Schultz, eds. *Showing Our Colors: Afro-German Women Speak Out.* Translated by Anne V. Adams. Amherst: University of Massachusetts Press, 1992.

Peña, Rosemarie. "Stories Matter: Experiences of Black German Adoptees in the U.S." In *Children of the Liberation: Transatlantic Experiences and Perspectives of Black Germans of the Post-War Generation,* translated and edited by Marion Kraft, 243–83. Oxford: Peter Lang, 2020.

Peterson, Judy. "Ming Quong: Once an Orphanage Now Modern Treatment Refuge." *Mercury News,* May 25, 2017. https://www.mercurynews.com/2017/05/25/lighting-the-way-orphanage-for-young-sex-slaves-is-now-modern-treatment-refuge/.

Pugach, Sara, David Pizzo, and Adam Blackler, eds. *After the Imperialist Imagination: Two Decades of Research on Global Germany and Its Legacies.* New York: Peter Lang, 2020.

"Radiant Light: Memories from the Ming Quong Home in Los Gatos." *The Museums of Los Gatos,* n.d. Accessed April 11, 2022. https://web.archive.org/web/20120328005506/http://www.museumsoflosgatos.org/site/2012/history-museum/ming-quong/.

"Restoration of German Citizenship: Federal Foreign Office." Germany.info, n.d. https://www.germany.info/us-en/service/03-Citizenship/restoration-of-german-citizenship/925120. Page discontinued, but see https://www.germany.info/us-en/service/03-Citizenship/german-citizenship-obtain/919576 and https://www.germany.info/us-en/service/03-Citizenship/-/2479488.

Rittenmeyer, Nicole, and Seth Skundrick, dirs. *The Third Reich.* US: New Animal Productions, 2010. 3 hr. DVD.

Rohrbach, Paul. *Deutsche Kolonialwirtschaft, Südwest-Afrika.* London: Forgotten Books, 2018.

Roseman, Mark. *Lives Reclaimed: A Story of Rescue and Resistance in Nazi Germany.* New York: Metropolitan Books, 2019.

Schilling, Britta. *Postcolonial Germany: Memories of Empire in a Decolonized Nation.* Oxford: Oxford University Press, 2014.

Sollors, Werner. *The Temptation of Despair: Tales of the 1940s.* Cambridge, MA: Belknap Press of Harvard University Press, 2014.

Steinmetz, George. *The Devil's Handwriting: Precoloniality and the German Colonial State in Qingdao, Samoa, and Southwest Africa.* Chicago: University of Chicago Press, 2007.

Stemmle, Robert A., dir. *Toxi*. Hamburg, Germany: Fono Film, 1952. DEFA Film Library, University of Massachusetts Amherst.

Stoecker, Helmuth. *German Imperialism in Africa: From the Beginnings until the Second World War*. London: Hurst, 1987.

Walther, Daniel J. "Racializing Sex: Same Sex Relations, German Colonial Authority, and Deutschtum." *Journal of the History of Sexuality* 17, no. 1 (2008): 11–12.

Washington State Department of Social and Health Services. "What the Difference between Legal and Undocumented Immigrants?" https://www.dshs.wa.gov/faq/what%E2%80%99s-difference-between-legal-and-undocumented-immigrants.

Whitehouse, Rosie. "The Fight to Get Citizenship for Descendants of German Jews." *BBC News*, November 18, 2019. https://www.bbc.com/news/stories-50398227.

Wigger, Iris. *The Black Horror on the Rhine*. London: Palgrave Macmillan, 2017.

———. "'Black Shame': The Campaign against 'Racial Degeneration' and Female Degradation in Interwar Europe." *Race & Class* 51, no. 3 (2010): 33–46.

Yates, Frances A. *The Art of Memory*. Chicago: University of Chicago Press, 1966.

Zantop, Susanne. *Colonial Fantasies: Conquest, Family, and Nation in Precolonial Germany, 1770–1870*. Durham, NC: Duke University Press, 1997.

CHAPTER 8

Black Germans

Coming Home to Self and Community

ROSEMARIE H. PEÑA

In the aftermath of the Second World War, between 1945 and 1965, thousands of children were born in Germany to local women and Allied Occupation troops. Those fathered by Black American soldiers were socially constructed transnationally, as a special cause for concern. In the German imaginary, German, as a national identity, was invariably homogeneous and culturally white. Interracial marriage at that time was still illegal in many US states. After considerable debate over who should be responsible for their welfare, many of the children born of these unions were among the first whose natural lives would be interminably altered by transnational adoption. This chapter uses the terms *Black German* and *Afro-German* synonymously to refer to this finite, dual-heritage, generational cohort. Black Germans join other postwar Black European, British, and Asian groups as experiential pioneers of the juristic process effectuating multicultural families by awarding irrevocable guardianship of children born in one country to genetically unrelated persons living in another. For nearly three decades, Black German Americans who grew up in relative isolation in Germany, Denmark, the US, and the Caribbean are discovering a globally dispersed community as they reconnect with their first families and their bifurcated transcultural roots.

Black German Americans are contemporarily (re)constructing their personal and collective histories while negotiating their complex identities just as they are re-emerging as a topic of significant public interest and academic inquiry. As a cohort, most of the adoptees, whose ages now range from the mid-sixties to mid-seventies, are learning about their ancestral roots in Germany while engaging in dialogue with journalists, academics, and filmmakers who are just as eager to learn about them. As digital technologies have advanced dramatically since the 1980s, Black German studies, adoption studies, and the digital humanities have concomitantly flourished as interdisciplinary research fields—in conversation with, and in response to, Black German and adult adoptee activism, respectively. Adoptees are thereby reunifying in discourse and actuality with multiple generations of Black Germans having divergent family backgrounds, cultural heritages, and relationships to Germany. This chapter documents the role of reunifying adoptees in the ongoing development of a dynamic, international, Black German counterpublic that both contributes to and benefits from interdisciplinary scholarly discourses across race and nation. It also offers a detailed account of the routes and practices of searching, the challenges of reunion and the efforts toward community-building over the last three decades.

Contextualizing the Postwar Adoptions within Black German History

In order to grasp the intellectual and sociocultural ethos in which the multilayered reunifications are taking place, it is important to know something about Black people's history in Germany and the emergence of Black German studies as a multidisciplinary field of research. Fortuitously, for searching adoptees who are actively integrating their birth and adoption-constructed identities, academia and life-writing provide opportunities for simultaneously developing senses of a collective identity, historical continuity, and cultural belonging.[1] While the growing canon of literature reveals that Black people have a very long history in Germany, the children born to white German women and Black occupation troops after both world wars represent the most appreciable groups of dual-heritage Black children born on German soil. Tina Campt's *Other Germans* explores the fates of the so-called Rhineland children, who were fathered by French colonial soldiers occupying the Rhineland border after World War I.[2] The racist beliefs that led to the marginalization and sterilization of the children born under National Socialism informed German treatment of those born after 1945. Many of the same Nazis that worked in

---

1. For an example of such life-writing, see the contribution by Tracey Patton in this volume.
2. Campt, *Other Germans*.

German universities, schools, and child welfare institutions held the same jobs after World War II.

German historian Yara-Colette Lemke Muniz de Faria demonstrates how false conclusions drawn from anthropological studies on "race mixing," performed as early as 1908 by Eugen Fischer, were reinterpreted in studies involving the children born during the interwar years.[3] These studies culminated in racially biased measures that were later employed to evaluate the Black German American children born after World War II. With respect to the later research conducted by Walter Kirchner (1951) and Rudolf Sieg (1952), Lemke Muniz de Faria writes:

> Central to both studies was a conflict between the biologically based definition of racial difference and its social factors; This, however, remains unexamined. The basic social problem of the children, prejudice, was thus projected back onto the children themselves. In this way, the scientific discourse mimicked the social construction of race more generally, insofar as the category of race was constructed in a way which meant that the "stigma" of racial mixture was foregrounded and thereby transformed into a form of "racial Otherness." [. . .] The reductively racialized classification of Afro-German children led to their being seen as "different" and "Other"—a perception tantamount to a representation of them as "not really German," displacing them instead to a homeland with a predominantly black population where they were assumed to "really belong." An unhappy future was forecast for these children in Germany, as it was anticipated that they would be handicapped by discrimination and unfavorable treatment. Frequently, these two perspectives combined such that, on the one hand, the race of the children was viewed as biologically fixed and unchangeable, while on the other hand, the negative reaction of society to their appearance was understood as the primary focus of conflict.[4]

Statistics are unreliable in the Black German context, since the postwar German census does not keep an account of race, though Lemke Muniz de Faria estimates that 4,776 Black German children were born in Germany between 1945 and 1955. As many as 500 were adopted "by proxy" through a controversial initiative directed by Mabel Grammer, wife of Chief Warrant Officer Oscar Grammer, who was stationed at the US Army base in Mannheim, Germany. Mabel Grammer was a journalist for the *Afro-American* newspaper,

---

3. Lemke Muniz de Faria, "Black German 'Occupation' Children."

4. Lemke Muniz de Faria, "Black German 'Occupation' Children"; see also Sieg, *Mischlingskinder in Westdeutschland*; and Kirchner, *Eine Anthropologische Studie*.

through which she launched a campaign imploring Black American families living in the US to adopt children she saw in the St. Josef *Kinderheim,* an orphanage not far from the Mannheim-Käfertal Casern, a major military campus in the city of Mannheim, in southern West Germany. Mabel Grammer's compassion for the children was such that she and her husband adopted twelve themselves.[5] A street, the Mabel-Grammer-Ring, in Mannheim-Käfertal, was named in her memory in 2019.[6]

Lemke Muniz de Faria's groundbreaking scholarship brought to light the history of Black Germans born after 1945 and their adoptions, paving the way for other scholars, Heide Fehrenbach, for example, to write about the cohort from a historical vantage point.[7] Lemke Muniz de Faria's trilogy of texts explicate the transnational state responses to the children's births and describe the racialized social politics that ultimately led to German mothers irrevocably relinquishing their children, voluntarily and by coercion. At the time, children born to unmarried women automatically became wards of the German state. Fehrenbach contends that between 1945 and 1956 as many as 4,000 Black German children were adopted to the US, although children were adopted well into the 1960s to both Denmark and the US.[8] In "Black German Children," Nancy Rudolph writes:

> From the Bureau of Statistical Affairs, I learned that there were 150,000 illegitimate babies with American GI fathers born in Germany in the 1940s and 1950s, 9,000 of whom were black. In 1956, 17,500 occupation children were born in the Bavarian part of the American zone, and 1,700 of these children had Black fathers. In my research at the *Abendzeitung* [Evening News], I learned that 900 fathers had declared themselves fully responsible for the support of their children, and that a great percentage of these fathers who had come forward were Black.[9]

German literary scholar Marion Kraft contests the notion that the majority of the children were adopted outside of Germany, asserting that "in 1960 more than 70 percent of the so-called Black occupation children lived with their mothers—a fact that counteracts the once common assumption that

---

5. Lemke Muniz de Faria, "Reflections on the 'Brown Babies.'"
6. On Mabel Grammer and the history of Afro-German adoption after 1945, see also the chapters by Kori Graves and Silke Hackenesch in this volume.
7. Lemke Muniz de Faria, *Zwischen Fürsorge und Ausgrenzung.*
8. See Fehrenbach, *Race After Hitler.*
9. Rudolph, "Black German Children," 384.

these women were irresponsible and not able to raise children."[10] Kraft affirms, however, that many children also grew up in orphanages or were fostered and/or adopted by white Germans. It is highly unlikely that we will ever be able to accurately number or geographically locate the childhoods of all the members of this historical cohort. Since the 1990s, however, Black Germans reuniting with their original families on both sides of the Atlantic reveal a myriad of lived experiences and disparate perspectives with respect to their adoptions, national identity, and political and cultural affiliation. Organizations founded by adoptees have played a significant role in the advancement of Black German studies in the US and in the exponential growth of a multi-generational virtual community of globally situated persons who self-identify as Black Germans.

Identity and Belonging: (Re)Defining the Self

When Black Germans who were adopted to the US introduce themselves in community forums, they often remark that they grew up feeling isolated. Many only discovered that they are members of a named, historical, and circumstantially situated group when they began to search for their mothers. The secrecy surrounding adoption in the 1950s and 1960s meant that adoptees learned early on that their personal origin story was taboo and not an appropriate subject to discuss outside the immediate family. While most US adoptees were always aware of their adoption status, some were late-discovery, meaning they first learned that they were adopted as teenagers or adults. Peggy Blow, for example, whose reunion is central to Michaela Kirst's documentary, *Brown Babies: Deutschlands verlorene Kinder,* claims her adoptive mother denied that she was adopted, despite Peggy's awareness that she looked very different from her adoptive parents. Their skin was considerably darker than hers.[11] Adoptees vary in complexion and hair texture, from passing as white to appearing as though they are the biological children of their adoptive parents. Some adoptees never saw their birth certificates or adoption papers until after their adoptive parents passed away. Others still lack their original documents and are concerned that their US citizenship may be precarious. Afraid of deportation, they are hesitant to approach INS to ask for proof of naturalization.[12]

---

10. Kraft, "Coming In from the Cold," 6; see also Kraft, *Kinder der Befreiung.*

11. Kirst, *Brown Babies.*

12. On the issue of adoptees' citizenship status, see also the chapter by Eleana Kim and Kim Park Nelson in this volume.

Maria Watson, for example, whose reunion story is profiled in my essay "Stories Matter," passed away at age seventy-one in June 2019, without meeting Hermann, her older half-brother, whom she had left behind in Germany in the early 1950s.[13] The siblings' mother died shortly after giving birth to Maria, whose adoption to the US was facilitated by Mabel Grammer when she was a toddler. After I, in my role as president of the Black German Heritage and Research Association (BGHRA), helped Hermann locate Maria in 2012, he sent her an airline tickets so that she could come to Germany and meet him and her extended family. Maria was unable to produce the paperwork necessary to obtain a passport, and, regrettably, her fears, frustration, and ill health prevented her from pursuing the matter further. She passed away without ever realizing her dream of an in-person reunion with her elder brother.

Adoptees often hesitate to discuss their intentions to search for their genetic kin with their adoptive family members. Some who delay searching until after their adoptive parents have passed away learn in the end that both of their birth parents have also died. While all their adoptions were initially closed, changing regulations, DNA analyses, and the internet have made it relatively easy today for adoptees to locate family members in Germany, though this was not always the case. In some situations, except through DNA analysis and a bit of luck, it is easier to obtain identifying information about the German mothers than it is for the Black American fathers. Many fathers are unidentified on birth certificates or in the adoption records, and often living maternal relations, when locatable, have little or no information.

A Germany-based nonprofit organization, GI Babies Germany e.V., provides search and support services for persons seeking their birth fathers in the US and especially for adoptees having difficulty obtaining information through the US National Personnel Records Center (NPRC) in St. Louis, Missouri. To make matters worse, the US National Archives reports a "devastating" fire in 1973 that "destroyed approximately 16–18 million Official Military Personnel Files (OMPF) documenting the service history of former military personnel discharged from 1912 to 1964."[14] GI Babies e.V. offers hopeful searchers an information request form and a cover letter template with the opening text "Please may I ask for any information under the *War Babes Agreement*. I am trying to trace my father who I understand was an American serviceman stationed in Germany in [. . .] in the year(s) [. . .]." The War Babes Agreement to which the letter refers is the July 16, 1990, decision of US District Court, District of Columbia, resolving the class action lawsuit *War Babes, et*

---

13. Peña, "Stories Matter"; see also Peña, "Bedeutsame Geschichten."
14. Lawrence, "Archives Recalls Fire."

al., Plaintiffs, v. Don Wilson, et al., Defendants. The British plaintiffs won the right to request identifying information about their suspected fathers over military objections citing "unwarranted invasion of privacy." The introduction summary of the court's decision reads as follows:

> Association that represented British citizens and three of its members sought to acquire information that could help them discover American servicemen whom they believed to be their natural fathers. On cross motions for partial summary judgment, the District Court, Jackson, J., held that the National Archives and Records Administration (NARA) failed to demonstrate that it would be an unwarranted invasion of privacy to disclose home addresses of the servicemen. Plaintiffs' motion for partial summary judgment granted; Defendants' cross motion for partial summary judgment denied.[15]

There is no guarantee, however, that the NPRC will honor a German-born adoptee's request based on a decision favoring the British. Nevertheless, it sets a precedent should a similar class action suit be filed on behalf of German-born adoptees.

Today the proliferation of affordable DNA testing services and the heritage websites attached to them make it possible for almost anyone to find their genetic kin. Volunteer search angels who manage Facebook groups are often able to provide telephone numbers and addresses in both countries in a matter of minutes. One Facebook group, "GI Family International Search," has over 2,500 members. Black Germans have posted their searches there, though they are not the majority. Many people who come to the site are not adoptees but persons simply looking for distant relatives. Other, more discrete search angels accept cases by referral only, and their private Facebook groups are not discoverable through an internet search. Each group has their own rules about how to submit a search request and whether any specific details, documents, or photographs are to be shared within the group. Translation software embedded in social media networks has all but removed language barriers. Depending on the German state where they were born, adoptees can now request copies of original documents via email, and the search angels often provide instructions and translation assistance.

In response to my request for information from the BGHRA to Charles M. Huber, the first dual-heritage Black German member of the German Parliament, and for guidance on how Black Germans in the US should request their original adoption files, Caren Marks of the Bundesministerium für Familie,

---

15. US District Court, District of Columbia, *War Babes v. Wilson.*

Senioren, Frauen und Jugend [the Federal Ministry for Family Affairs, Senior Citizens, Women and Youth] wrote the following:

> German adoption proceedings are very reliably documented and the documents very well archived—the persons concerned therefore have a good chance of gaining information about the adoption proceedings in their individual cases. Until the 1970s, there was an obligation to retain adoption records for thirty years—this period was then extended to sixty years and later, in 2015, to [a] hundred years. It also applies retrospectively to past adoption placements, to make sure that adopted people, who often only begin to trace their roots an advanced age, are able to access their records. [. . .] There is one caveat here, however: We have been told by the central adoption agency in one state that some children were taken to the USA in the 1950s in groups, sometimes with involvement from U.S. attorneys, and only placed for adoption once they arrived. In many such cases no records will exist in Germany.[16]

While it is impossible to verify how many Black German children were adopted to the US, we do know that many left Germany from Mannheim beginning in 1952 as part of Grammer's "Brown Baby Plan." Adoptees who grew up in the US sometimes still return to Mannheim in search of their maternal family roots and personal histories. Inge Groos, the current director at St. Josef, maintains a small collection of photographs depicting some of the Black German children who stayed there in the 1950s, along with a few contemporaneous news clippings. Because the children's individual case files from the 1950s no longer exist, adoptees and staff members alike are disappointed when there are no personal recollections or photos memorializing the presence of the visiting adoptee in St. Josef's humble archive.

While directing me on a tour of the facility and grounds, Jürgen Hoffman, the house manager, mentioned that when Peter Grammer, one of Mabel Grammer's adopted sons, visited, he experienced a sense of déjà vu, sharing shadowy memories of the obtrusive pole that extends from the floor to the ceiling in the tiny infant nursery. Although the paint and furniture have been updated, the smallest children living in St. Josef still sleep in the same room today. I myself also likely slept here as an infant, though I have no memory of my time in the orphanage. Peter Grammer found the old oak tree that still stands in the garden just outside the main structure also familiar, where Hoff-

---

16. As translated by Dr. Christine Kaiser, Mr. Huber's office manager, in an email communication to me received March 31, 2017. The "caveat" could be read as a reference to Mable Grammer and the by-proxy adoptions facilitated through her "Brown Baby Plan."

man says the nuns attended to the youngest children at play and often read stories to them. Those who return are routinely invited to pose for photos on the front steps with Hoffman to commemorate the event. Prints of these digitally captured images are now also kept in binders along with the original Polaroid and lab-processed photographs of the children who lived there in the 1950s.

The black-and-white photographs have no information or dates written on them, although, according to the staff, a few adoptees pictured have returned to visit and recognized themselves. Similar photos have also appeared on adoptees' social media timelines that are not in the archive but seem to have been taken at St. Josef and at other German children's homes in the 1950s. The girl holding a doll in one of the photographs just recently published her memoir, *Too Brown to Keep: A Search for Love, Forgiveness, and Healing.*[17] We cannot know from these photographs how the children they portray were treated before and after the holiday celebrations, or how long each was there, or how many were eventually adopted, but according to Lemke Muniz de Faria, as noted in her 2012 BGHRA keynote, Germany paid reparations to the children who grew up in institutional care during this time on the basis of the abuse they endured from their caregivers. While there are a few news clippings and official letters from the US military, all other records in the archive from the relevant period, according to Director Groos, have been purged. Most adoptees seeking hard evidence of their presence in or adoptions from Mannheim must look elsewhere.

It is unfortunate that many of the adoption records from the 1950s that were archived in the *Jugendamt* (Child Welfare Office) in Mannheim, along with the index to the entire collection, were destroyed in a flood. Alexandra Mähringer, the office manager, advised me in 2017, when I went to retrieve my own file, that surviving records are technically available to adoptees on request—provided one has their *Aktenzeichen* (case number). This number appears on adoptees' original German birth certificates, which some have never seen. Fortunately for me, I was able to produce my case number, 285, and Mrs. Mähringer provided me a copy of my complete file, as sparse as it was, while I was there. As was the custom at the time, all postwar adoptions were closed, and original birth documents were amended and sealed. A note, often handwritten in an obsolete cursive script called *Sütterlinschrift*, appends the original birth record advising that the child has been adopted. The notation also provides the name and *Wohnort* (city of residence) of the adoptive parents. A new English-language document referred to as an international

---

17. Fambrough-Billingsley, *Too Brown to Keep.*

birth certificate (IBC) is then issued by the court as *if* the child were the biological offspring of his or her adopters. When German mothers relinquished custody of their children, they also waived their rights to ever pursue contact with them. All legal ties between the child and mother were irrevocably severed.

Searching for Family and Finding Community

When adoptees searching for their birth parents in the 1980s discovered each other, a sense of community developed among those who wanted to connect transnationally and share their life experiences. Though the path to family reunification is never uniform and outcomes vary, US-based adoptees offered each other practical advice and emotional support. Before the internet revolution, the obstacles to adoptees' bifurcated searches between Germany and the US were legion, and the process was painfully slow.[18] Long-distance phone calls were costly, and most requests for information were handled by traditional mail. In the mid-1980s, the Red Cross and other adoptee advocacy services routinely referred US adoptees to German birth mother and search angel Leonie Boehmer. In the debut issue of his newsletter, *Geborener Deutscher* [Natural Born German], German-born, US adoptee William Gage wrote about his personal journey and his partnership with Boehmer and encouraged other adoptees to contribute the reunion stories to encourage others. Gage sent out the first issue by traditional mail on April 14, 1988, a month after his own search ended with the disappointing news that his mother had already died. Gage described his newsletter as "a new adoptee/birth parent periodical named *Geborener Deutscher* (Natural Born German) because it is designed to meet the needs, answer the questions and otherwise provide a forum for discussion of topics of concern to German born adoptees and birth parents, particularly those residing in the United States of America." Gage promised his readers that future issues would offer a search workshop, profiles of adoption reformers, and first-person "search journals" and progress updates. One may fairly assume that Gage's first subscribers and contributors were adoptees who had contacted Leonie Boehmer for assistance in finding their birth parents.

Evidently, Gage had enough Black Germans on his mailing list, or Boehmer had enough inquiries, to warrant her front-page cover essay in 1991, "Biracial Adoptees Can Expect a 'Mixed' Reaction," warning them of the high

---

18. Peña, "From Both Sides of the Atlantic"; see also Cain, "Rockford, Il, Adoptee Finds Mother."

probability that their mothers would refuse contact. Boehmer writes, "To this day, I, as a German-born birth mother, am ashamed to say that the attitude of Germans towards people with other-than-white skin has not changed."[19] Archived issues of *Geborener Deutscher* are a unique source that documents early efforts of exchange and community-building among German adoptees in the US and thus their collective sense of alienation and quest for belonging. Gage eventually stopped mailing the newsletter and engaged his readers online in a Yahoo group by the same name. Though he recently repatriated to Germany, Gage still offers advice to searching adoptees. The Yahoo group was founded on December 26, 2000, and had 482 members in 2019, when it closed, not long before Yahoo discontinued the feature in 2020. It is unascertainable how many of his subscribers were Black, but they are likely the minority. Searching Black adoptees often identified themselves in their introductory messages when joining the group. Gage and other list members customarily advised those who did identify as dual-heritage of resources available to them through Black German organizations in Germany and the US. Though Gage's forum is inactive today, the original printed newsletters have been digitized.[20] Over fifteen years and fifty-seven issues, five Black German search and reunion stories were profiled in the *Geborener Deutscher* printed newsletter, and previously isolated adoptee readers learned that Black Germans, who submitted stories from both Germany and the US, were searching for their bifurcated genealogical roots.

Jenny Jansen's profile in the second issue of *Geborener Deutscher* (1988) demonstrates how reunifying, in all its relevant forms, is a fluid experience subject to change. Gage authored the narrative of Jenny's front-page reunion story. He described how Jansen found her birth parents and discovered the Black community in Germany. In 2017, however, Jansen learned through DNA that Willie Booth, the man with whom she had "reunited" in the earlier article, was not her father after all. Jansen subsequently launched a social media campaign reviving her search and, in 2018, when she ultimately reunited with her half-siblings, posted photos on Facebook. Jansen's birth father had already passed away by then. Early subscribers to *Geborener Deutscher* have been able to follow Jansen's search over time, though it is important to mention that reunion is just the start of a new phase of adopted life.[21]

---

19. Boehmer, "Biracial Adoptees Can Expect a 'Mixed' Reaction."

20. The issues are currently being cataloged for display as a searchable collection in the forthcoming BGHRA digital archive under construction at http://www.blackgermans.us.

21. Gage, "Profile: Jenny Jansen." See also Gindler-Price, "'A Little Brown Baby': An Afro-German Adoptee's Story."

As the community grew and social network technology advanced over the years, the virtual culture evolved accordingly. The Black German Cultural Society's (BGCS) first online forum, created on July 26, 1999 (also now defunct), was, like *Geborener Deutscher,* a rudimentary Yahoo group.[22] Members were in conversation with Black organizations in Germany, specifically the *Initiative Schwarze Menschen in Deutschland* (ISD) [Initiative of Black People in Germany] and ADEFRA, a Black feminist organization in Germany. The relationships established among members of these organizations effected the construction of a transnational counterpublic. Globally situated persons identifying as Black Germans having diverse backgrounds, life experiences, and relationships to Germany who met in the early years continue to network in online spaces today.

The virtual network was from the outset multigenerational, multicultural, and experientially diverse. When new members introduced themselves in the early years, many who identified as Black Germans, especially adoptees, were astonished to learn that there were so many others with similar backgrounds and experiences. Many found the term *Black German* to be revelatory. Some in Germany were shocked to learn about the postwar adoptees and initially expressed confusion at the existence of a Black German community rooted in the US. Over time, the membership included multiple generations of persons identifying as Black German. In "Stories Matter," I explain how the US adoptees' childhood experiences were divided along military and civilian lines.[23] Adoptees who grew up on military campuses often had non-adopted Black German classmates whose fathers brought their mothers back with them when they left Germany. Many of the interracial families socialized together; however, often the secrecy surrounding adoption and the exclusivity of the social groups meant that the young adoptees were deprived of the sense of a dual-heritage cultural community that their non-adopted peers enjoyed.

Between the Obama campaign and 2008 election, there was a significant surge in activity. Subscribers on both sides of the Atlantic posted hundreds of links to articles and videos during this time. The transnational community celebrated President Barack Obama's historic victory together. Prominent author, activist, and performer Noah Sow, widely known for her book *Deutschland Schwarz Weiß: Der alltägliche Rassismus* (2008) [Germany in Black and White: Everyday Racism], led the celebratory chorus by posting a selfie from Hamburg, Germany, announcing "Wir sind Präsident!" [We are

---

22. See the BGCS website at http://www.afrogermans.us.
23. Peña, "Stories Matter."

president!]. James Sanders, an award-winning Black German photographer from Atlanta, Georgia, also known as Jimi Flix, accurately predicted a decline in the vibrancy of the dialogue after Obama took office in January 2009. There is no way to know how often members connected privately or met offline; however, occasional photographs evidenced that small groups met casually at restaurants and cafés. Some that began as virtual encounters in the early years have developed into important, long-term offline relationships. Arguably, the election of Barack Obama provided an experience through which the historically transnational community could bond in the present. The next step would be to organize in person after spending so many years together online.

Reunifying in Diaspora: Establishing New Traditions

Since described as a watershed event, the inaugural BGHRA conference created a space for multilayered conversations. Many in attendance were already virtually acquainted for more than a decade on the various social networks and were meeting face-to-face for the first time. As reflected in the theme, "Strengthening Transatlantic Connections," the event, held in August 2011, symbolically celebrated the reunification of Black Germans in the diaspora.

On the first morning of the three-day event, a delegation of Black Germans representing the US, Germany, and South Africa met with representatives of the Congressional Black Caucus on Capitol Hill at the invitation of Congressman Alcee Hastings of the Commission on Security and Cooperation in Europe, also known as the US Helsinki Commission. Policy Advisor Mischa Thompson facilitated the conversation on prior interventions related to anti-Black racism in Germany and the obstacles confronting those seeking original birth and adoption records. Adoptees articulated their desire for a centralized mechanism for finding families that would mediate for language, economic, and bureaucratic barriers. Though fully aware that this was not the appropriate forum through which they could realistically expect any direct intervention, adoptees expressed a desire for an unfettered path to dual citizenship, US/Germany, without complicated procedures or economic penalties. These first moments on Capitol Hill defined the political ethos in which the diaspora community officially made a unified public debut. Black German scholarship and activism emanating from Germany in the 1980s paved the way for the adoptees' voices to be heard for the first time in such an important forum. The conversation among the delegates and officials affirmed that the social justice concerns of the Black community in Germany and those of the transnational adoptees were inextricably linked.

The enthusiastic audience included many prominent authors who write about Black Germans and a multigenerational group of Black Germans with diverse ethnic and cultural backgrounds. The primary goal of the event was to bring this group together face-to-face; in this respect, it was a tremendous success. Noah Sow gave the inaugural keynote.[24] Sow and I developed a close relationship beginning in 2008 when, on her invitation, I attended the annual Black German community retreat called the ISD *Bundestreffen* [federal meeting] in Hellmarshausen, Germany. It was my first trip back to Germany since leaving with my adoptive parents in 1958. A thank-you letter I wrote to Sow is published in context in Hellmuth Karasek's *Briefe bewegen die Welt* [Letters Move the World].[25] The message Sow conveyed in her exegesis with soft, subtle humor was more *for* Black Germans than *about* them. She frequently referenced and addressed the adoptees directly in her talk. Sow's hour-long presentation, "Geteilte Geschichte" [Shared/Divided History], reflected on the ties between Afro-Germans who were displaced and sent to live in the US via transnational adoptions and Afro-Germans who remained but were "internally displaced." Sow emphasized how the systematic deportation of Black German children in the 1950s and 1960s contributed to the isolation of their siblings and peers who were left behind. Sow argued that ensuing generations were challenged with negotiating a collective identity for themselves in a predominantly white German society that still cannot seem to understand itself as multicultural:

> The German word *geteilt* has different meanings, some of which are actually opposites. Geteilt means shared and at the same time it also means divided, separated. It is our geteilte Geschichte, our shared history, which also divided us. The word Geschichte means history. This is the history we share. Step by step, we are coming to understand that there is a reason, a link to why our older generations in Germany grew up isolated, alienated from other Black people—with the same pain and the key question that could not and cannot be safely enunciated, "you all do not identify with me. Where can I find somebody who does? And whom I can identify with?" We are coming to understand why this has been so. Why most of the Black German kids in the 1970s and 1980s didn't have anybody to turn to. Because they had taken you away. You would have been our sisters, our mothers, our aunts. Our teachers, our deans, our doctors, our librarians, our social workers, our judges, our pilots, our nurses, our neighbors. We've been missing you a great deal.[26]

24. Sow, *Deutschland Schwarz Weiß.*
25. Karasek, *Briefe bewegen die Welt.*
26. Sow, "Geteilte Geschichte."

After providing an overview of Black history in Germany since medieval times, Sow acknowledged the work that contemporary Black German scholars and activists have accomplished. Highlighting the significance of community for Black people in Germany, Sow showed a short video clip celebrating the twenty-fifth year of the ISD Bundestreffen. In recognition of the shared history, Sow explained:

> Though we have different experiences, we now know that they are closely connected. We have all been displaced. Some of us were physically abducted from our own country. Some of us were expelled from the country, internally. We have been divided so forcefully, ruthlessly, that even most of us, Black Germans, are not aware, or are just now beginning to realize, that our whole history, including our own personal history, has been obscured. I think right now we are at the point where we've been meeting a long-lost sister for the first time, and now we'll have to decide how and where the relationship should go. Of course, I have an idea about how I want it to go. And hopes and dreams about us in the future.[27]

Subsequent BGHRA conference programs reflect the organization's aim to amplify the visibility of Black German Americans while encouraging the advancement of Black European studies internationally. More recently, the organization is engaging with scholars and activists representing Black populations beyond Germany and including other countries in Central, Eastern, and Northern Europe. What sets the BGHRA events apart from many other academic conferences is that many audience members are the subjects of panel presentations given by scholars who most often do not identify as a group member. The BGHRA conference provides a platform for those who are living / have lived the experiences being explored in the scholarship to speak back—to express their own perspectives in conversation with or in response to the researchers. It is important for Black German Americans, who are relative newcomers to the academic discourse inspired by and dominated by Black voices emanating from Germany, to learn from these experiences as they begin to educate others about their own. There are just a few memoirs and controversial documentaries that illuminate the lives of the adoptees, who have thus far been written about mostly by historians.[28] No ethnographic or quantitative analysis yet centers on the lived experiences of Black German adoptees, and nonadopted Black German Americans are virtually silent in

---

27. Sow, "Geteilte Geschichte."
28. See Griffin, *Brown Babies*.

the literature; therefore, each year, in a different way, American perspectives are highlighted. Adoptees are always invited to share their personal stories on oral history panels, along with others who are disparately situated geographically and have various family backgrounds and migration histories. When Yara-Colette Lemke Muniz de Faria gave the second keynote address in 2012, "'In Their Best Interest': Afro-German Children in Postwar German Children's Homes," the esteemed historian mentioned how important it was for her to have met in person the adoptees she wrote about from archival sources years before. Adoptees were likewise delighted to meet the person who first brought their stories into the light. Other Black European and reverse adoption experiences have also been represented over the years; for example, Rosemarie Äikäs, a Black Finn, shared with the audience what it was like to grow up in an orphanage in post-WWII Finland.

The BGHRA is committed to scholarly activism, to Black German studies research that emanates from the globally dispersed and culturally diverse community and for the amplification of its social justice initiatives. Fostering open dialogue between the intellectual and experiential communities is a critical intervention in this regard, and the ensuing discourse responds to advancements as well as tensions that arise within groups and subgroups. Perhaps most importantly, BGHRA conferences provide an existential space for Black Germans displaced by adoption and/or migration, as well as those who may feel culturally displaced and isolated within Germany, to belong. For many, the conference is a safe space where they can reconstruct and articulate complicated individual and collective identities amid an international sociopolitical ethos that is hostile to them.

Black German studies is, since the 1990s, unveiling to the world a shared history that, because of the secrecy surrounding their closed adoptions, the adoptees in particular were never supposed to know. For some, for whom reunification with their mothers is impossible and/or for whom the obstacles to learning about their individual origins seem insurmountable, the transnational counterpublic may provide some measure of comfort. The multimedia archives maintained on the organization's website, Facebook page, and YouTube channel reveal the multilayered conversations about and by Black Germans that are ongoing in both the activist and academic realms. While the videos are used in university classrooms internationally for teaching purposes, they also provide an opportunity for adoptees and their families who are unable to attend the events to learn about Black German life and history and to locate themselves contemporaneously, within the diaspora community. Maria, the adoptee who passed away before meeting her brother Hermann, left children and grandchildren behind who can learn something about their mother's ancestral history and their own through this work. Black Germans are in many ways actively making history as they excavate their individual and collective pasts.

Black German Americans in general, and the adoptive cohort in particular, remain underrepresented in the bodies of literature that compose the rapidly expanding canon of Black German studies as both authors and subjects. Similarly, in adoption studies, Black transnational adoptee voices are only beginning to emerge in a burgeoning field where Asian transnational adoption and domestic transracial adoption dominate the discourses. In the realm of Black German studies, many living in the US believe that at this point, and considering the advancement of the field, the absence of Black German American stories and voices is evidence of active and intentional erasure. Current initiatives of the BGHRA and its newly organized Black Transnational Adoption Consortium respond emphatically to these silences. The BGHRA exemplifies adoptee agency and resistance by insisting that we fill in our own knowledge gaps. With the growing number of activists and scholars situated globally who are working in solidarity with us since 2011, we are doing just that.

Bibliography

Boehmer, Leonie. "Biracial Adoptees Can Expect a 'Mixed' Reaction." *Geborener Deutscher: A Newsletter for German Born Adoptees and Their Birth/Adoptive Families*, Autumn 1991.

Cain, Henriette. "Adoptee Finds Mother and Three Half Brothers in Virginia." *Geborener Deutscher: A Newsletter for German Born Adoptees and Their Birth/Adoptive Families*, vol. V-2 (1992): 1–4.

Campt, Tina. *Other Germans: Black Germans and the Politics of Race, Gender, and Memory in the Third Reich*. Ann Arbor: University of Michigan Press, 2005.

Fambrough-Billingsley, Judy. *Too Brown to Keep: A Search for Love, Forgiveness, and Healing*. Judy Billingsley, 2019.

Fehrenbach, Heide. *Race after Hitler: Black Occupation Children in Postwar Germany and America*. Princeton, NJ: Princeton University Press, 2005.

Gage, William. "Profile: Jenny Jansen." *Geborener Deutscher: A Newsletter for German Born Adoptees and Their Birth/Adoptive Families*, June 14, 1988.

Gindler-Price, Shirley. "'A Little Brown Baby': An Afro-German Adoptee's Story." *Geborener Deutscher: A Newsletter for German Born Adoptees and Their Birth/Adoptive Families*, Spring 2000.

Griffin, Regina, dir. *Brown Babies: The Mischlingskinder Story*. United States, 2011.

Karasek, Hellmuth. "Rosemarie Peña and Noah Sow." In *Briefe bewegen die Welt, Bd 2: Liebe, Schicksal, Leidenschaft*, by Hellmuth Karasek, 133–41. Kempen: teNeues Verlag, 2011.

Kirchner, Walter. "Eine Anthropologische Studie an Mulattenkindern in Berlin unter Berücksichtigung der sozialen Verhältnisse." PhD diss., Freie Universität Berlin, 1952.

Kirst, Michaela, dir. *Brown Babies: Deutschlands verlorene Kinder.* BR/ARTE/WDR, Germany, 2011.

Kraft, Marion. "Coming In from the Cold: The Black German Experience, Past and Present." New York: Rosa Luxemburg Stiftung, July 2014.

———, ed. *Kinder der Befreiung: Transatlantische Erfahrungen und Perspektiven Schwarzer Deutscher der Nachkriegsgeneration.* Münster: Unrast, 2015.

Lawrence, Kerri. "Archives Recalls Fire That Claimed Millions of Military Personnel Files." *National Archives,* July 19, 2018. https://www.archives.gov/news/articles/archives-recalls-fire.

Lemke Muniz de Faria, Yara-Colette. "Black German 'Occupation' Children: Objects of Study in the Continuity of German Race Anthropology." In *Children of World War II, the Hidden Enemy Legacy,* edited by Kjersti Ericsson and Eva Simonsen, 249–65. Oxford: Berg, 2005.

———. "Reflections on the 'Brown Babies' in Germany: The Black Press and the NAACP." Accessed April 28, 2022. http://afrogermans.us/wp-content/uploads/2013/09/Reflections-on-the-Brown-Babies-in-Germany.pdf.

———. *Zwischen Fürsorge und Ausgrenzung: afrodeutsche "Besatzungskinder" im Nachkriegsdeutschland.* Berlin: Metropol, 2002.

Peña, Rosemarie. "Bedeutsame Geschichten: Kontextualisierung der Erfahrung(en) Schwarzer Deutsch-Amerikanischer Adoptierter." In *Kinder der Befreiung: Transatlantische Erfahrungen und Perspektiven Schwarzer Deutscher der Nachkriegsgeneration,* edited by Marion Kraft, 223–60. Unrast, 2015.

———. "From Both Sides of the Atlantic: Black German Adoptee Searches in William Gage's Geborener Deutscher (Born German)." *Genealogy* 2, no. 4 (2018): 13–20.

———. "Stories Matter: Contextualizing Black German American Adoptee Experience(s)." In *International Adoption in North American Literature and Culture: Transnational, Transracial and Transcultural Narratives,* edited by Mark Shackleton, 197–220. Cham: Palgrave Macmillan, 2017.

Rudolph, Nancy. "Black German Children: A Photography Portfolio." *Callaloo* 26, no. 2, 2003, 383–400.

Sieg, Rudolf. *Mischlingskinder in Westdeutschland: eine anthropologische Studie an farbigen Kindern.* Baden-Baden: Kunst und Wissenschaft, 1956.

Sow, Noah. *Deutschland Schwarz Weiß. Der alltägliche Rassismus.* München: Bertelsmann, 2008.

———. "Geteilte Geschichte." Keynote Address, Black German Heritage & Research Association Inaugural Conference, August 21, 2011, German Historical Institute, Washington, DC.

US District Court, District of Columbia. *War Babes v. Wilson.* Civ. A. No. 88-3633, 16 July 1990. Court Listener, https://www.courtlistener.com/opinion/2129562/war-babes-v-wilson/.

One Million Children Moving

Seventy Years of Transnational Adoption since the
End of World War II

PETER SELMAN

Although intercountry adoption is often seen as beginning with the adoptions from South Korea after the end of the Korean War in 1953, there were
many adoptions during and following World War II. Other examples of the
historical movement of children are the "orphan trains" in the US, and in Britain the story of child migrants to Australia, Canada, and New Zealand from
the nineteenth century to the 1960s. In his magnificent book *Uprooted*, Roy
Parker gives a detailed historical account of the "Shipment of Poor Children
to Canada, 1867–1917," of which he writes: "With hindsight, a damning ver-
dict is inescapable."[1] There were also many movements of children during the
Second World War, for example the *Kindertransport* of Jewish children to the
UK, and the evacuation of Finnish children to Sweden, which continued after
the war.[2] Writing about Germany, Textor reminds us that during the Third
Reich, many children "born to Aryan [*sic!*] women in occupied countries and
fathered by German soldiers were brought to the 'fatherland' and placed in
adoptive families."[3] So the period from 1948 to 2020 is just a small part of
the demographic of children moving for international adoption. This chapter
concentrates on international adoptions after the end of World War II, when
Germany was a major *exporter* of children for adoption in foreign lands, espe-

---

1. Parker, *Uprooted, 123*.
2. Hodge, *Rescuing the Children*; Serenius, "Silent Cry"; Saffle, *To the Bomb and Back*.
3. Textor, "International Adoption in West Germany."

cially to the US. It looks at transnational adoption dynamics on a global scale and provides several tables illustrating my and other scholars' data.

Sources of Data for Historical Estimates of International Adoption, 1948–2018

Few countries sending children for ICA (intercountry adoption) have kept detailed records of outgoing adoption. An exception is Korea, whose Ministry of Health and Welfare records 169,000 international adoptions since 1953. There are also detailed statistics available for India from CARA (the Central Adoption Resource Authority). Pilotti has good detail on adoptions from Latin America to the US and Sweden, and Kane gives detailed statistics from Colombia in the 1980s.[4]

For receiving states, the longest accessible sequences are for the US (1948 to date) and Sweden (1940–68, and annually 1969 to date). The US data are summarized for 1948 until 1967 by Altstein and Simon, in more detail for 1948 to 1981 by Weil, and in a series of factbooks published by NCFA (National Council for Adoption).[5]

In the Netherlands, the first Adoption Act was passed in 1956, and international adoptions by state of origin are recorded from 1957.[6] Intercountry adoptions are also recorded in detail for Denmark from 1970 and for Norway from 1966 with details on states of origin from 1979. Switzerland has annual totals with key states of origin from 1979, and detailed annual figures for France are available from 1980, although it is known that ICA dates back at least to 1968.

For the 1980s we have data for fourteen countries, using statistics gathered by Saralee Kane, and before that on data from the US, the Netherlands, and Scandinavian countries (Denmark, Norway, and Sweden) together with data from Korea about adoptions to Belgium, France, Germany, and Switzerland between 1967 and 1979.[7]

The smaller number of receiving countries reflects the late involvement in the practice by many countries but also a lack of recording of data, which suggests that estimates for these earlier periods may be too low. No official data are available for the UK before 1993, but we know there were adoptions from Korea in the 1970s and have survey data showing adoptions from Asia and South America in the 1980s. Feast et al. identified a significant number of

4. Pilotti, *Intercountry Adoption*; Kane, "Movement of Children."
5. Weil, "International Adoptions"; Altstein and Simon, *Intercountry Adoption*.
6. Hoksbergen, *Kinderen die niet konden blijven*.
7. Kane, "Movement of Children."

adoptions from Hong Kong to England in the 1960s, which were later followed up in a study of a hundred adoptees in 2008.[8]

My estimates for 1998 to 2019 are based on data from twenty-one to twenty-seven receiving states; for 1990 to 1997 on eleven to nineteen, the numbers rising following the entry into force in 1995 of the 1993 Hague Convention; but there are indications of many adoptions from Romania in 1990 and 1991 that are not officially recorded. The chapters in this volume by Graves, Hackenesch, Patton, and Peña reveal significant numbers of adoptions from Germany, including many Black German children.[9] These are discussed in greater detail later in this chapter alongside aggregate data on international adoption from Germany from 1950 to 1987, provided by Textor.[10]

Intercountry Adoption, 1948–1969

This period is perhaps the most challenging in terms of accurate data on international adoption and the most crucial in terms of explaining a new pattern that was to grow significantly in the following twenty-five years leading to the 1993 Hague Convention.

Adoptions to the US are summarized by Howard Altstein and Rita Simon, who list 19,230 between 1948 and 1962: 22 percent from Korea, 16 percent from Greece, 13 percent from Japan, and 10 percent from Germany.[11] They suggest seeing the period in two phases: 1948 to 1952, when 5,814 visas were granted for 1,808 children adopted from Europe, especially Greece[12] and Germany, and 2,418 adopted from Asia—mainly Japan. In the second phase, from 1953 to 1962, they estimate 13,416, marked by growing numbers from South Korea but a continuation of adoptions from Germany, Greece, Italy, and Austria. A more detailed picture of this period is given by Richard Weil, who provides data for over twenty states of origin, the majority from Europe.[13]

In the next seven years (1963–69), Altstein and Simon record a further 11,901 adoptions—a third from Korea and more than 2,000 from Germany,

---

8. Feast et al., *Adversity, Adoption and Afterwards.*

9. Fehrenbach, *Race after Hitler.*

10. Textor, "International Adoption in West Germany."

11. Altstein and Simon, *Intercountry Adoption,* 14.

12. The story of these early adoptions from Greece was revisited in a 2019 book by Van Steen that reveals some major scandals, including the sale of babies by a prominent New York magistrate, Stephen S. Scopas. Hoksbergen notes that ICA in the Netherlands starts in the early 1960s with the adoption of children from Greece, Austria, and Germany (see "Intercountry Adoption Coming of Age," 142).

13. Weil, "International Adoptions."

making a total of over 31,000 adoptions for 1948 to 1969.[14] Ruggeiro has an estimate of 20,688 between September 1957 and June 1969.[15] Table 9.1 lists the countries sending the most children to the US between 1948 and 1969. As it is recognized that not all adoptions were registered, a total for the period of more than 33,000 intercountry adoptions to the US seems reasonable.

TABLE 9.1. Intercountry Adoptions to the US, 1948–69 [with 2 header rows]

SOURCE	WEIL (1984)			ALTSTEIN AND SIMON (1991)			WEIL[†]
COUNTRY	1948–52	1953–62	1948–62	1948–62	1963–69	1948–69	1963–75
South Korea	0	4,162	4,162	4,162	3,531	7,693	14,684
Greece*	1,246	1,920	3,166	3,166	544[‡]	3,710	932
Japan	0	2,987	2,987	2,987	699	3,686	1,460
Germany	1,156	636	1,845[†]	1,845	1,609	3,454	2,976
Italy	568	2,007	2,575	n/a[‡]	739[‡]	3,314	1,137
Austria	169	575	744	744	—	—	—
South Vietnam	—	—	—	—	—	—	2,110
Canada	—	—	—	—	—	—	1,906
China	1	465	466	—	—	—	793
Colombia	—	—	—	—	—	—	802
All States	4,066	15,165	19,231	19,230[†]	11,901	31,131	34,568

* Adoptions from Greece are affected by the aftermath of the Greek Civil War (1946–49) as well as World War II.
† Weil's total for Germany is the same as Altstein and Simon's, but period subtotals add up to only 1,792. Weil offers only aggregate totals for 1963–75, but I include these because they indicate that Korean and German adoptions were increasing more rapidly.
‡ Altstein and Simon omit Italy from their top five states of origin—their total for all states is one less than Weil's. 1963–69 totals for Greece and Italy are incomplete.

Estimating the number of adoptions to other countries is more difficult. Swedish data record 1,031 international adoptions in 1969 (182 from Korea) and an estimate of 4,291 in the previous twenty-eight years, which includes significant numbers from Korea and Germany, and 632 from Finland, dating back to 1941. Other countries listed include several European countries, Denmark, Norway, Greece, Hungary, Poland, and Austria, as well as India and Iran. Adoption was legalized in the Netherlands in 1956, and a total of 843 international adoptions are recorded between 1957 and 1969.

---

14. Altstein and Simon, *Intercountry Adoption.*
15. Ruggeiro, "Adoptions in and to the United States."

International adoptions from Korea are recorded to several other countries so that, in light of these figures, it seems that the best way to explore this period may be to look in more detail at the pattern of international adoption from Germany and South Korea from 1950 onwards—concentrating in the latter case on the period 1953–69, for which the Korean Ministry of Health and Welfare has detailed records.

Intercountry Adoption from South Korea, 1953–2019

I begin with the demographic history of Korean adoption. I have already noted that South Korea has the largest number of recorded intercountry adoptions since the 1950s. These began in 1953 following the end of the Korean War and initially were mainly the adoption in the US of the children of Korean women and American soldiers but continue today despite the country moving from a poor war-torn country to one of the richest and most developed countries outside of Europe and the Americas.

Eighty-seven percent of the 9,065 adoptions in the years 1953 to 1969 recorded by the Korean Ministry of Health and Welfare are from the US.[16] The adoptions to Sweden, Norway, and other countries are largely from the late 1960s.

The growth in annual numbers is most striking in the 1970s and 1980s, reaching a peak at more than 9,000 in 1985 and 1986. By this time, those adopted were no longer mainly the "mixed race" offspring of American GIs but increasingly the children of unmarried women who faced stigma and poverty.[17] In the 1970s there were more adoptees who were the children of single mothers than described as "abandoned," and from 1980 these were a clear majority: 72 percent from 1981 to 1990, 92 percent from 1991 to 2000, and about 98 percent in the new millennium.[18]

Annual numbers peaked at more than 8,000 for 1985 to 1987, but when Korea hosted the Olympic Games in Seoul in 1988, this level of international adoption generated much adverse publicity about the huge numbers of children being sent, primarily to the US, and in the next five years, numbers fell dramatically. The Korean government announced that it planned to end intercountry adoption. Thirty years later, Korea remains one of the top ten "sending" countries (see table 9.13). Korea finally signed the 1993 Hague Convention

---

16. In chapter 3 in this volume, Eleana J. Kim and Kim Park Nelson discuss the issue of large numbers of Korean adoptees deported because they never attained US citizenship.

17. Sarri, Baik, and Bombyk, "Goal Displacement."

18. Kim, *Adopted Territory,* 25.

in 2013 but as of this writing has yet to ratify it, and no one seems clear as to when (or whether) they will. They remain one of only three such countries (the others are Nepal and the Russian Federation). In 2018 there were 321 adoptions from Korea, placing them fifth in the ranking of states of origin.

How Many Children Were Adopted Internationally, 1948–1969?

Viewing this period from the perspective of the receiving countries, we can say that at least ten received children from South Korea. Table 9.2 shows that most went to the US, but Korean children were also adopted to Sweden and Norway beginning in 1955; to Canada, Denmark, and Germany since the mid-1960s; and to Australia, Belgium, France, and the Netherlands since the late 1960s. We can assume that Australia, Belgium, Canada, and France also adopted children from other countries. We can assume a minimum of 33,000 to the US alone.

TABLE 9.2. Intercountry Adoptions from South Korea, 1953–2019 (with Top Five Receiving States)

YEAR(S)	US	FRANCE	SWEDEN	DENMARK	NORWAY	OTHER[†]	TOTAL
1953–69	7,931	45	689	25	124	251[§]	9,065
1970–74	8,911	583	2,707	1,878	1,053	3,005[‡]	18,137
1975–79	16,003	2,634	1,410	1,948	1,039	4,864	27,898
1980–84	19,152	3,634	1,316	1,930	1,278	3,083	30,393
1985–89	26,919	2,888	1,271	1,518	940	3,582	36,118
1990–99	17,545	958	990	989	1,149	1,294	22,925
2000–2009	14,785	384	998	435	756	1,987	19,345
2010–19*	3,960	39	367	84	213	696	5,409
1953–2019	114,206	11,165	9,748	8,807	6,562	18,812	169,290

* Data for 2010–19 are estimates based on statistics provided by receiving states, as detailed figures for country of origin were not available from Korea for this period.
† All data recorded from 1953 to 2009 are from the Korean Ministry of Health and Welfare. Other countries receiving large numbers of children over this sixty-five-year period are the Netherlands (4,099), Belgium (3,697), Australia (3,555), Canada (2,639), and Germany (2,352).
‡ There were ca. 1,000 adoptions to Germany and Switzerland in the 1970s, and in the 1980s a further 1,200 to Germany and 600 to 700 to Luxembourg.
§ From 1960 to 1969, adoptions are also recorded to Switzerland, Japan, Australia, France, Belgium, and the Netherlands.

Altstein and Simon give a total of 7,693 adoptions from Korea in this period, accounting for about a quarter of all adoptions recorded between

1948 and 1969.[19] There were at least four other countries sending more than 2,000 children to the US in these years, accounting for a further 43 percent of the total. Germany sent 3,454 children, Japan sent 3,686, Italy sent 3,314, and Greece sent 3,710 (see table 9.1). All four countries experienced high levels of intercountry adoption in the period 1948–62, gradually diminishing in the mid- and late 1960s, except for Germany, which sent more children to the US than Korea in 1967 and a total of over 1,500 in the 1970s. Adoptions from Italy also continued into the 1970s to some countries such as Switzerland. Adoptions to the US are also recorded from Hong Kong, Taiwan, and the Philippines, the number from the latter increasing, along with adoptions from Canada and Vietnam, which began in the late 1960s.

The only other countries for which we have reliable data before 1970 are Sweden, which records more than 1,000 in 1969, the majority from Europe, and a total of over 5,000 between 1950 and 1969; and the Netherlands, for which Hoksbergen records a total of 843 between 1957 and 1969, most from Greece, Germany, and Austria.[20] As Germany features in the top states of origin for both Sweden and the US and continues to do so in the 1970s, and is also the focus of other chapters in this volume, I look at their experience before turning to global trends in the 1970s.

Intercountry Adoption from Germany, 1950–1979

Intercountry adoption from Germany begins earlier than from Korea—in the aftermath of World War II—but ends by the 1980s and is now rare. Instead, Germany has become a receiving state and is one of the top ten receiving countries in the period 1990–2018.

Altstein and Simon record 1,845 children adopted from Germany in the period 1948–62, less than the number recorded as adopted from Greece (3,116), Japan (2,987), or Italy (2,575) under special US legislation in that period.[21] A further 3,200 are recorded in the next seventeen years, with Germany sending more children than any country other than Korea for the period 1963–75.[22]

Textor records more than 30,000 children adopted from Germany between 1950 and 1969—mainly to the US, Scandinavian countries, Belgium, and the Netherlands.[23] He notes that from 1960 onwards, these numbers fell as a growing number of German couples sought to adopt children. By 1969 the

---

19. Altstein and Simon, *Intercountry Adoption*.
20. Hoksbergen, *Kinderen die niet konden blijven*, 65, table 2.
21. Altstein and Simon, *Intercountry Adoption*; Weil, "International Adoptions."
22. Weil, "International Adoptions."
23. Textor, "International Adoption in West Germany."

annual number was 743; beginning in 1980, fewer than 300 outgoing international adoptions are recorded each year; and the number of children adopted by German couples from Third World countries rose to over 1,000 a year by 1989, most of these "private" adoptions. Table 9.3 compares these figures with recorded adoptions in the US, Sweden, the Netherlands, Denmark, and Switzerland. No data were accessible for Belgium or Norway or for Sweden in the 1970s, but it is likely that more than a hundred may have been adopted, taking the total postwar adoptions to over 6,000.[24] My estimate of more than 7,000 shows the significance of Germany as a state of origin in the twenty-five years after the end of World War II and fits well with observations by the scholars in this volume about the adoptions of the children of Black American GIs.[25]

TABLE 9.3. Intercountry Adoptions from Germany to Five Countries, 1948–89

YEAR(S)	US	SWEDEN	NETHER-LANDS	DENMARK	SWITZER-LAND[§]	TOTAL (5 STATES)	TEXTOR[‖]
1948–62	1,845	284+[‡]	150	n/a	n/a	4,000+	22,481
1963–69	1,609	—	—	n/a	n/a	—	7,805
1970–79	2,148	n/a	187	192	77[§]	2,600+	4,631
1948–79	5,602*	500+	187	192	500	7,000+	34,917
1980–89	33[†]	—	7	—	71	105	2,139[‖]

* Verrier (1993) says that 6,578 children were adopted in the US during the period 1963–81. My figures for 1948–79 are estimates, including years not recorded.
[†] Weil records twelve adoptions from Germany to the US in 1981 but offers no evidence from 1981 to 1989.
[‡] Swedish data are aggregates for 1958–68 for one agency and probably underestimate the total number of children adopted from Germany in this period.
[§] Swiss data from 1970 to 1979 are for 1979 only—but include intrafamilial adoption.
[‖] Textor's data cover the period 1950–87.

In Textor's table, the largest annual totals of at least 2,000 adoptions occur from 1955 to 1959. One of those adopted in this period was Peter Dodds, born in June 1955 and adopted from an orphanage at age two and a half in 1958 by an American couple stationed in the Federal Republic of Germany, who later moved back to Georgia. In 1997 he published his story, *Outer Search Inner Journey: An Orphan and Adoptee's Quest,* and has spent much of the subsequent years campaigning against international adoption.[26]

---

24. The discrepancy between Textor's data and the estimate derived from adoptions recorded by receiving states is huge, and I have not been able to find a reason for this, so any suggestions from readers are welcome.

25. See the contributions by Graves, Hackenesch, Patton, and Peña in this volume; Siek, "Germany's Brown Babies."

26. See, for example, Dodds, "Parallels between International Adoption and Slavery."

Dodds's story is that of a white German boy whose parents were both German citizens. But many of the children adopted from Germany were the children of American GIs, and for those of dual heritage—the so-called brown babies—the stories are often even more complicated.[27] Rosemarie Peña was one such child, who, like Dodds, was adopted to the US in 1958 at age two and writes about Black German adoptees and their stories in chapter 8 of this volume. Tracey Patton also shares the story of her adopted Black German mother, in chapter 7.

Intercountry Adoption, 1970–1979

A difficult decade. We have reliable data from the US, the Scandinavian countries, and the Netherlands, which has detailed records from 1970. We also have evidence of adoptions from Korea to other receiving states such as Belgium, Canada, France, Germany, and Switzerland, and adoptions from Korea in the 1970s are also recorded to England, New Zealand, and Japan.

TABLE 9.4. Recorded Intercountry Adoptions for Five Countries, 1970–79 (with Korean Data in Brackets)

COUNTRY	1970	1973	1975	1977	1979	1970–79
US[†]	2,409	4,323	6,290	6,854	4,864	48,636
[from Korea]*	[998]	[2,329]	[2,995]	[3,711]	[2,347]	[24,914]
Sweden[‡]	1,150	1,314	1,517	1,864	1,382	14,819
[from Korea]	[340]	[618]	[308]	[355]	[169]	[4,117]
Netherlands[§]	177	417	1,018	1,119	1,290	7,548
[from Korea]	[96]	[182]	[307]	[282]	[171]	[2,172]
Denmark[‖]	226	687	770	715	491	5,883
[from Korea]	[126]	[555]	[246]	[460]	[406]	[3,826]
Norway[#]	115	294	296	412	275	2,906
[from Korea]	[71]	[259]	[109]	[302]	[112]	[2,092]
Total	4,077	7,035	9,891	10,964	8,302	79,792
(5 States) >	[1,631]	[3,943]	[3,965]	[5,100]	[3,205]	[37,121]

* Figures for Korean adoptions are taken from their Ministry of Health and Welfare.
† US data taken from Altstein and Simon (1991) and NCFA.
‡ Swedish data from Central Authority MIA (now MFOF).
§ Dutch data from Ministry of Justice.
‖ Danish data from AdoptionsNaevnet.
Norwegian data from Statistics Norway.

---

27. Siek, "Germany's Brown Babies."

On this basis we can say that there were at least 80,000 recorded inter-country adoptions during this period, but there is clear evidence of adoptions to many other countries, for example Belgium, Canada, France, Germany, and Switzerland, including over 8,000 from South Korea, of which 3,262 were to France. During this decade Korean adoptions are also recorded to Australia, New Zealand, and Japan. In table 9.5, I try to estimate the number of international adoptions for a further seven countries, using data provided by the Korean Ministry of Health and Welfare.

This suggests that the decade total should be raised to over 100,000. If this estimate is correct, many other countries must have been involved; I explore this in the next section. Korea is clearly the major source of children for international adoption in this decade, but data from the US, Sweden, Denmark, and the Netherlands indicate that at least ten other countries sent significant numbers of children.

TABLE 9.5. Top States of Origin for Four Countries, 1970–79

COUNTRY	US	SWEDEN	NETHERLANDS	DENMARK	4 STATES
Korea	24,914	4,274	2,172	3,826	35,186
NEXT TEN COUNTRIES					
Colombia	3,334	611	765	32	4,742
India	501	2,143	669	332	3,645
Vietnam	2,499	66	77	2	2,644
Philippines	2,334	52	39	13	2,438
Thailand	853	1,076	93	79	2,101
Canada	1,916	n/a	3	3	1,922
Chile	593	917	72	25	1,607
Germany	1,114	n/a	187	192	1,493
Indonesia	n/a	284	1,119	28	1,431
Sri Lanka	n/a	811	77	214	1,102
Subtotal	13,144	5,960	3,090	920	23,125
Top 11 [incl. Korea]	38,058	10,234	5,262	4,746	58,300
Total	48,636	14,819	7,548	5,883	76,876

Adoptions from Canada, Germany, the Philippines, and Vietnam were mainly to the US, those from Sri Lanka and Thailand were to Sweden, and 75 percent of the adoptions from Indonesia were to the Netherlands. Adoption from Vietnam began in the later stages of the Vietnam War and is often remembered through the airlifts of thousands of children after the fall of Saigon in April 1975, and especially the first flight of Operation Babylift, which crashed shortly after takeoff, killing seventy-eight children.

Seven of the top eleven countries are Asian, and two are Latin American. However, another five countries were sending more than 500 children, and three of these—Mexico, Costa Rica, and El Salvador—were Latin American, accounting for ten of the top fifteen states of origin in the 1980s. In contrast, four of the top six states of origin between 1948 and 1969 were European.

Intercountry Adoption in the 1980s

For this decade, I rely largely on the work of Saralee Kane, who obtained data from fourteen countries that she believed received most of the children adopted in this decade.[28] Data sent amounted to 163,000 (47 percent from the US), but Kane estimates a minimum of 170,000 to 180,000 for the decade, allowing for incomplete data for Canada, Finland, Germany, and Spain and no statistics available for the UK, Austria, Ireland, and Israel. The decade totals match those I have received from receiving states—where there are differences, these are discussed in notes to table 9.6.

Kane estimates that the data she collected represented 90 to 95 percent of the actual number, and that 170,000 to 180,000 moved in this decade. Her estimate seems reasonable given the missing years and limited coverage for Canada (where only Quebec provided data). No data were obtainable from the UK, Ireland, Israel, and Austria, although all four were known to be receiving children for adoption. Adoptions from Korea to Luxembourg are also recorded for this period.

It is noticeable that the annual number of international adoptions to the US, Sweden, and the Netherlands declines sharply after 1987, largely because of the decline in adoptions from Korea in that period. Altstein and Simon saw this as "the beginning of the end of wide-scale ICA"—with the high numbers of adoptions from Romania in 1990 seen as "a momentary addition to the world's pool of children available for adoption by foreigners."[29] This view was undermined by the advent of China as a major source in the 1990s and a sharp rise in adoptions from many African countries in the new millennium.

Kane provides estimates of the number of children sent abroad for intercountry adoption in this decade by fifty states of origin.[30] Only Ethiopia and

---

28. Kane, "Movement of Children," 331, table 4.
29. Altstein and Simon, *Intercountry Adoption*, 191. See also table 9.10.
30. Kane, "Movement of Children," 330, table 3.

TABLE 9.6. Top Ten Receiving States, 1980–89 (Kane, 1993)

COUNTRY	1981	1984	1986	1988	1989	1980–89*	RATIO‡ 1989
US	4,868	8,327	9,286	10,097	7,948	77,606	2.0
France	1,256	1,906	1,995	1,735	2,383	18,501	3.0
Sweden	1,789	1,493	1,560	1,355	883	15,788 [14,524]†	9.4
Netherlands	1,643	965	1,297	872	642	11,526	3.7
Italy	206	779	1,150	1,602	2,332	10,055	3.8
Switzerland	868	535	544	492	509	6,157	6.7
Denmark	658	441	693	523	468	5,818	8.5
Belgium	386	594	679	662	771	5,443	6.6
Norway	344	501	477	566	578	4,637	11.0
Australia	n/a	417	480	516	349	3,561	1.4
All States* [Number]	11,997 [8]	16,184 [11]	19,611 [12]	19,327 [14]	18,195 [14]	162,661 [161,456]	n/a
Decade Estimate with Missing Data	n/a	n/a	n/a	n/a	n/a	170,000– 180,000	n/a

* Data for Germany were available for 1988 and 1989 only—in these years the total number of adoptions was similar to that for Sweden.
† Kane's published total for Sweden from 1980 to 1989 is higher than the aggregate of individual years—see total in brackets. The decade total is also too high—see bracketed figure. The latest Swedish data give a decade total of 15,055.
‡ The adoption ratio is the number of adoptions per 1,000 births. In Sweden this means one adoption for every hundred live births. In 1980 the ratio would have been over 2.0.

the islands of Madagascar and Mauritius featured among countries sending over one hundred children.

Table 9.7 shows the top ten countries, all from Asia or Latin America, and each sending at least 2,000 children. The next five include one European country, Poland. The table also shows the totals for 2000 to 2009 for these countries and compares the adoption ratio in 1989 with the ratio fifteen years later.

TABLE 9.7. Top Ten States of Origin, 1980–89, and Comparative Rank, 2000–2009 (Kane, 1993)

COUNTRY	RANK, 1980–1989	TOTAL ADOPTIONS	RATIO, 1989	RANK, 2000–2009*	TOTAL ADOPTIONS	RATIO, 2004
Korea	1	61,235	5.4	5	19,713	4.7
India	2	15,325	< 0.1	9	10,589	0.04
Colombia	3	14,837	2.5	7	16,908	1.8
Brazil	4	7,527	0.5	15	4,451	0.14
Sri Lanka	5	6,815	1.0	—	—	0.2
Chile	6	5,243	3.0	33	865	0.2
Philippines	7	5,167	0.4	12	4,664	0.2
Guatemala	8	2,242	0.8	3	30,834	8.2
Peru	9	2,205	1.1	24	1,523	0.2
El Salvador	10	2,178	1.0	—	—	0.3
All countries	n/a	162,661	—	—	382,232	n/a
Top 10 States	n/a	122,774	—	—	296,627	n/a

* Data for the later date range (2000–2009) are taken from table 9.9, which is based on data from 14–22 receiving states (see table 9.13) and so may be an underestimate.

Adoption Irregularities in the 1980s and the Hague Convention

In the last three decades, there has been growing concern about and evidence of irregularities in adoptions from Asia and Latin America in the 1980s that were not recognized at the time. Two examples are Sri Lanka and Chile, ranked fifth and sixth in the 1980s, when each sent about 8,000 children for international adoption. Concern over such irregularities were a major factor in the decision to develop a Hague Convention on the topic.[31]

The Hague Convention seeks to ensure that intercountry adoption is regulated by governments through designated "central authorities" and the use of accredited bodies, requiring careful assessment of prospective adopters and ensuring that children placed are free for adoption. Ten thousand children were adopted from Sri Lanka in these twenty years, more than half in the five years from 1983 to 1987. Over the whole period, 80 percent went to three countries—Sweden, the Netherlands and France. There have been reports that most were not orphans, and that corruption and baby-selling were widespread.[32]

31. Van Loon, *Report on Intercountry Adoption.*
32. McVeigh, "'There Were a Lot of Baby Farms.'"

There were also issues in a number of Latin American countries.[33] Argentina responded to the discovery of illegal adoptions in the 1980s by imposing a minimum five-year residency requirement on adopters that effectively halted international adoption.[34] In contrast, the full story of adoption and stolen children under the Pinochet regime (1973–90) is only now becoming clear.[35] As with Sri Lanka, it is linked to a remarkable rise in numbers in the late 1970s (see table 9.5) and throughout the 1980s, when there were more than 1,000 adoptions to France, Sweden, and the US, followed by a rapid decline from the early 1990s.

Intercountry Adoption in the 1990s

During this decade 223,000 children are recorded as adopted to fifteen countries (rising to twenty-two by 1999), many from China and Russia after 1992. It is thought that thousands of children were adopted from Romania in 1990 and 1991—2,800 are recorded in the US; 1,000 in France, 100 in Sweden, but *Defense for Children International* (DCI/ISS 1991) estimate at least 2,000 to other countries including Germany, Ireland, Israel, Italy, Spain, and the UK.[36]

Data were obtained for eighteen to twenty-two countries from 1994 to 1999 and for eleven to fifteen countries for 1990 to 1993. There were no data that I could access for some countries in the latter period, but I have made some estimates which I use in later discussion of global data since World War II.

These estimates are later highlighted in table 9.9 and consider the number of adoptions in 1989 reported in Kane's 1993 article. My 1990 figure is lower than Kane's 1989 total—largely because of the absence of data for Italy and Germany, who recorded 3,400 adoptions in Kane's data. But by 1994 the annual total for the fourteen countries in her study was over 20,000, and by 1998 the total was over 30,000. This was largely due to the sharp increase in adoptions in the US and France in the late 1990s and the inclusion of full data for Canada from 1992 on. In contrast, the decade totals for Sweden and the Netherlands show a decrease in numbers of over a third. The decade total of 223,000 recorded adoptions is nearly 40 percent higher, and my estimate below—238,500—shows a similar increase to Kane's.

This is an interesting decade for changes in the countries from which children moved for intercountry adoption and for considering the impact of the

33. Briggs, *Somebody's Children*.
34. Cantwell, *Sale of Children and Illegal Adoption*.
35. Agoglia, "'Irregular Adoptions.'"
36. Defence for Children International/ISS, *Romania*.

1993 Hague Convention, which came into operation in 1995. Critics, especially in the US, have argued that the tighter regulations introduced are a major reason for the current decline in intercountry adoption, but table 9.8 shows a steady rise in annual numbers from 1993 to 1999, which continued until 2004. Annual numbers had been falling since 1988, following South Korea's decision to limit intercountry adoption, which continued until 1992 after a brief increase in adoptions from Romania in 1990 and 1991, whose number is not fully understood because many were not recorded.[37] The main drivers of the subsequent rise were the arrival of China and Russia as states of origin, while Korea continued to send more than 2,000 children a year, despite initial assertions that it would end the practice.

TABLE 9.8. Top Ten Receiving States, Recorded Adoptions, 1990–99

COUNTRY	1990	1993	1995	1997	1999	1990–99
US	7,055	7,358	9,384	12,596	15,717	102,037
France	2,956	2,790	3,035	3,537	3,597	31,704
Italy	1,700	1,696	2,455	2,095	3,123	15,791 21,000+*
Canada	210	1,896	2,161	2,019	2,177	15,695
Sweden	1,113	934	895	834	1,019	9,670
Netherlands	830	574	681	686	993	7,369
Denmark	427	509	629	507	688	5,791
Norway	578	543	605	534	527	5,748
Spain	100	250	815	942	2,006	5,606 7,000+
Germany	800	800	871	833	977	5,241 8,500
Other†	1,385	1,812	1,514	2,332	2,598	19,422
Total Recorded	14,391 (11)	17,743 (15)	23,415 (19)	26,681 (20)	33,265 (22)	224,024
Estimated	18,000+	19,000+	—	—	—	237,500

* When two numbers are provided, the bottom figure represents my estimate of decade totals given the absence of data for these countries in some years.
† There are 12 other countries recording adoptions in this decade. Australia, Belgium, Finland, New Zealand, and Australia record 2,000+; the UK and Ireland 1,000+; and Cyprus, Iceland, Israel, Luxembourg and Malta less than 500.

37. Defence for Children International/ISS, *Romania*.

Table 9.9 shows the top ten states of origin from 1990 to 1999 using data collected from the statistics recorded by fifteen to twenty-two receiving states. Totals include decade aggregates for some countries and should be seen as minimum estimates, as data are missing for some years.

TABLE 9.9. Top Ten States of Origin, Selected Years, 1990–99

COUNTRY	1981	1983	1984	1985	1986	1989	1990–99
China	123	747	1,479	3,140	4,838	5,945	27,548
Russia	n/a	940	1,904	2,377	4,975	6,157	25,996
South Korea	2,197	2,290	2,262	2,180	2,057	2,409	22,925
Colombia	1,414	1,450	1,308	1,575	1,173	1,750	14,871
Romania	3,382	421	493	1,401	1,202	2,345	13,455
India	949	1,116	1,374	1,385	1,403	1,633	13,277
Vietnam	159	570	1,031	1,192	1,509	1,862	10,915
Brazil	944	1,483	889	1,024	674	558	8,536
Guatemala	398	591	615	655	1,237	1,494	7,371
Philippines	519	711	629	528	305	371	4,988
Top 10	10,085	10,319	11,984	15,457	19,373	24,524	148,970
World Total	16,698	17,743	20,484	23,415	26,681	33,265	224,024

Intercountry Adoption in the Twenty-First Century

More than 382,000 children were adopted worldwide to more than twenty-three countries between 2000 and 2009. Even here the total is likely an underestimate due to incomplete data for Austria and Portugal and no information on adoptions to Greece, Japan, Singapore, or the Gulf States. There were nearly 143,000 international adoptions in the next ten years, making the total 525,000 for the period 2000–2019. The total of 382,000 adoptions is the highest for any decade since 1950, but it masks a rise in annual numbers to over 45,000 in 2004 followed by a decrease to less than 30,000 by 2009. The next ten years saw a steady decline to a low point of 6,530 in 2019, a decline of 86 percent from 2004. Data for 2020 were incomplete at the time of writing but suggest a further decrease to under 4,000. The sharp decline is found in all major receiving countries but is most striking for France, Spain, and Germany, where it is over 90 percent. In these later years, Italy adopts far more children internationally than France and Spain and becomes a clear second to the US as a receiving state after 2010. Table 9.10 shows the rise and fall of ICA from 2000 to 2019 with detailed numbers for the top eight receiving countries, ranked by the total number received over these years.

TABLE 9.10. Top Eight Receiving States, 2000–2019 (Countries Receiving 10,000+ Children for Intercountry Adoption, Totals Are for 22–24 Countries)

COUNTRY	2001	2004	2007	2010	2013	2016	2019	2000–2019
US	19,647	22,988	19,601	12,149	7,094	5,372	2,971	264,274
Italy	1,797	3,402	3,420	4,130	2,825	1,872	1,205	52,380
Spain	3,428	5,641	3,648	2,891	1,191	574	370	51,203
France	3,095	4,069	3,155	3,508	1,343	956	421	48,237
Canada	1,774	1,949	1,715	1,660	1,243	790	576	28,045
Sweden	1,044	1,109	800	728	450	342	170	13,393
Netherlands	1,193	1,154	782	705	401	214	145	13,643
Germany	854	744	783	513	288	196	85	10,172
All States	36,685	45,482	37,295	28,751	16,177	11,081	6,532	531,117
% to US	54%	50%	53%	42%	44%	48%	46%	50%

The US accounts for 50 percent of global adoptions in this period, and the next four countries, Italy, Spain, France, and Canada, contribute a further 33 percent, although their relative ranks vary from year to year (see table 9.10). Four more countries, Switzerland. Norway, Denmark, and Belgium, record over 5,000 international adoptions since 2000.

There are much more dramatic changes in the ranking of states of origin by year or by decade. Table 9.11 shows the top ten states of origin ranked by number of adoptions between 2000 and 2019. China and Russia are the top two, accounting for 41 percent of all adoptions, and Guatemala stands out as a major contributor to the adoption boom in the early years of the century, especially in the US, which received 97 percent of adoptions from that country in 2007. All totals are based on data provided by receiving states.

TABLE 9.11. Top Ten States of Origin, 2000–2019 (Countries Sending 15,000+ Children for Intercountry Adoption)

COUNTRY	2001	2004	2007	2010	2014	2019	2000–2019
China	7,724	13,412	8,749	5,429	2,949	1,062	126,070
Russia	5,689	9,440	4,925	3,426	1,057	228	77,332
Ethiopia	781	1,534	3,041	4,369	1,087	22	35,406
Guatemala	2,007	3,425	4,852	58	32	5	31,028
South Korea	2,491	2,239	1,225	1,127	507	259	25,122
Colombia	1,891	1,749	1,643	1,828	536	607	25,082
Ukraine	2,470	2,119	1,623	1,098	610	365	24,018
Vietnam	1,297	492	1,691	1,260	409	240	17,540
Haiti	741	1,170	822	2,502	572	252	15,661
India	1,508	1,067	987	607	361	548	15,563
All States	36,685	45,482	37,295	28,751	13,567	6,532	531,117

China is the main country of origin, followed by Russia, but numbers fall more sharply in the latter beginning in 2014, so that by 2019 it is ranked eleventh. Ethiopia takes third place because of numbers rising from 2004 to 2009, when elsewhere the annual totals were falling, and continuing at a higher level until 2013. In contrast, Guatemala, which ranked third between 2005 and 2009, experienced a very rapid decline after 2009, having initially been a strong replacement for falling numbers elsewhere. If we look at the standardized measures, measuring adoptions per 1,000 live births in the peak years, China has the lowest ratio apart from India, and Guatemala emerges as the top state, with one child adopted for every hundred born. The ratio is also high in Korea despite the decline in adoptions since the 1980s (see table 9.2); in 1985 the ratio was 13.5. For all ten countries, the number of adoptions is lower in 2017 than in 2010. Worldwide the decline is two-thirds (67 percent), but in Russia and Ethiopia it has been about 90 percent and in Guatemala 93 percent, resulting in its replacement by the Philippines in the top ten. But despite this dramatic decline, the new millennium has already seen a global total of at least 530,000 international adoptions, which is about half the total I have been able to find documented since 1948. In the next section I spell out the process by which I reached this conclusion.

Conclusion: Intercountry Adoption 1948–2019—One Million Children Moving

In this section I draw together the various data estimates from previous sections to make an overall estimate of the minimum number of international adoptions in the seventy years since the ending of World War II and consider what the future trends may be. Tables 9.12 through 9.14 summarize my estimates from previous sections, indicating at least one million intercountry adoptions since 1948.

TABLE 9.12. Recorded Intercountry Adoptions in the US, 1948–2019
(Using Identifiable Data Only)

PERIOD	NUMBER OF ICAS RECORDED	SOURCE
2010–2019	66,436	FY Annual Reports—in 2010 includes 1,090 humanitarian visas
2000–2009	197,838	State Dept. website
1990–99	102,037	NCFA
1980–89	77,586	NCFA and Kane
1970–79	48,636	NCFA/Altstein
1948–69	31,131	Altstein and Simon (1991); Weil (1984)
1948–2019	523,632	—

TABLE 9.13. Total Recorded Intercountry Adoptions, 1948–2019
(Using Identifiable Data Only)

PERIOD	NUMBER OF ICAS RECORDED	NUMBER OF RECEIVING STATES
2010–19	148,865	24–25 States
2000–2009	382,232	21–27 States
1990–99	223,407	14–22 States
1980–89	161,456	14 States [Kane, see table 9.6]
1970–79	79,792	5 States [USA, Sweden, Denmark, Norway, and Netherlands
1948–69	37,296	3 States [USA, Sweden, and Netherlands]
ALL STATES 1948–2019	1,033,068	
US 1948–2019	523,632 [51%]	

TABLE 9.14. Revised Estimate of Minimum Likely Number of Intercountry Adoptions Worldwide (Allowing for Missing Data)

PERIOD	NUMBER OF ICAS ESTIMATED	NUMBER OF RECEIVING STATES	NOTES
2010–19	149,000	24–25	Does not include adoptions from Greece, Japan, or the Middle East; Austria and Portugal in some years only
2000–2009	382,800	21–27	n/a
1990–99	237,500	14–22	Additional 11,000 from Italy, Germany, and Spain, and unrecorded from Romania
1980–89	180,000	14+ [Kane]	Increase allows for missing years and countries
1970–79	100,000	10+	Recognizes other countries with no data who have adopted from Korea
1948–69	45,000+ (incl. all Korean)	5–10	Assumes some adoptions to Belgium, France, Italy, Switzerland, and Japan, and more from Germany
ALL STATES 1948–2019	1,094,300		
US 1948–2019	523,700 [48%]		

There remain many unanswered questions about the number of international adoptions before 1970, with suggestions that not all Korean adoptions are recorded by their Ministry of Health and Welfare and the possibility of more adoptions from Germany, as noted earlier.

Top Receiving States and States of Origin since World War II

It is clear from tables 9.12 through 9.14 that the US has been the major receiving country, accounting for half of all recorded intercountry adoptions. Determining the order of the other receiving countries is more difficult. Spain, Italy, and France are the key countries in the new millennium, followed by Canada, but for earlier years things are less clear, with Sweden and the Netherlands having larger numbers of recorded adoptions and Spain appearing to be a latecomer. Norway also has a long history of international adoption, with at least an estimated 20,000 adoptions since 1960. These nine countries seem to be the most important receiving states, accounting for more than 85 percent of the recorded international adoptions since World War II. When it comes to assessing the countries that have sent the most children, Korea is clearly the front-runner with its long history and a continuing practice even though its peak numbers were reached in the 1980s. My estimate, based largely on the figures provided by the Korean Ministry of Health and Welfare, is a total of nearly 169,000 since 1953 (table 9.2).

At one stage it looked as if China might outstrip Korea, but recent drops in annual figures and the ending of the one-child policy mean that this may never happen. Russia also has been a strong contender, but the decrease in its annual numbers has been more dramatic. These are clearly the top three states of origin, sending over 100,000 children each and together accounting for about 40 percent of the total. Two other countries, Colombia and India, have sent at least 40,000 children, and a further six, Ethiopia, Guatemala, Vietnam, Ukraine, Brazil, and the Philippines, have sent at least 20,000. If we accept Textor's figures, discussed earlier, Germany could also be in this category.

Some Final Thoughts

My estimate in table 9.14 suggests that the number of international adoptions passed the million mark in the 2010s, but the downward trend in annual numbers has continued for fifteen years since 2004, and few would predict any reversal in this trend, so that many foresee a virtual ending of international adoption in the years ahead. The global total for 2019 is 6,532 to twenty-six countries, and predictions for 2020 have been further complicated by the international crisis of the COVID-19 pandemic. Even before this downturn, David Smolin had argued that evidence of international adoption being tied to child trafficking meant that it should end unless reformed and that history may label the entire enterprise a "neo-colonialist mistake," just as child migration was seen by Parker and others as a terrible episode.[38]

More than half of my estimated total has been recorded since 2000, which means that many of those adopted are now approaching young adulthood. Even if international adoption numbers continue to fall and the practice ends in the coming decade, these adult adoptees will need much support at a time when agencies are closing and funds available from an ongoing process are diminishing. The experience of more than 160,000 Korean adoptees indicates that adopted children do grow up and have need for support. What postadoption support should we offer to the Chinese girls adopted from the 1990s to the early 2000s as they reach adulthood in the years ahead?

---

38. Smolin, "Intercountry Adoption."

Postscript: Transnational Adoption in 2020—The Impact of the COVID-19 Pandemic

From the available data, we can say that the annual total for most countries will be substantially lower than in 2019, thus continuing the downward trend of the previous fifteen years, and at an accelerating rate. The interpretation of these numbers is more problematic, as they are clearly affected by the COVID-19 pandemic.[39] Five major receiving states—the US, France, Italy, Spain, and Sweden—have shown a decline of 42 to 48 percent. Other receiving states have shown higher rates of decline (for example, Finland at 60 percent) or less change (for example, Australia at 35 percent), and recent data submitted to the HCCH by Ireland show that a rise in numbers can be found if the data are based on the number of children arriving in the country as opposed to when their adoption was confirmed. My latest global total is 3,300 transnational adoptions to twenty-one receiving states, an overall decline of 44 percent since 2019.

There is also variation in the patterns shown by those states of origin that have provided data. The number of adoptions from the Philippines fell by 53 percent, the number from Colombia by 35 percent. Statistics from receiving states suggest much larger decreases in the number of children adopted from China, but this drop is harder to interpret, as it coincided with the introduction of a three-child policy, replacing the one-child policy, which initially led to China's rise as the most important state of origin in terms of the number of children sent for adoption.

It is possible that 2021 will see a recovery if the declines are due to delays in the transnational adoption process, and that there will be a compensating increase as these difficulties are overcome. On the other hand, the sharp fall may be the beginning of a final, more rapid decline with the possibility that this is the beginning of the end to transnational adoption, as more and more states of origin realize that many children can be placed domestically and the evidence of malpractice in previous decades becomes more evident, a pattern recognized by the major states of origin—Congo RDC, Ethiopia, Kenya, and Russia—that have imposed moratoria following such evidence.

---

39. It has been impossible to bring the data presented up to date as the 2020 statistics for some countries had not been published at the time the final version of this chapter was submitted in December 2021.

Bibliography

Agoglia, Irene S. "'Irregular Adoptions' in Chile: New Political Narratives about the Right to Know One's Origins." *Children & Society* 33, no. 3 (April 2019): 201–12.

Altstein, Howard, and Rita Simon, eds. *Intercountry Adoption: A Multinational Perspective.* New York: Praeger, 1991.

Briggs, Laura. *Somebody's Children: The Politics of Transracial and Transnational Adoption.* Durham, NC: Duke University Press, 2012.

Cantwell, Nigel. *The Sale of Children and Illegal Adoption.* Den Haag: Terre des Hommes, 2017.

Defence for Children International. *Romania: The Adoption of Romanian Children by Foreigners.* Geneva: DCI/ISS, 1991.

Dodds, Peter F. *Outer Search Inner Journey: An Orphan and Adoptee's Quest.* Puyallup, WA: Aphrodite, 1997.

———. "The Parallels between International Adoption and Slavery." *Sociology Between the Gaps: Forgotten and Neglected Topics* 1 (Fall 2014–Summer 2015): 76–81.

Feast, Julia, Margaret Grant, Alan Rushton, John Simmonds, and Carolyn Sampeys. *Adversity, Adoption and Afterwards: A Study of Women Adopted from Hong Kong.* London: BAAF, 2013.

Fehrenbach, Heide. *Race after Hitler: Black Occupation Children in Postwar Germany and America.* Princeton, NJ: Princeton University Press, 2007.

Hodge, Deborah. *Rescuing the Children: The Story of the Kindertransport.* Toronto: Penguin Random House, 2012.

Hoksbergen, Rene. *Adoption in Worldwide Perspective.* Lisse: Swets and Zeitliger, 1986.

———. "Intercountry Adoption Coming of Age in the Netherlands: Basic Issues, Trends and Developments." In *Intercountry Adoption: A Multinational Perspective,* edited by Howard Altstein and Rita Simon, 141–60. Santa Barbara, CA: Praeger, 1991.

———. *Kinderen die niet konden blijven: zestig jaar adoptie in beeld,* Soesterberg, NL: Uitgeverij Aspekt, 2012.

Kane, Saralee. "The Movement of Children for International Adoption: An Epidemiologic Perspective." *The Social Science Journal* 30, no. 4 (1993): 323–39.

Kim, Eleana J. *Adopted Territory: Transnational Korean Adoptees and the Politics of Belonging.* Durham, NC: Duke University Press, 2010.

McVeigh, Karen. "'There Were a Lot of Baby Farms': Sri Lanka to Act over Adoption Racket Claims." *The Guardian,* September 20, 2017. https://www.theguardian.com/global-development/2017/sep/20/baby-farms-sri-lanka-admits-adoption-racket-claims.

Parker, Roy. *Uprooted: The Shipment of Poor Children to Canada 1867–1917.* Bristol: Policy, 2008.

Pilotti, F. *Intercountry Adoption: Trends, Issues and Policy Implications for the 1990s.* Inter-American Children's Institute, 1990.

Ruggeiro, Josephine A. "Adoptions in and to the United States." In *Adoption: Global Perspectives and Ethical Issues,* edited by Jagannath Pati, 103–36. New Delhi: Concept, 2007.

Saffle, Sue. *To the Bomb and Back: Finnish War Children Tell Their World War II Stories.* New York: Berghahn Books, 2015.

Sarri, Rosemary, Yenoak Baik, and Marti Bombyk. "Goal Displacement and Dependency in South Korean-United States Intercountry Adoption." *Children & Youth Services Review* 20, no. 1 (January–February 1998): 87–114.

Serenius, Mona. "The Silent Cry: A Finnish Child During World War II and 50 Years Later." *International Forum of Psychoanalysis* 4, no. 1 (December 2007): 35–47.

Siek, Stephanie. "Germany's Brown Babies: The Difficult Identities of Post-War Black Children of GIs." *Spiegel Online.* October 13, 2009. https://www.spiegel.de/international/germany/germany-s-brown-babies-the-difficult-identities-of-post-war-black-children-of-gis-a-651989.html.

Smolin, David. "Intercountry Adoption as Child Trafficking." *Valparaiso University Law Review* 39, no. 2 (2004): 281–325.

Textor, Martin R. "International Adoption in West Germany: A Private Affair." In *Intercountry Adoption: A Multinational Perspective,* edited by Howard Altstein and Rita Simon, 109–26. Santa Barbara, CA: Praeger, 1991.

Van Loon, J. H. A. *Report on Intercountry Adoption.* The Hague: The Hague Conference, 1990.

Van Steen, Gonda. *Adoption, Memory, and Cold War Greece: Kid Pro Quo?* Ann Arbor: University of Michigan Press, 2019.

Verrier, Nancy Newton. *The Primal Wound: Understanding the Adopted Child.* Baltimore, MD: Gateway Press, 1993.

Weil, Richard H. "International Adoptions: The Quiet Migration." *International Migration Review* 18, no. 2 (Summer 1984): 276–93.

CONTRIBUTORS

LAURA BRIGGS is a professor of women, gender, and sexuality studies at the University of Massachusetts Amherst and an interdisciplinary scholar of reproductive politics and the US relationship to Latin America, trained in history and American studies. She has written numerous articles and published in diverse venues, from law reviews to history journals to popular books. Her most recent book is *Taking Children: A History of American Terror* (2020). She is also the author of *Somebody's Children: The Politics of Transracial and Transnational Adoption* (2012), which won the Rawley Prize on Race Relations from the Organization of American Historians, and *Reproducing Empire: Race, Sex, Science and U.S. Imperialism in Puerto Rico*. Her PhD is from Brown University's Department of American Studies, 1998.

KORI A. GRAVES is an associate professor of history at the University at Albany, SUNY. Dr. Graves's research interests allow her to pursue questions that evaluate the significance of political and popular representations of gender, race, nation, and family. Her book, *A War Born Family: African American Adoption in the Wake of the Korean War* (2020), tells the story of the first African Americans who adopted Korean children and the ways their efforts revealed the contested nature of adoptive family formation across racial and national color lines. She teaches courses that consider gender and women's history, the history of marriage and family, and histories of the body, beauty, and identity politics in the US, with a specific emphasis on the histories of motherhood and transracial and transnational adoption. Dr. Graves has won awards for teaching excellence, and she is committed to efforts that support the recruitment and retention of students who are members of historically underrepresented populations, first-generation students, and students with special needs.

SILKE HACKENESCH (EDITOR) is an associate professor at the Institute of North American History at the University of Cologne, Germany. She specializes in twentieth-century family and adoption studies, African American history, critical race and gender studies, and Black diaspora studies. She received her PhD from the Free University Berlin in 2012. Her publications include *Chocolate and Blackness: A Cultural History* (2017) and "'I Identify Primarily as a Black German in America': Race, Bürgerrechte und Adoptionen in den USA der 1950er Jahre," in *Kinder des Zweiten Weltkrieges* (2016). Currently, she is finalizing her second book manuscript, which explores the contentious debates among nonprofessional adoption advocates, social workers, and civil rights activists on the adoption of Afro-German children to the US after World War II. Her research has been supported by the German Academic Exchange Service (DAAD), the Thyssen Foundation, the German Research Foundation (DFG), the Society for the History of Children and Youth (SHCY), the Alliance for the Study of Adoption and Culture (ASAC), and the German Historical Institute in Washington, DC.

ELEANA J. KIM is a cultural anthropologist and the author of *Adopted Territory: Transnational Korean Adoptees and the Politics of Belonging* (2010). Her essays on transnational Korean adoption have appeared in several journals and edited volumes, including *Anthropological Quarterly, The Cambridge Handbook of Kinship, Cultures of Transnational Adoption,* and *The Journal of Korean Studies.* She is an associate professor of anthropology at University of California, Irvine.

KIM PARK NELSON is an educator and researcher whose work uses adoption as a lens through which to understand race and culture. Her work has contributed to building of the field of adoption studies and Korean adoption studies in the US and internationally. Dr. Park Nelson has authored or co-authored several published articles on adoption cultures and communities. Her book *Invisible Asians: Korean American Adoptees, Asian American Experiences and Racial Exceptionalism* was published in 2016. The book is based on her ethnographic research exploring the many identities of adult Korean adoptees, as well as the cultural, social, historical, and political significance of sixty years of Korean adoption to the US. She is the director and associate professor of ethnic studies at the Winona State University.

TRACEY OWENS PATTON is professor of English in the Department of English; adjunct professor in African American & Diaspora Studies in the School of Culture, Gender, and Social Justice; and affiliate faculty in the Creative Writing MFA Program in the Department of Visual & Literary Arts at the University of Wyoming. She also served as the director of the African American & Diaspora Studies Program from 2009 to 2017 at the University of Wyoming. She earned her PhD in communication at the University of Utah. Her area of specialization is critical cultural rhetorical studies and communication, critical media studies, feminist and womanist theory, and transnational studies. She has published numerous journal articles, published a co-authored book titled *Gender, Whiteness, and Power in Rodeo: Breaking Away from the Ties of Sexism and Racism* (2012), and is working on a second book involving race, memory, rejection, and World War II.

ROSEMARIE H. PEÑA is founder and president of the Black German Heritage and Research Association (BGHRA) and adjunct professor of German in the Department of Central, Eastern, and Northern European Studies at the University of British Columbia in Vancouver. She holds bachelor's degrees in psychology and German from Rutgers University in Camden, New Jersey, where she also earned her MA and PhD in Childhood Studies. Her research explores the historical and contemporary intersections of transnational adoption and child migration. Rosemarie is contributing author in several edited volumes published in both German and English. Her peer-reviewed articles appear in *The Encyclopedia of Children and Childhood*, *Genealogy Journal*, and the *Journal of Adoption and Culture*. Rosemarie's most recent essay, "Stories Matter: Contextualizing the Black German American Adoptee Experience(s)," appeared in Marion Kraft's edited volume *Children of the Liberation: Transatlantic Experiences and Perspectives of Black Germans of the Post-War Generation* in 2019.

PAMELA ANNE QUIROZ is executive director of the Inter University Program on Latino Research (IUPLR) and the director of the Center for Mexican American Studies and professor of sociology at the University of Houston. Professor Quiroz has been a fellow at the Center for the Advanced Study of Behavioral Sciences, Stanford University; a visiting research associate at the Autonomous University of Barcelona; and a research fellow at both the Institute for Research on Race and Public Policy and the Great Cities Institute. She earned her PhD from the University of Chicago in 1993 and has received grants from the National Science Foundation, the American Sociological Association, the US Department of Education, and the Society for the Scientific Study of Sexuality. She served as editor of *Social Problems,* a prominent journal in sociology that focuses on the pursuit of social justice, and she has served as North American editor for the interdisciplinary journal *Children's Geographies*. She also served on the board of directors for the Council on Contemporary Families (2013–18). Her book, *Dating, Mating, Relating: Personal Advertising and Modern Romance,* is forthcoming.

PETER SELMAN is a visiting fellow in the School of Geography, Politics & Sociology at the Newcastle University, UK, where he was head of the Department of Social Policy until his retirement in 2002. He is editor of *Intercountry Adoption: Development, Trends and Perspectives* (2000) and has written many articles and chapters on adoption policy. His main research focus in recent years has been on the demography of child adoption with a special emphasis on transnational adoption. He has made regular presentations on this topic and convened a thematic group on "Agencies and the HCIA" at the Forum on International Adoption and Global Surrogacy in Den Haag in August 2014. Peter has acted as research consultant to international organizations such as the UN Population Division, the Hague Conference on Private International Law, and the Innocenti Research Centre in Florence. His data are published on the Hague Intercountry Adoption website. After leaving university, he worked for three years as a childcare officer, specializing in adoption, in Oxfordshire Children's Department. He has continued to be involved with domestic adoption since then and was a member of Newcastle's Adoption Panel until 2018. From

1995 to 2013, he was chair of NICA (Network for Intercountry Adoption) and from 1999 to 2013 a member of the board of trustees and the research advisory group of BAAF (British Association for Adoption & Fostering).

AMY E. TRAVER is a professor of sociology at Queensborough Community College, the City University of New York. Her research interests include student success in community colleges, as well as intersections of adoption, race/ethnicity, religion, and gender in American family life. She has published articles on these topics in *Teaching Sociology, Internet and Higher Education, Qualitative Sociology, Sociological Focus, International Journal of Sociology of the Family, The Journal of Education Policy,* and *Qualitative Inquiry.* Traver is also the co-editor of four scholarly volumes: *Humanistic Pedagogy across the Disciplines* (with Leshem, 2018); *Poetry across the Curriculum* (with Jacob and Kincaid, 2018); *Service-Learning at the American Community College* (with Perel Katz, 2014); and *Women, Family, and Class: The Lillian Rubin Reader* (with Kimmel, 2009). Her research was recognized by a 2019–2020 Mellon/ACLS Community College Faculty Fellowship.

INDEX

FORMATIONS: ADOPTION, KINSHIP, AND CULTURE
EMILY HIPCHEN AND JOHN McLEOD, SERIES EDITORS

This interdisciplinary series encourages critical engagement with all aspects of non-normative kinship—such as adoption, foster care, IVF, surrogacy, and gamete transfers—especially as they intersect with race, identity, heritage, nationality, sexuality, and gender. Books in the series explore how these constructions affect not only those personally involved but also public understandings of identity, personhood, migration, kinship, and the politics of family.

Adoption across Race and Nation: US Histories and Legacies
    EDITED BY SILKE HACKENESCH

The Politics of Reproduction: Adoption, Abortion, and Surrogacy in the Age of Neoliberalism
    EDITED BY MODHUMITA ROY AND MARY THOMPSON